ALASKA

POINT BARROW

ARCTIC OCEAN

BUE SOUND

ENINSULA

NULATO

YUKON RIVER

TANANA

YUKON RIVER

PORCUPINE RIVER

FAIRBANKS

TANANA RIVER

EAGLE

DAWSON

CANADA

Mt McKINLEY

VALDEZ

PRINCE
WILLIAM
SOUND

CORDOVA

COOK INLET

SEWARD

YAKUTAT

SKAGWAY

SHELIKOF STR.

KODIAK IS.

THREE SAINTS

GULF OF ALASKA

JUNEAU
DOUGLAS

ALEXANDER PENINSULA

STR.

WRANGELL

KETCHIKAN

OCEAN

THE STORY OF
A L A S K A

C. L. ANDREWS

Author of

STORY OF SITKA

WRANGELL AND THE GOLD OF THE CASSIAR

NUGGETS OF VERSE PANNED FROM THE
GRAVELS OF THE PAST

THE STORY OF ALASKA

Alexander Andreevich Baranof
Chief manager, Russian American Company from 1790 to January 11, 1818.

THE STORY OF
ALASKA

BY

C. L. ANDREWS

Illustrated

The CAXTON PRINTERS, Ltd.
Caldwell, Idaho
1944

First printing, April, 1938
Second printing, July, 1938
Third printing, January, 1940
Fourth printing, June, 1942
Fifth printing, March, 1943
Sixth printing, February, 1944

Printed and bound in the United States of America by
The CAXTON PRINTERS, Ltd.
Caldwell, Idaho
60640

Dedication

To THOSE WHO ARE ENDEAVORING to develop the last of Uncle Sam's farms, and who are conquering the last frontier, giving their lives to that service, this volume is dedicated.

Preface

OUT OF A FRIENDSHIP EXTENDING BACK OVER A LONG SPAN
of years when he and I were young fellows working in the
pioneer town of Seattle, it is a pleasure to write this prefatory
message of commendation for Clarence L. Andrews and his
book, *The Story of Alaska*.

Few men known to me are so well equipped as Mr.
Andrews for the task he has here completed. He first visited
that interesting Northland in 1892. Five years later he was
with the party of the Duke of Abruzzi in the famous ascent
of Mt. St. Elias. At the conclusion of that successful and
historic undertaking, Mr. Andrews accepted a position with
the United States Customs Service in the District of Alaska.
Beginning in 1897, he continued that work for twelve years.
The intimate knowledge of the entire District acquired under
such favorable circumstances was recognized when he was
drafted for work in 1909 with the Alaska Department of the
Alaska-Yukon-Pacific Exposition in Seattle. There followed
two years of work with the *Alaska-Yukon Magazine* and five
other years of newspaper work and photography in Alaska.
During the World War he served with the Red Cross, Northwest Division. At the end of the World War, he accepted
work with the Alaska Bureau of the Seattle Chamber of
Commerce. From 1923 to 1929 he was again active in Alaska,
part of the time in the northernmost reaches. This work was
with the Bureau of Education and Reindeer Service. Official
reports and photographic records show a remarkable range
of service for the natives.

With an interest in history from boyhood, it was perfectly
natural that Mr. Andrews should have developed a keen interest in the early days of each section visited in his various
duties and travels. This resulted in his becoming familiar
with the Russian language, in his collection of many books
and documents, and in acquaintance and interviews with
pioneers.

It is clear that such a man with such unusual opportunities for observation and study should be well equipped to write the story of Alaska. His choice of a title for the book is most appropriate. No equal portion of the earth's surface has a history with more glamor, more adventure, more call for elemental courage. Alaska's history certainly is a story.

Space limits have favored terseness and compactness in style. This has by no means injured the book. Readers will find each paragraph valuable in its store of dependable information.

The story begins, naturally enough, with the Russian voyages of discovery and ends with a discussion of present-day conditions and prospects. The great gold rush receives ample treatment and the other resources of the "Republic's Treasure House" are by no means neglected.

One convincing portion of the book is a careful comparison of Alaska's possibilities with those of Northwestern Europe. It is a logical array of facts and figures. Under the heading, "Alaska is the Greater Scandinavia," is this compact argument: "Alaska is a greater area than that of Norway, Sweden, Finland, and Denmark combined. They have nearly sixteen million people, while Alaska has about sixty thousand. They have been drawing on their natural resources for hundreds of years. Alaska is almost a virgin country. Alaska has almost every resource that those lands have and yet others that they have not."

Thus to the value of the book as history we have added this challenge to the future which the author has epitomized in five words: "Alaska has room for millions."

EDMOND S. MEANY.

Contents

PART TWO
1867-1937

List of Illustrations and Maps

There is a Land with gold and copper and coal

WITH VAST FORESTS AWAITING THE AXE OF THE lumberman, a place for millions of people, with broad acres for the dairyman. It has more white coal than has New England to smelt its mineral and to drive the wheels of industry. It is asking for homemakers who will work.

It is ALASKA.

In 1845, Captain Gordon, brother of the Earl of Aberdeen, then Prime Minister of England, came to Victoria, B. C., with a party of officials who were investigating this country. During his stay he said: "I would not give the most barren hills in the Highlands of Scotland for all I see around me."

The answer to his opinion is expressed in Seattle, Vancouver, B. C., and Portland, Oregon, situated in the garden spot of the world today.

Congressmen are saying that Alaska is valueless, and advise the removal of the Government Railroad, forgetting that Daniel Webster gave an opinion that California was not worth a dollar as indemnity for the cost of the Mexican War.

The answer will be, in the future, with an Oslo, a Stockholm, and a Copenhagen in the Scandinavia of America, Alaska.

Foreword

MORE THAN TWO BILLION DOLLARS HAS BEEN THE TRADE OF
Alaska with the United States in the period of a little over
seventy years which has elapsed since the territory was
acquired from Russia.

At the time of the purchase there were men in Congress
who called it "An inhospitable, wretched, and God-forsaken
region." It was bought for less than two cents an acre, and
men railed at the price. Since that time one mine has paid in
gold nearly ten times the cost of the whole country; one small
group of islands has yielded more than fifty millions in furs;
one fishing company has declared in dividends more than
was paid for the territory. Alaska was called barren by those
who did not know. The Guggenheims did not think it barren
when they built a railway there at a cost of twenty million
dollars, and they have since shipped twenty millions in copper
over that road in a single year. The salmon packers do not
think it barren when they ship fifty millions of canned
salmon in a year. The traveler does not think it barren when
he sees miles of waving grass and flower-clad slopes, and looks
over the thriving farms of the Tanana or the Matanuska.

The story of Alaska, historically and industrially, has not
been told in full for more than thirty years. Dall, in his
Alaska and Its Resources, outlined it in 1879. Bancroft, in his
History of Alaska, detailed it in 1886. Since Bancroft completed his work, history of a vivid sort has been in the making.
The modern industrial development of the amazing country
has taken place almost wholly within forty years.

In the earlier years the search for the soft-furred skins
led adventurers over sea and land; the Russian domain was
built by one of the greatest organizers in the history of the
world's frontier; among the managers of the Russian American Company were princes and barons who ruled with almost
imperial sway over a land as broad as an empire. The story
of the delving for the golden treasures of the mountains is

one of the great romances of history; the development of the industries of the present is one of the notable achievements of modern times.

No land in history has poured out its wealth more bountifully than has this, and none has retained less within its boundaries for the upbuilding of itself. Scores of millions of dollars annually have been taken from its fisheries and its mines, but the golden harvest has passed to the United States, and Alaska has not retained even a tithe for herself. Beautiful buildings have been built in nearly every city of the West from the proceeds of Alaskan gold. Rich farms in nearly every valley of the West have been purchased with wealth brought from the Northland, but what has remained in Alaska? This is not the theme of this book, the aim of which is to sketch impartially the course of development and to show its present value, but it forms an outstanding and astonishing feature that colors, of necessity, much of Alaskan life and to every true Alaskan is of vital importance, for he must live there and suffer by its limitations.

"The physiognomy of a government can best be judged in its colonies, for there its characteristic traits usually appear larger and more distinct," says DeToqueville. Perhaps our nation may benefit by a study of its acts in Alaska.

I have been identified with the life of Alaska for more than a quarter of a century. I have looked into the cheery faces of the Eskimos on the shores of the Arctic Sea and wondered at their fortitude; I have counseled with the Thlingits of the Sitkan Archipelago concerning their hereditary fisheries and listened to their traditions; my heart has gone out to the long-suffering Aleuts in their grass-covered *barabaras* on the western islands. I have hunted with the caribou hunters of the Yukon, have shoveled gravel into the sluice boxes at Nome, and have pulled an oar alongside the fishermen of the coast. I have lived the life of the North and I love it, and if this story brings a little better understanding of our Northland province to the reader I shall be satisfied with my work.

I wish to acknowledge the assistance and encouragement of the late Dr. Alfred H. Brooks, Alaska Division of the U. S. Geological Survey; Dr. Edmond S. Meany of the University of Washington, Seattle; Philip S. Smith of the U. S. Geological Survey; Carlyle Ellis, of New York; John W. Troy, Editor, Juneau *Empire,* Juneau, Alaska; Chas. W. Hawkesworth, Office Ind. Aff.; Chas. D. Garfield, Seattle Chamber of Commerce; W. T. Lopp, of Seattle; Ward T. Bower, Agent of the Bureau of Fisheries for Alaska, and others. Also to Mrs. Julia Krenov, a Russian, whose residence in London, Paris, and Berlin gave her a knowledge of languages that made clear many of the obscure passages in the Russian volumes of 100 to 150 years ago.

PART ONE
1728-1867

1

Russian Voyages of Discovery

THE NAME ALASKA WAS DERIVED FROM A WORD IN USE BY the Aleutian islanders at the time of the coming of the Russians, *Alyaska,* or *Alaksu,* and by them applied to the mainland of the peninsula of Alaska. By the Russians it was spoken of as "Our Possessions in America," or "The Colonies," while on our maps of sixty years ago it was designated as Russian America, and after it became a dependency of the United States the name Alaska was adopted by Congress. There was bitter contention over the purchase, the acquisition was strongly opposed, and many opprobrious epithets were applied to the land, "Walrussia," "Land of Icebergs," and "Seward's Folly" being among them.

The area is 586,400 square miles, equal to nearly one fifth of the area of the rest of continental United States. It is larger than the original thirteen colonies, or than the combined area of Norway, Sweden, and Finland. The length of the coastline is about 26,000 miles.

At the close of the first quarter of the eighteenth century, the whole of the northern part of the Pacific Ocean was a mystery. Drake, in his voyage in the *Golden Hind,* had reached the coast of what he termed New Albion, on the American coast, and the Russians had reached and coasted along the shores of the Sea of Okhotsk. Between these points an unknown ocean washed the shores of an unknown land.[1]

Tales were heard among the sailors of the fabled Straits of Anian, the voyage of Juan de Fuca, and of the mythical Gamaland lying to the northeast of Japan.

On the continent of North America the French had penetrated no farther from the eastern coast than to the headwaters of the Mississippi, and the most westerly post of the English was on Hudson's Bay. More than three quarters of a century were yet to elapse before the memorable journey of Lewis and Clark to the mouth of the Columbia River. In

New England the Colony of Massachusetts was waging a border war with the Indians of Canada, and Boston was only a town of eighteen thousand inhabitants.

Such were the conditions surrounding the territory now called Alaska when the Russian Emperor planned the first expedition to make explorations on the eastern shores of Asia.

Peter the First, greatest of all the czars, the dynamic, erratic, passionate Russian in whose eyes blazed the fires which were of genius or of madness, looked toward the confines of the East and dreamed of what lay beyond it. The Cossacks had followed the hunters, *promishleniki* they were called, to the Sea of Okhotsk, to collect the *yassak,* or tribute of fur. From the Chukchee people, the strange, warlike nomads who followed their reindeer over the hills of eastern Siberia and fought back the Russian advance, came stories of a people farther on who had ivory teeth in their cheeks. Peter heard and was fired with a desire to know what lay beyond the Sea of Okhotsk, and to know if Asia and America were separated by an ocean.

He chose Vitus Bering, a Dane, captain in the Russian Navy, to command an expedition to explore this *terra incognita.*[2] Alexei Chirikof, a Russian lieutenant, and Martin Petrovich Spanberg, also a lieutenant of the Navy, were appointed his assistants.

Peter the Great died January 28, 1725,[3] only fifty-three years of age when his impetuous energies were stayed by death, but this did not alter the carrying out of the enterprise. His successor, Catherine the First, the daughter of a clergyman, whom Peter found following his Army and made his queen, took up the work he had begun, and on February 5 the last party of the expedition left St. Petersburg for the shores of the Pacific, six thousand miles away.[4]

Bering's forces arrived at Tobolsk, Siberia, on March 15, took boats on the river in May, went down the Irtish, up the Ob and the Ket, then up the Tunguska and the Ilim. They arrived at Ilimsk on September 29, spent the winter there, and in the spring went to Yakutsk, the capital of eastern Siberia, then a town of three hundred houses, where they arrived in June. From this place their route lay across the Stanovoi Mountains, a region of intense cold in winter,[5] 580 miles to Okhotsk, at which place Bering arrived in October, but it was July of the next year before the last of Chirikof's division appeared with the cordage and other materials for the ship's stores.

A small boat, the *Fortuna*, was at once built at the mouth of the river, and on it, and on an old vessel formerly constructed for tribute gathering, they sailed to the *Bolshaya Ryeka*, or Big River, and landed at Bolscheretsk, on the west side of the Kamchatka Peninsula.

During the winter the supplies were taken across the peninsula, and down the Kamchatka River to *Nizhne Kamchatsk*, twenty miles from the Pacific Ocean, where there were forests of timber suitable for shipbuilding, and there a ship was built, launched, and named the *St. Gabriel*.

Bering sailed from the mouth of the Kamchatka River on July 13, 1728. His course lay along the coast to the northeast, usually in sight of land. On August 11 he sighted land to the east and named it St. Lawrence Island, then going to the northeast he passed through the strait afterward named for him, past the Diomede Islands, into the Arctic Ocean. The coastline of Siberia disappeared to the northwest and on the 16th they reached 67° 18′ N. Lat. Then Bering decided that he had passed the extreme eastern point of Asia, and had demonstrated that Asia and America were separate continents. He turned back, repassed the Diomedes,[6] but did not see the American coast, although the headlands of East Cape, Siberia, and Cape Prince of Wales, Alaska, are only fifty-five nautical miles apart. He followed the coast, reached the mouth of the Kamchatka River on September 2, and the first voyage from the Pacific to the Arctic was completed.

Bering spent the winter of 1728-9 at the Kamchatka *Ostrog*, or fort, sailed in the spring to search for land to the eastward, went to sea about one hundred miles, then, finding none, he rounded Cape Lopatka, the lower point of Kamchatka, went to Okhotsk, and from there overland to St. Petersburg. He reached the capital on March 31, 1730, after an absence of five years. He had located and charted the eastern Siberian shore through thirty degrees of longitude, and through thirteen degrees of latitude, had discovered and named the Diomede Islands and St. Lawrence Island, had entered the Arctic Ocean, and had established the fact that Asia and America were separate continents.

While Bering was absent on his voyage, Afanasius Shestakof, a Cossack officer of eastern Siberia, presented to the Russian Government a plan for the subjugation of the Chukchee people. He was given permission to make the attempt, and forces were placed at his disposal for the purpose. He returned to Siberia, equipped two expeditions, one by land, the other by sea. His land forces were defeated in battle, Shestakof was killed, and the campaign ended in failure. The sea force sailed on a ship, the *St. Gabriel,* which Bering had built, and left Kamchatka on July 12, 1732. One Jacob Hens was in command, and Ivan Fedorof was his lieutenant, but through their illness, the navigation of the ship fell on Michael Spiridinovich Gvozdef, the geodesist of the expedition.

They sailed to the northeast, passed Cape Chukotski, and came to an island, presumably one of the Diomedes, where the natives opposed their landing; but at a second island (Little Diomede) they landed and saw land to the east. On August 21 they sailed eastward to the land, skirted the coast but were unable to go ashore, and voyaged to the southeast for five days when, on account of the shallowness of the water, they were compelled to stand offshore, so they sailed for Kamchatka. This is the first expedition that sighted the American mainland, and it is supposed, from the scant accounts of their voyage which are extant, that they coasted from near Cape Prince of Wales, southeast to the vicinity of St. Michael. The Diomede Islands were sometimes called Gvozdef's Islands by the Russians on account of this voyage.[7]

Bering had enemies at the Russian court who hated him as a foreigner, and who were jealous of his being the commander of Russian expeditions. They questioned the veracity of his records, and his journals were not fully accepted as authentic by many until Captain Cook verified the results in 1778. Bering answered their attacks and proposed to make further explorations to confirm his discoveries by reaching America. He also suggested other explorations and surveys.

In December, 1732, the Senate approved the plan for a second expedition, made Bering commander, and added other duties to those outlined by him. These included surveys of the Arctic coast and an expedition to Japan.

The first detachment of Bering's command left St. Petersburg in February, 1733; the others followed later. Bering was promoted to the rank of Captain-Commander and given supervision over all the different undertakings. Chirikof, promoted to Captain-Lieutenant,[8] and Spanberg,[9] also promoted to the same rank, were assigned to the task of assisting him. A scientific corps, equipped with libraries and instruments, accompanied the expedition.

Bering went to Tobolsk, built a boat for the first Arctic expedition and sent it down the Irtish River to the Arctic coast in May, 1734. He then went to Yakutsk where he built two boats, which he sent down the Lena in June, 1735, to the Arctic to make surveys there, then he went to Okhotsk.

The last stretch of the journey was the most difficult and trying. The freight was lined[10] up the swift mountain streams by men who waded in the rivers or followed the banks. It was then packed over the divide by horses and floated down the Urak River to Okhotsk. At one time more than a thousand men were employed. The hardships were extreme. Many were drowned, and some were frozen.

At Okhotsk the expedition for Japan was equipped and placed in charge of Spanberg. Bering then prepared for the American voyage. Ships were constructed from the timber in the forests, and in June, 1740, two vessels were ready for sea, named the *St. Peter* and the *St. Paul*. In September they left Okhotsk, rounded the lower point of Kamchatka, entered the Bay of Avacha, and landed in a small harbor on the north side, where they founded a town which they called Petropaulovsk, or the town of Peter and Paul.

On June 4 of the next year the ships sailed for America. Bering was on the *St. Peter* with a crew of seventy-seven men including Lieutenant Waxel, Shipmaster Khitrof, and the scientist, George Wilhelm Steller.[11] Chirikof was in command of the *St. Paul* with a crew of seventy-six men, including Marine Officers Chegatschof and Plautin, and the scientist, Louis Delisle de la Croyere.

They sailed eastward together, but on the night of the 19th the ships separated. Chirikof left Bering, sailed in a general east-northeasterly direction, and on the 15th of July sighted land near Cape Addington, on the west side of Prince of Wales Island. Drifting to the northwest, he entered a bay on the 17th, which his observations placed in 57° 15′ N. Lat., and which is supposed to be the Sitka harbor of today.[12]

Chirikof anchored his ship in the bay and sent Abraham Dementief, the mate, ashore with ten men armed with muskets and a small brass cannon, in the long boat. Several days passed and they did not return, so the boatswain, Sidor Savalief, went with three sailors in the remaining boat to recall them. Neither returned, but the next day two small boats with natives came out to the ships. These natives shouted some words in their own language, then returned to the shore.

After waiting a few days longer Chirikof gave up all hope for his men. He had no other boats with which to land and was compelled to set sail for Petropaulovsk. He went to the northwest, sighted high mountains near the entrance to Cook Inlet, turned south, passed along the east side of Kodiak Island, turned west along the Peninsula of Alaska. On September 4 he saw land, and on the 20th entered a bay where he met natives of the islands.

Chirikof and many of his men were sick with the scurvy so they pressed on with all possible speed for Avacha Bay, were fortunate enough to miss the storms which delayed the St. Peter, and on October 9 reached the port of Petropaulovsk. Twenty of the crew had died, and so many of the living were disabled by the disease that the pilot, Yelagin, was the only navigating officer able for duty. De la Croyere died on being brought to the fresh air on the deck of the ship.

In May of the following year Chirikof went to sea in search of Bering's ship, passed near the island on which it was wrecked, but not sighting it he returned to Avacha Bay, and from there went to St. Petersburg to make his report to the Government.

When Bering became separated from his consort he searched for Chirikof three days, then gave up the fruitless quest and took his course to the E. N. E. until about noon of July 16 when the lookout reported a high peak above a range of snow-covered mountains. This was Mt. St. Elias.

On the 19th he was close to the south point of Kayak Island, known as Cape St. Elias, with its sharp pinnacle rock offshore, called by the Russians a *kekoor*. He anchored between Kayak Island and Wingham Island, and he named Kayak as St. Elias Island in honor of the saint of the day.[13]

Khitrof explored and charted St. Elias Island while Steller searched on shore for objects of natural history and for evidences of human habitation. He collected some plants and found houses containing articles of household use, some of which he took on board the ship.

On the 21st Bering prepared to return. Steller and some of the ship's officers opposed him, but he was determined to sail. He was on a strange and dangerous coast, with scant provision and was twenty-five hundred miles from his base of supplies. He was wiser than he knew, for he was in one of the worst storm centers of Alaska. There is not a safe harbor within a hundred miles of his anchorage, and he knew nothing of the dangers of the long chain of reefs and rocks along the Aleutian Islands that stretched away between him and the coast of Kamchatka.

He stood to the westward; the rain fell incessantly, and his course was determined by soundings. He fortunately escaped the Sea Otter Rocks and other dangers almost in his track, skirted the eastern side of Kodiak Island, sighted a point which he called St. Hermogenes, drifted at night through Douglas Passage, and on August 2 discovered and named Tammanoi, or Foggy Island (Chirikof Island) as his officers placed it on their chart. On the first of August they saw two peaks on the mainland, and the next day discovered the Semidi Islands, and called one of them Endoiefski. On August 30 they landed on an island to bury Shumagin, the first one of the sailors who died of scurvy, and named the island for him. Bering was too ill of the same disease to leave his cabin, and from this time onward this dread scourge of the seas pursued them incessantly.

They sailed to the westward on September 6, but the delay cost them dearly. On the 24th they were struck by a storm and driven back to the southeast nearly three hundred miles into the Pacific Ocean. For seventeen days they were beaten and baffled by adverse winds off the south shore of the Aleutian Islands.[14] They then went on their course till November 4 when they saw land which they supposed to be Kamchatka.

A council of officers was called to decide whether they should land, or try to make Petropaulovsk. They were in a most deplorable condition. The storms of rain had changed

to sleet and snow which froze on the decks and tackle. The
rigging was rotting and breaking from the fastenings, and so
many seamen were sick of the scurvy that there were hardly
enough men to man the watches.[15] All who were able to
crawl dragged themselves to the cabin to hear the decision.
Bering advised making Avacha Bay at any cost, but Waxel
and Khitrof opposed him and decided to land. It was a fatal
decision for Bering.

Steller and Waxel went ashore to reconnoitre. They
found the land snow covered, with no wood save driftwood
from the sea. On the 8th they began to land the sick, some
of whom died on being brought to the air on the deck, and
others on reaching the land. Blue foxes thronged around
them in such numbers that with difficulty were they kept
from mangling the dead or from injuring those who were too
ill to protect themselves.[16] In the bank of a ravine, pits, or
caves, were dug. These were covered with driftwood and
canvas, and into these the sick were carried.

Bering was brought ashore, but rapidly grew weaker.
Proper food and care were not to be had, although all was
done that his unfortunate shipmates could do. On December
8 he died, and he was buried on the island which bears his
name, one of the Commander Group, which lies west of the
Aleutians. But poor Bering, lying in the pit, with the sand
rolling down on his feet as he died, could not know that his
memory would be perpetuated through the centuries in the
land he had discovered for the world.

The *St. Peter* lay at anchor in a curve of the eastern shore
of the island until a November storm drove her ashore, a total
wreck.

With the coming of the New Year the spirits of the survivors rose. There were no more deaths, and all busied themselves with some duty. Steller found the island a rich field
for investigations and to his stay we owe some most interesting material which has made his name known over the world
with a fame second only to that of the commander. The sea
otter were on land in droves. The fur seal abounded. There
was a multitude of foxes, and over sixty were killed in one
day. The great mammal, the rhytina, or sea cow, was found
there, and its flesh was one of the chief resources for food
during the winter.[17]

The following spring the survivors constructed a forty-foot boat from the wreckage of the ship, into which they loaded their baggage and the furs they had saved during the winter from the animals they slew, and they sailed away from the ill-starred spot on the 12th of August. On the 27th forty-six of the seventy-seven men who sailed out of Petropaulovsk the previous year, returned to that port and were greeted as though risen from the dead, for all hope of their surviving had long been abandoned.

The importance of the discoveries was not at once recognized. Russia did not publish the account of the voyage as did England when Vancouver and Cook sailed to these shores. The mainland of America, the country we call Alaska, had been reached for the first time. The first definite knowledge of the northern part of the Pacific Ocean was obtained. The basis for Russian claims to their possessions in America had been laid. The way was opened to the hunters and fur traders, the Russian *promishleniki,* who later swept along the coast and explored every bay and inlet until finally permanent settlements were established which completed the title of the Czar to his holdings in the colonies in America. When the news reached the other nations, which it tardily did, it spurred the Spanish and the English to new ventures in the North Pacific. Bering and Chirikof had outlined the headlands and islands from Sitka to Bering Island; they had broken the mystery of the unknown and blazed the way across three thousand miles of uncharted seas, more than sixty years before Lewis and Clark crossed the continent of North America.

2

THE INTEREST OF THE RUSSIAN GOVERNMENT IN THE newly discovered possessions seemed to vanish after the return of Bering's expedition. The coasts to the east would likely have been abandoned, as far as Russia was concerned, had it not been for the furs brought by the survivors of the voyage, among which were many skins of the rich, beautiful fur of the animal known as the sea otter, called by the Russians *bobri morski,* or sea beaver. Of these pelts nine hundred were brought to Petropaulovsk by the survivors of the *St. Peter* on their return from Bering Island. The best skins brought from thirty to forty rubles in Kamchatka, and at the great fur market at Kiachta more than twice that sum was realized, or an equivalent of from seventy-five to eighty dollars each.[1]

The skins that Bering's men threw into the little forty-foot boat among their baggage were worth nearly thirty thousand dollars at the port at which they landed. When the news reached the *promishleniki,* or fur hunters, of Siberia, who had been following the sable across Asia for a century for its fur, it caused an excitement second only to the fever for gold that more than a century and a half later drove the thousands to the mines of the Klondike.

The Russian furs of that time were generally sold in China, and beaver and other skins were even brought from Canada, transported through St. Petersburg, and sold to the Chinese. The convention called the Treaty of Kiachta, made between Russia and China, by which the ports of Kiachta and Zuru-chiaitu were opened for trade between the two nations, was made in 1728. The former of these two ports soon absorbed the greater part of the traffic. Through it were exported from Russia, furs and peltry, cloth, leather, hides, cattle, provisions, etc., while from China were imported silk and cotton, tea and porcelain, rice, rhubarb, etc., amounting in the aggregate to about three million rubles during 1777.[2] The trade was entirely through barter, as the Chinese would receive nothing but bullion silver, and Russia forbade the export of coin.

The town of Kiachta stood on the bank of a brook which marked the international boundary south of Irkutsk. Two posts were near the bank of the stream. One was the Russian fortress known as Kiachta, the other was the Chinese town of Miamatschin.[3] From there the great tea caravans wound over the hills and steppes to St. Petersburg (now Leningrad), for all the tea trade of the vast Russian Empire was at that time by land, it being believed that the delicate aroma of the herb was impaired by being carried by sea.

The furs from the Aleutian Islands and the Alaskan coasts went to Okhotsk and from there by pack trains, or caravans, to Kiachta, until the opening of the direct trade by sea with Canton in the early part of the nineteenth century. During the whole of the Russian occupation of Alaska certain furs were sent to China through this port.[4]

The furs of the Bering party and the reports of the abundance of the fur animals along the islands that they had discovered, opened such a possible source of profit that ships were at once fitted out for the trade. The hunters who had followed the fur animals across Siberia for their precious pelts now embarked on a new element in search of wealth. It was an adventurous profession, one that had taken them to the icebergs of the frozen ocean for the capture of the polar bear, and that had lured them along the borders of the Mongolian desert for the striped skin of the fierce Siberian tiger. Now they were to face new dangers on the waters of the eastern ocean on the small, badly constructed, poorly equipped vessels built of the materials to be had on the shores of the Sea of Okhotsk.

The profession was beset with dangers, but it offered fabulous profits to the successful adventurer. For a ship to return to port, after a year or two of absence, at the time of the glory of the trade, with a cargo of fur valued at a hundred thousand rubles was not at all unusual. The *Fish*, owned by Trapeznikof, during 1757 brought no less than 354,900 rubles in value, and among the cargo were 4,573 sea otter, 1,493 silver fox, 2,115 cross fox, and 1,278 red fox. At the prices of the present day this cargo would be valued at no less than $2,500,000.

The *promishleniki* were to that country what the mountain men and traders of the West, the Joe Meeks and the Manuel Lisas, were to our frontiers. Before them the wild life disappeared as it did before our hunters and trappers.[5] The Aleutian natives soon found that the only protection an aboriginal people have against the avarice and lust of civilized man is absolute poverty, both of person and property. The hunters opened the way to settlement of the country; but for them it might have remained unknown for another century.

As the news of the fur from the islands passed from mouth to mouth among the *promishleniki* scattered through the forests of Siberia, everyone was fired with a desire to go to the great eastern ocean, to embark on its waters, and to reach an island where such a source of wealth lay waiting for the taking. From far and near they toiled toward the sea, over the steppes and through the passes of the mountains, until they came out from the dark, sombre evergreen forest that fringed the shore of the Sea of Okhotsk and sought a craft on which to ship for the voyage. Merchants of Moscow, and merchants of Irkutsk and of Rilsk invested their capital in financing ventures in that far distant trade. When the wealthy fur dealers of St. Louis planned their ventures in the early part of the last century as far as to the Rocky Mountains, or to the headwaters of the Snake River, they felt that they were reaching out to distant lands, but compared to the far-reaching projects of the Siberian traders they were dealing near at home.

Pack trains laden with cordage and ships' stores, with material and provisions, toiled over the mountains. In the edge of the forest on the Sea of Okhotsk and along the Kamchatka Peninsula men were felling the trees in the forest and hewing them into timbers and planking. As the ragged, footsore hunters reached the sea they clamored to sign for the voyage, taking as their pay a share in the results of the venture.

Poorly built, scantily equipped ships, sometimes with the timbers lashed with withes, set out upon the sea, steered for Bering Island to lay in a store of the meat of the sea cow for food, and the next year, coasting from island to island, they worked to the eastward on the hunt for fur.

The first who sailed was Sergeant Emelian Basof, in 1743 in the sewed boat, or *shitik*,[6] *Kapitan*, and who made three voyages for which he was well paid, although he went no farther than to Bering Island. On one of these he took 1,600 sea otter, and the whole cargo was worth 112,000 rubles.[7]

Michael Nevodchikof, a silversmith who was with Bering on his last voyage, sailed to a group of small islands, probably the ones now known as the Near Islands.[8] The name is likely derived from their proximity to the Siberian coast, yet the language was unknown to the Russians or to their Kamchatkan interpreter. Nevodchikof and his crew during their stay abused the islanders, killed some of them, thus initiating the career of rapine that long continued,[9] then left for Kamchatka and were wrecked on Kraginski Island, where twelve men were drowned.

Serebrennikof sent a ship in 1753 that discovered a new group, probably the Rat Islands, and there the vessel was wrecked.[10] The crew reached the shore and from the wreckage during the next year they constructed a new boat and in it reached Kamchatka. Trapeznikof sent out the *shitik St. Nicholas,* which went to the east to still another island, and returned with a cargo valued at 187,268 rubles. Two years later Andrean Tolstykh visited some of the Aleutian Islands and on his return gave the most accurate account of them yet received. Other adventurers sailed out on the eastern ocean, and met with varying results. Stephen Glottof went as far as to the Fox Islands in 1759 and made the first exploration of that group. Gavril Pushkaref soon after sailed to the mainland of the Peninsula of Alaska, called *Alaksu* by the natives, and was well received by the inhabitants until he attempted to seize some girls when a fight ensued in which several Russians were killed.[11] In retaliation the Russians killed some of the hostages whom they had exacted from the natives, then sailed from Umnak, taking with them six men and twenty-five girls. At a landing they sent some of the girls on shore to pick berries; two ran away, one was killed, some of the rest drowned themselves; then, in order to remove witnesses to the tragedy, Pushkaref threw all the rest into the sea, with the exception of two boys. After his arrival in Siberia a rumor of the outrage leaked out which reached the authorities. An investigation was had, with the result that only a warning was issued that such outrages would not be tolerated.[12]

Andrean Tolstykh went to the islands in 1760, explored a group, and on his return wrote a description of them, from which they became known as the Andreanof Islands.[13]

Thus voyage by voyage the hunters and traders, the *promishleniki,* as they were known, sought out and made known the different units of the long chain of the Aleutians until they reached the continent of America.

During the earlier years they went to the Commander Islands the first season, killed the sea cow and prepared its meat for food, dried or buccaned it much as did the buccaneers of the Spanish Main at the same period of history, then fared forth upon the defenseless islanders much as Morgan and his pirates fell upon the peoples along the shores of the Caribbean Sea. They had no knowledge of navigation, coasted from island to island, sometimes losing their way and sailing far out to sea through mistaking the side on which land lay. Golofnin in his writings records an instance of a ship sailing so far to the south that the pitch melted in the seams before they turned north again and found the chain of islands. They took no observations, made no surveys, and the world received little knowledge of their voyage beyond the record of the furs taken at the port of arrival on their return.

A tribute (called *yassak)* of one tenth of the fur was exacted by the Russian Government during the early years of the trade from all the subjugated tribes. It was collected by Cossacks, one of whom went on each ship for that purpose. This was not always correctly accounted for, and it was so often used as an excuse for abuses that the Emperor later ordered it discontinued.[14]

On landing at a village hostages were exacted from the natives, generally the wives and daughters of the principal men; the men were given fox traps, *kleptzi,* with which to go out for furs. Then the Russian *promishleniki* lived the winter in the enjoyment of the primitive pleasures of a petty sultan of a barbarian harem. In the spring the furs were received from the trappers. If enough were not produced by the natives to satisfy the demand of the exacting masters, death was dealt out with as little compunction as it would be to any of the hunted animals. The traps were taken in, a few beads were given to the women; then sail was set for Kamchatka, and the ship and crew disappeared into the misty distance to the westward. A year or so later another ship came and repeated the abuses until the Aleuts, long-suffering, patient, and merry-natured though they were, became embittered under the wrongs. They conspired to drive the invaders from their soil, and a confederation against the Russians seems to have been formed from the Peninsula of Alaska to Umnak Island.

3

The Rebellion of the Aleuts

FIVE RUSSIAN SHIPS SAILED IN 1762 TO THE *Lyssie Ostrova*, or Fox Islands, so named from the multitudes of black, red, and cross foxes found there at the time of their discovery. Of these ships but one returned to Kamchatka; the others, with their crews, fell into the hands of the outraged Aleuts and were destroyed by them.

One of these, the *Andrean and Natalie*, Stephen Glottof, master, made one of the most remarkable voyages of the time, going east past the Fox Islands and the Alaska Peninsula as far as to the hitherto unvisited island now known as Kodiak.[1] The language was strange, differing from that of the Aleuts, but communication was had through an Aleut boy who had been in captivity among the Kodiaks. The natives were more warlike than the Aleuts. The ship was soon attacked by war parties that attempted to destroy it by fire, approaching under cover of shields or breastworks which protected them from the musketry of the Russians. They were finally defeated in a hand-to-hand battle with a sally party from the vessel and withdrew to the hills. The Russians feared to go far from their ship during the winter and consequently suffered greatly from inaction and scurvy.

There is a tradition among the Kodiak Islanders of a ship coming to the south side of the island, near Alitak, and which is presumably this vessel. They tell that the natives went to the Russians to trade furs for beads and other goods, and were there set upon and many of them killed while all of their furs were taken from them.[2]

In the spring Glottof sailed westward to Umnak Island to trade in the region he had formerly visited.

During Glottof's voyage to the eastward the other ships had gone into winter quarters. The *Holy Trinity*, under Ivan Korovin, anchored near Kosheega at the west side of Unalaska Island, Medvedef's ship went to the north side of

Umnak, while Alexei Drushinin with the *Zacharias and Elizabeth* discovered the harbor of Unalaska, sailed up to the head to what is known as Captains Harbor, where he hauled his ship ashore. The fourth boat went farther to the east to Isanotski Strait.

At Captains Harbor the natives appeared to be friendly, brought furs to trade, told where the other ships were located, and offered hostages as was usually exacted by the Russians; so Drushinin sent out parties, one to Kalekhta, another to Biorka, where he later went in person. In October an attack was made on the party remaining at the ship, the Aleuts falling on the Russians with knives and spears while they were untying packages of furs, and every man was murdered. The creek near which the boat lay was long known as *Ubienna,* or Massacre Creek.[3] At Biorka, on the same day, the Aleuts attacked the party and killed all but five Russians. Gregory Shavarin, with four companions, reached a *barabara,* or underground hut, where they kept the enemy at bay for four days, then secured a *bidar*[4] and went to Kalekhta, only to find that the Russians at that place had met the fate of their unfortunate companions. They then went to Captains Harbor where they found all were dead at the ship, so they took such articles as they could use from the remaining stores and went to the mountains above the bay where they remained for over nine months. In August or September of the next year a friendly Aleut told them that Korovin's ship was near Makushin Bay. They made a small *bidar* from the leathern sacks in which provisions had been stored and made their way to Makushin where they went on board the *Holy Trinity.*

Korovin reached Kosheega on August 15 after leaving Kamchatka, where he anchored but later moved his ship to Makushin, took hostages from the natives, and went into winter quarters. The destruction of his boat was planned by the Aleuts at the same time as the attacks were made on the other ships but he was warned by a friendly Aleut and successfully defended his ship although he was so harassed that he was compelled to move offshore. Confined to the ship, they suffered from scurvy and lack of food, which was fast weakening them when the survivors of Drushinin's ship arrived. Then all sailed for Umnak to join Medvedef but were wrecked on the shore of that island; the crew escaped the sea to be attacked by the Aleuts, when two Russians and three of their hostages were killed, while the other hostages escaped. Nearly all the Russians were wounded and in desperate straits, but drove away the assailants, constructed a small *bidar* and continued their search for Medvedef's vessel, which they expected to find on the north side of Umnak. After ten days' search they found the remains of a ship that had been burned, an empty Russian dwelling, and twenty dead men, among them Medvedef. With heavy hearts they buried the dead, then looked about them for means of escape from their perilous situation, when, almost providentially it seemed to them, Glottof's ship hove in sight on his return from Kodiak.

Sixty years after, many details of the destruction of the ships were gathered by Father Veniaminof, who was the priest at Unalaska for a number of years. Out of the traditions of the past he learned that at the boat which went on the north side of Umnak there was a *peredovchik* named Jacob who was so strong that with one hand he could raise an anchor. Jacob abused the Aleuts, even killing some of them. When the boat was attacked they assigned five men to kill Jacob, but by his unusual strength he pulled a spear from one of his assailants, killed some of them, and burst through the men around him, but, being mortally wounded, he fell dead beside the ship. Veniaminof also tells that the crew of the ship in Isanotski Strait heard that the natives contemplated hostilities and they forestalled the expected trouble by destroying the native villages and killing the people. They were successful at four villages but at the fifth they were defeated, and retreated to their ship, where, harassed by the natives and weakened by scurvy, they passed the winter. In the spring they fell an easy prey to the enemy and all were killed. Neither the name of the ship or of the master is known.[5]

Ivan Solovief, one of the navigators and traders who plied along the islands who heard of the fate of the unfortunate Medvedef and his companions, took on himself the mission of revenge and proceeded to wreak his vengeance on the islanders without discrimination between innocent and guilty. Hearing that three hundred natives were fortified in a village, he advanced against them with his *promishleniki,* fought them until their arrows were exhausted, then he placed gunpowder in the walls of their *barabaras* and blew up the structures, and with muskets and cutlasses killed the survivors who crouched amidst the ruins of their homes.[6] Under the pretext of avenging the death of his countrymen he destroyed their villages and murdered the natives, nearly without exception, on the southern side of Umnak, as well as Samalga and the Islands of Four Mountains. Besides this he destroyed two *bidars* of Unimak Aleuts who were on the way to visit their relatives, and finally he found the inhabitants of several villages assembled on Egg Island and killed all, even to the women and children.

Solovief was not the only butcher who made the motive of revenge an excuse for licentious cruelty, for Russians on another ship destroyed four large villages on Unimak, keeping only the young women, with a few young men for slaves. This vessel was probably commanded by Glottof, who is reputed by some to have been as bloody as Solovief.

It is told of Solovief that he at one time tied a dozen Aleuts together in a row to use them for a target and to see how far a musket ball would penetrate their bodies. The bullet is said to have stopped in the body of the ninth man.[7] He executed his purpose in as relentless and bloody a manner as Judge Jeffreys carried out the Bloody Assizes in Merrie England. For generations the Aleut mothers are said to have frightened their children to silence with the name of Solovief, and he so completely crushed the spirit of the islanders that they never after made any resistance to wrongs but became a people changed in nature and disposition, from a merry, cheerful people to a gloomy and dejected race.

It is a strange coincidence that in the same year in which the Aleuts arose against their oppressors, and in their desperation flung themselves against the Russians, Pontiac, almost at the other end of the continent, was trying to stay the flood that was overwhelming his people.

4

Later Russian Voyages

THE FAME OF THE FUR COUNTRY AND THE SHEEN OF THE pelts of the lustrous black foxes of the islands of the eastern ocean reached St. Petersburg, so when a present of a royal robe of the velvety skins was presented by the merchants to the Czarina she was delighted and her interest was excited to know more of that far dominion. She asked that some of the merchants come to the capital in person, so Vasili Shilof came, was granted an audience at court, presented a map of the islands, informed her of the manner of conducting the trade, and gave a glowing account of the riches to be realized there.

To make official investigations the Empress sent Lieutenant Synd of the Royal Navy on an expedition in 1764. He sailed from Okhotsk in the *St. Catherine*, seems to have touched at St. Paul Island, laid down and named St. Matthew Island on his chart, then continued to near the present site of Nome, where he claims to have made a landing. His map is badly distorted, the latitude and longitude incorrect, and his results are of small value, for he added little to the existing knowledge of the new lands.[1]

The Empress ordered another expedition, and two ships, one under Captain-Lieutenant Peter Kumich Krenetzin, the other commanded by Lieutenant Michael Levashef, sailed in June, 1768, after much ill fortune, the smallpox in Kamchatka delaying the departure, and shipwreck at Okhotsk adding to their difficulties. Krenetzin wintered on Unimak Island at Isanotski Strait, while Levashef made his winter quarters at Unalaska in Captain Harbor, so named because of his stay. The next year they returned to Kamchatka after accomplishing little. Ill fortune pursued them to the end, for Krenetzin was drowned while crossing the Kamchatka River in a small boat.[2]

Along the coast of the islands sailed an expedition in 1771 that was strange enough to excite comment even in those

days of rash undertakings. Among the varied crowd of
exiles who were banished to Siberia and reached even the
farther coasts of the Pacific, was one Maurice August
Benyowski, a Polish nobleman, who had been sent to Siberia
for political reasons. He was one of the courtly, polished,
reckless adventurers, daring in action, and as boastful as
daring, who would have been a fit subject for the pen of a
Dumas. He planned a conspiracy at Bolscheretsk, organized
a secret society of adventurers as desperate as himself, overpowered the authorities, killed the Commandant, seized a
ship, and sailed out on the Pacific. The story of the venture is
a volume in itself, but it relates to Alaska in but a limited
way, for he only touched at Bering Island, landed on Kodiak
Island, a thousand miles to the east, then touched at a few
points on his return to the Asiatic shores along the China
coast. His exploits, however, put a fear of pirates into the
hearts of the Russian colonists that was not removed for
many years.[3]

Under the persistent hunting by the natives and Russians
the fur animals were decreasing in many localities and new
grounds must continually be sought. Instead of a voyage
a year to the Commander Islands, yielding a cargo valued at
a hundred thousand rubles, they were now compelled to
equip for a voyage of from three to seven years, with a consequently greater expense. This led to the formation of
companies. A merchant would organize a company, divide
the capital into shares, retain the majority for himself, sell
most of the remainder, and put out a few shares to special
persons, as high government officials, the Church, the tribute
gatherer, the shipmaster, or other who might distinguish
himself in the service of the expedition, thus propitiating all
the powers that might bring success. The gratuitously distributed shares were termed *dry shares*.[4]

A few among these voyages will suffice for a view of the
whole.[5] The merchant, Kolodilof, equipped a ship in 1772,
and sent her out under Dmitri Polutof, who sailed to Unalaska, traded for two years, then went to Kodiak, where he
found the natives hostile, so returned to Atka, then later to
Kamchatka. Potap Zaikof sailed from Okhotsk, September
22, 1772, in the *St. Vladimir*, went to Isanotski Strait, traded
on the Alaska Peninsula and the adjacent islands, made sur-

veys, and after seven years returned to Okhotsk with a cargo valued at over three hundred thousand rubles.[6]

Zaikof was at Unalaska at the time Captain Cook landed there in 1778, when he heard of Prince William Sound with its wealth of furs and determined to visit this part of the mainland. Three vessels went under his leadership in 1783, the *St. Alexei,* in command of Eustrate Delaref; the *St. Michael,* under Polutof; and the *Alexander Nevski,* of which Zaikof was the master. They went first to the vicinity of Kayak Island, and on August 18 the *bidarshik* (canoemaker), Nagaief, returned from an expedition along the mainland to report the discovery of a large river, the Copper River of today, and that he had ascended it for some distance.

The ships then entered Prince William Sound, where they established winter quarters and sent out hunting and trading parties. The sound was called the Chugach Gulf by the Russians, the native name, and the mountains above it still retain the name of the Chugach Mountains. The natives were hostile, probably because of the conduct of some of the trading parties; there were numerous encounters in which the Chugaches held their own with at least equal success with the invaders, and the trading was not successful. The ravages of the scurvy, combined with the losses in the battles with the natives, reached the number of nearly half the crews of the ships before spring, so the Russians returned to the Aleutian Islands.[7]

The depletion of the fur animals of the Aleutian Chain led to the discovery of the Pribilof Group, the Seal Islands they are often called, in 1786. Gerassim Pribilof, one of the navigators of the Lebedef-Lastochkin Company had been cruising along the Aleutian Islands in the ship *St. George,* with poor success. He, in common with others, noted the multitude of seals that went north through the passes of the Aleutians and returned with their young in the fall of the year. There was also a tradition of a native, Enghadeer, who had been cast away on an island to the north, and who on his return described the multitudes of sea animals he saw there. Pribilof believed that there must be land to the north and went in search of it. He was fortunate enough to sail almost directly to the island which[8] he named St. George, after his ship, and landed there on June 12, 1786.

He left a party of hunters on shore to kill fur animals during the winter, then sailed his ship to the Andreanof Islands, as there was no safe harbor on St. George. On June 29 of the next year the hunters saw land to the northwest, and as it was the Day of the Saints Peter and Paul the new discovery was named after them, but the name has since been shortened to St. Paul Island. Efim Popof, the *peredovchik,* at once made his way to the new discovery in a *bidarka.*[9]

These islands were uninhabited by man, but there were multitudes of sea otters, walruses, foxes, sea lions, and especially seals, all of which had been undisturbed for ages and had practically no fear of man. The Arctic, or white, fox was so tame that they might be caught with the hands. Literally millions of seals were on the rookeries, and the Russians killed until they were satiated with the slaughter. In a small bay on the west side of St. Paul Island were found a sword hilt, a clay tobacco pipe, and the remains of a fire, indicating the visit of Europeans at some time, probably relics of the voyage of Lieutenant Snyd.

5

The First Russian Colony in America

GRIGORII IVANOVICH SHELEKOF, A MERCHANT OF RILSK, became interested in the trade of the Kurile Islands, later fitted out a ship for the Aleutian trade in 1777, and extending his operations in company with Solovief and others sent out the *Barfolomei i Barnabas* to the islands. These ventures were successful, and he invested in different companies, owning stock in the Lebedef-Lastochkin Company when their navigator, Pribilof, discovered the Seal Islands. He saw the declining condition of the fur trade and noted the depletion of the finest hunting grounds, in consequence of which he formed the plan of a permanent settlement on the islands and of the organization of the business on a permanent basis.

To accomplish these objects he founded the Shelekof-Golikof Company in 1783. The company fitted out three ships that put to sea August 16 of that year with a total of 192 men on board. Natalie Shelekof, wife of the adventurous merchant, was on board the ship *Three Saints,* with her husband, the first white woman to sail these northern seas. She was a woman of rare courage and ability, a worthy partner of her distinguished mate, and was later specially honored by order of the Empress.

The ships became separated. The *Three Saints* and the *St. Simeon* wintered on Bering Island; from there in the following spring they sailed eastward and landed on Kodiak Island. The third ship met many disasters and did not arrive until two years later.

At Three Saints Bay, so named by Shelekof in honor of his ship, in the southeastern part of Kodiak Island, a place now almost forgottten by geographers, the first Russian colony in America was planted in August, 1784. Storehouses, offices, and dwellings were soon erected for a factory, as such a post is often termed in the trading country, all fortified in a rude fashion against attacks by the natives. Conciliatory messages were sent out to the inhabitants, who were invited

Печ. Дарлингъ.

Рис. Смирновъ.

GRIGORII IVANOVICH SHELEKOF
First organizer of the fur trade in Alaska under Russian rule.

to come to the settlement to trade. A defiant answer was returned, so Shelekof determined to teach them a lesson of the Russian power. A large number were gathered together on a high, detached rock, off a headland, called a *kekoor* by the Russians, probably a native name, where they fancied themselves secure. Shelekof surrounded them with boats and demanded a surrender. On their refusal he swept the rock with grapeshot from his cannon, and the terrified natives, panic-stricken at the sound of the artillery and its horrible effect, plunged headlong into the sea, where many of them drowned, and the others were captured by the Russians and held as hostages.[1]

Exploring parties were then sent out to Cook Inlet, to Prince William Sound, and to the western side of the island, where the strait was discovered which now bears the name of the founder of the colony. Trading stations were placed at Cook Inlet, Afognak, Karluk, and other places.[2] Karluk was occupied by reason of its wonderful fishing, the greatest red salmon stream in the world for many years, in later times the site of seven great canneries, where the *yukali*, or fish dried without salt by the natives for food, was prepared for the settlement.

Shelekof completed the organization of the colony, placed a *peredovchik*, or leader of hunters, named Samoilof, in charge of the post, then returned to Siberia, leaving Three Saints on May 22, 1786. His instructions to Samoilof show able foresight and have the appearance of fairness and justice toward the native inhabitants. His plans for the future were ambitious and far reaching, contemplating the extension of the posts to the east and southeast even as far as to the present coasts of Oregon and California, the region then known as New Albion.[3]

He landed at Petropaulovsk, hurried on to Russia by dog-sled and horse sleighs, going around the Sea of Okhotsk and across Siberia in winter, for he had important matters to accomplish: the combining of the fur companies into one corporation, the procuring from the Government of the exclusive rights to the trade in the possessions in America, the extension of the Russian dominion, and first of all, the selection of a competent agent for directing his colonies. During his absence in the colony, his partner, Golikof, had been occupied with advancing the interests of the company with the Empress by presenting her with a chart of the islands, outlining the plan with special emphasis on the advantages to be derived by the empire through the settlement of the new domain. Upon his reaching St. Petersburg, both Shelekof and Golikof were granted an audience by the Empress, and decorations for distinguished service were presented to them. The collection of tribute was discontinued, and soon after a ukase was issued granting them exclusive rights to the trade of the country actually occupied by them.

The cries of the Aleuts against the abuses inflicted on them by the traders also faintly reached the ears of the Empress across the nearly ten thousand miles of intervening land and sea. In 1787 she issued two orders in reference to these injustices, denouncing the practices and warning all navigators and traders against a repetition of the acts.[4] The situation was such that it had given rise to the saying: "Heaven is high and the Czar is far away."

The Empress desired more information about the distant lands and sent Joseph Billings, an Englishman who had been with Cook on his last voyage, in the ship, *Glory of Russia* on "A Secret Geographical and Astronomical Expedition," to those shores.[5] Billings sailed from Okhotsk in September of 1788, but shipwreck and other delays consumed nearly two years. From Petropaulovsk he passed along the Aleutian Islands, made a landing at Unalaska, and of the traders at that place, Mr. Sauer, the secretary of the expedition, says: "These people lord it over the inhabitants with more despotism than generally falls to the lot of princes, keeping the islanders in a state of abject slavery." The ship reached Three Saints, June 20, 1790. The conditions there were more agreeable than in the other places visited. The garrison consisted of about fifty Russians, including the officers of the company and the tribute gatherer, Ismailof. Two vessels were hauled out near the water, armed and well guarded against attacks of the natives.

The first marriage ceremony according to the rites of civilization was performed by the priest from the ship, a Russian being united with one of the native women. Home life was beginning to be enjoyed in the colony, for Sauer mentions that: "Several of the Russians have their wives and

THE HARBOR AT THREE SAINTS
From Sauer-Billings Expedition.

children with them, and keep gardens of cabbage and potatoes, with cows and goats." The beginnings of agriculture
were being made in the new domain.[6]

From Three Saints, Billings went to Prince William
Sound,[7] then to Kayak Island, afterwards returning to Petropaulovsk, where he wintered in 1791-2. A small boat, the
Black Eagle, had been built as a consort, and both ships sailed
for Unalaska, where they passed the next winter. Scurvy
afflicted them grievously, from which many of the crew died.
They then sailed to the Siberian shore, where Billings landed
for an overland expedition in Siberia, and returned to Kamchatka, having accomplished but little, although Lieutenant
Sarychef, one of the officers, was acquiring a knowledge of
the northern ocean which later enabled him to publish the
first atlas of those waters.[8]

Eustrate Delaref,[9] a Greek who had been at Unalaska for
a number of years, and who had been to Prince William
Sound in 1781 with the first Russian ships in those waters,
took charge of the colony in 1788. To combat the British
traders who were encroaching on the hunting grounds, and to
seek for new fields for fur gathering, Delaref dispatched the
navigator, Bocharof, on the ship *Three Saints,* to the eastward
in 1788, and he visited Middleton Island, Prince William
Sound, Yakutat, and Lituya Bay.[10]

The traders and hunters of the Lebedef Company came
into the port on the ship *St. Paul* in 1786, and asked to be
directed to the sea-otter grounds. In order to get rid of the
unwelcome visitors as easily as possible they were advised to go
to Cook Inlet, where they went and placed a post at the
Kisselof River.[11] A more ill-advised suggestion could hardly
have been given to them, for the rival company took all the
trade of the Inlet from the Shelekof Company and soon became a grievous thorn in the side of the Kodiak colony.
Meanwhile the people of Three Saints with anxiety awaited
the arrival of the new manager who was to be sent by
Shelekof.

When Shelekof left Three Saints his mind was filled with
a great plan for vast Russian dominion in the New World. It
covered, first, the organizing of all the fur trade of the northwest coast of America under the one great company, of
which he was to be the head. Then, as a result of this, the

establishing of the rule of the Fatherland over the shores of the Pacific from California to the Arctic.

The era of exploration had nearly passed. The shore lines from the Spanish possessions to the line of the ice pack of the Arctic Ocean had been vaguely outlined; it only remained to fill in the few scattering intervals.

The time of ruthless outrages on the natives and the unbridled grasping for the furs by the lawless *promishleniki* was nearing the end. Until Shelekof came no permanent plan had been outlined, no stable settlement had been made. It had been a reckless scramble for the richest gathering places of the fur animals, a place where the fairest maidens could be had for the harems, while the husbands and brothers brought in the pelts of fox and sea otter with hearts filled with rancor and impotent rage.

In the future was to be colonization, of extension of posts and dominion, to the east and south, the conquering of fierce, wild tribes, and the combating of strong forces that were reaching out from the eastward for the rich fur trade of the northwest coast of America. Vast distances must be crossed, great natural obstacles overcome, fierce and hostile enemies vanquished, all to be done at a far distance from the base of supplies, with meagre equipment and supplies, and with few, inferior, and turbulent men. It was a task to daunt the most fearless spirit, but a man was coming who rose to meet the emergency.

6

Other Nations on the Northwest Coast of America

OTHER EUROPEAN NATIONS BEGAN TO TAKE NOTICE OF what Russia was doing in the distant regions of the North. The Russian Government did not give the publicity to the results of the voyages of Bering and others that were made in the Pacific that properly should have belonged to them, yet the truth slowly filtered through to the world.[1] The Spanish at that time claimed the whole western shore of the continent as her special possession, relying perhaps on the papal bull that gave North America to Spain, and soon they made preparations to extend their discoveries and surveys northward from Mexico. Their most northerly accurate exploration had been made by Vizcaino in 1603. In 1769 they sent colonists to San Diego and Monterey, and they established a base for marine operations at San Blas on the Gulf of California.

The first Spanish expedition for northern waters sailed January 24, 1774, under command of Juan Perez, in the ship *Santiago*. On July 18 he sighted land in 54° N. Lat., approached the shore but found no safe anchorage, and to the headland at the northwest of what is now Graham Island he gave the name of Santa Marguerita. Northward he saw land, now known as Prince of Wales Island, Alaska, and called it Santa Maria Magdalena. He fell into difficulties in the violent tide rips off the cape. His vessel almost capsized in the powerful currents, and these perils of the sea cooled his ardor until he turned southward without making further discoveries.[2]

Two vessels, the ship *Santiago*, and a small schooner but thirty-six feet in length, the *Sonora*, were sent out in March of the next year. Lieutenant Juan Francisco de la Bodega y Quadra commanded the schooner, and his pilot was Antonio Maurelle. Off the coast of what is now Washington a storm struck the ships, the commander of the *Santiago* turned back to port, but the *Sonora* under the intrepid Quadra kept her northward course until land was sighted on August 16 near what is now Sitka, and a mountain was named as Mt. San Jacinto,[3] which is described so particularly in the account of the voyage as to leave no doubt that it was Mt. Edgecumbe. Quadra anchored in Krestof Bay on the following day,[4] later sailed farther north, visited a port, probably Bay of Islands, or Salisbury Sound, on the 21st reached 57° 57' N. Lat., and was then compelled to return on account of the ravages of the old enemy of the sailor, the scurvy. On his way south he entered and named Bucareli Bay in Prince of Wales Island.

The English, always interested in the far regions of the earth and desirous of extending their dominion, could not, with inaction, long pass by the progress of the Russians on the western ocean. A settlement on that coast would interfere with her westward development in Canada, and there was the unsolved question of a northeast passage from the Pacific to the Atlantic or to Hudson Bay.

Captain James Cook, the great mariner, fresh from his service before Quebec under Wolfe, had been sent to the southern seas for his famous voyages of discovery, and was now called for his third and last voyage to go to the northern Pacific Ocean. He sailed from Plymouth, England, July 12, 1776, in the ship *Resolution*, accompanied by the *Discovery*[5]. On his way he discovered the Sandwich Islands (Hawaiian), and entered Nootka Sound, which had been discovered by Perez.

Cook reached the Alaskan coast on May 1, 1778, passed and named Mt. Edgecumbe,[6] sighted and named Mt. Fairweather, and designated Yakutat Bay as Bering Bay, supposing it to have been the anchoring place of that navigator.[7] He landed on Kayak Island, which he named Kayes Island,[8] discovered and named Prince William Sound, entered Cook Inlet, explored it to the head, hoping it might prove to be the long-sought northeast passage, but meeting with disappointment he named it the River Turnagain.[9] He then sailed southwest, passed through Unalga Strait, entered a bay called Samghanooda, now English Bay, in Unalaska Island, turned northeasterly to Bristol Bay, which he named in honor of the Earl of Bristol, then went north to the Arctic Ocean. At Icy Cape his way was barred by the Arctic ice pack, so he retraced his track, entered Norton Sound, then went to

Unalaska Island, where he beached his vessel for repairs. Russian traders from the vessel lying in the harbor of Unalaska visited Cook. The commanders compared charts, exchanged courtesies as well as possible under the difficult conditions of the different languages, each informing the other of his explorations. Cook went to the Sandwich Islands for the winter, where he was killed by the natives on February 14, 1779.[10]

Captain Clerke took command of the expedition, went back to the Arctic Ocean in July of the next year, but the ice pack again barred their way. They then began their return voyage for England by the way of the Cape of Good Hope. The crew sold the furs obtained in Alaska for about ten thousand dollars in the Chinese ports, an astonishing amount of wealth for the sailors to receive, which almost caused a mutiny on board the ships, the seamen threatening to desert in order to return to the land of furs. When they reached England they told their story of easy profits and spread a desire to equip expeditions to the Ultima Thule of the far west.

The Spanish again essayed a voyage of discovery in 1779, sending two ships, the *Princesa,* under Captain Ignacio Arteaga, and the *Favorita,* in command of Quadra. They reached Bucareli Bay May 2, made surveys, and refitted the ships,[11] then sailed to Prince William Sound, and from there to Cook Inlet, where they landed on a small island and took possession for the King of Spain with elaborate ceremonies. On August 7 they departed for Mexico. Like the Russians, the Spaniards concealed the results of the voyages in their archives where they lay unpublished for years.[12] The interest of the Spanish was easily dulled, and it was a decade before they again visited the North, although they later made a settlement at Nootka Sound.

The French Government took an interest in the new region, instructing Jean Francois Galoup de LaPerouse, who was conducting an official exploring expedition in the Pacific with the ships *Astrolabe* and *Boussole,* to continue his work to parts of the northwest coast which had not been examined by Cook. On June 3, 1786, he came in sight of Mt. St. Elias, attempted to enter Yakutat Bay, but failing in his purpose he went to the bay now known as Lituya, where he anchored on July 3 and named it Port des Francais, or Frenchmans Bay. It was a disastrous discovery for him, for on the survey of the bay the falling tide swept two of his boats into the breakers where they were swamped and the crews drowned. A third boat escaped and brought the ill-starred tidings to the commander, who, in memory of his men, erected a monument on the island in the entrance and called it Cenotaph Island, then departed for the south. He afterward went to Petropaulovsk, sent his journals to Paris across Siberia, and turned southward to the southern seas, touched at Botany Bay, and from that time all trace of the distinguished Frenchman was for years lost, for both ships vanished among the maze of coral reefs of the southern ocean.[13] Some of the wreckage was later recovered, but nothing more is known of the fate of the mariners.

The story of the fur and the profits to be had in dealing with the unsophisticated inhabitants of the northern wilds reached the traders of France. Etienne Marchand, in the ship *Solide,* entered Sitka Sound on August 12, 1791, anchored his ship in Krestof Bay, calling it *Tchinkitinay,* a name derived from the natives, to trade with the Sitkas. He was not fortunate in his bargaining, for other traders had been there before him. In the ears of one young man he saw two copper coins of Massachusetts worn as pendants, showing that the Yankee traders had preceded him. The natives had evidently profited by experience and had learned to drive a sharp bargain, for he says on leaving: "The modern Hebrew would perhaps have little to teach to these savages."[14]

The sailors of Cook's expedition told tales that fired the adventurers of England with desire to participate in the lucrative and alluring trade for the soft-furred peltry. To promote an expedition to that sea involved some intrigue, for the monopoly of the business by the way of the Cape of Good Hope had been given to the East India Company, while the South Seas Company controlled the trade by way of Cape Horn. The ships of other companies that attempted to pass into the Pacific were in danger of seizure and confiscation, which caused the ventures to be fitted out under the flag of some other nation, as the Portuguese, or under special license from the corporations holding the charters for the trade.

The ships *Captain Cook* and *Experiment* came to Prince William Sound in 1786, but the commander of neither of these added anything to the existing knowledge of the country. Captain Nathaniel Portlock, in the ship *King George,* and Captain George Dixon, in the ship *Queen Charlotte,* both belonging to the King George Sound Company, reached Cook Inlet the same year, sailing under the flag of the East India Company.[15] They were piloted into Port Graham by the Russian hunters; there they traded with the natives and made surveys of the harbor, after which they went to Prince William Sound, but failed to make the entrance and went to the Sandwich Islands for the winter, returning in April of the next year. They anchored in Port Chalmers, there learning of the miserable plight of the crew of the ship *Nootka,* who were in a small bay farther up the sound, they sent assistance in the way of men and supplies to the unfortunate voyagers. Captain Dixon went to Yakutat Bay, visited Sitka Sound and called it Norfolk Sound, a name by which it had sometimes been known, then went to Dixons Entrance, to which he gave the name it bears, ignoring the Spanish name of Estrada de Perez.[16] Captain Portlock traded with the Chugaches, but lost much property through theft, even some of his ship's boats being plundered of the clothing of the sailors. He surveyed and named Port Etches, then went to Chichagof Island, where he entered and named Portlock Harbor.[17]

Captain James Meares, in the ship *Nootka,* came to Cook Inlet in 1786, found the Russians established there, and went to Prince William Sound, where he expected to meet the *Sea Otter,* under Captain Tipping. He did not find her, for she was lost at sea with all on board. Meares anchored in a cove well up the sound, unfortunately choosing one which was in a location that froze full of ice later in the season. Scurvy attacked the crew; many of them died, and at one time there were hardly enough well persons to bury the dead. They cut holes through the ice and sank the bodies in the water. When the natives brought fresh fish for trade in April the better fare restored the health of the survivors, and later in the season assistance from Captain Dixon enabled Captain Meares to put to sea on June 21 after losing more than half his crew. Other ships came from England, among them the *Iphigenia,* under Captain Douglas, sailing under the Portuguese flag.[18]

The merchants of the Atlantic seaboard sought for commerce for their shipping after the close of the Revolutionary War, and turned to the Pacific to engage in the lucrative fur trade. So many ships sailed from the port of Boston that on the northwest coast the name "Boston man" became synonymous with American, in distinction to the term "King George man," which was applied to the English, wherever the trade language of the region, the *Chinook* jargon, was spoken. Captain Gray, famous as the discoverer of the Columbia River, extended his voyages as far north as 55°43' N. Lat. in 1789 in the *Washington*, and in 1791 in the *Columbia* he entered the inlet afterward named by Vancouver as Portland Canal. At a place called Massacre Cove, Caswell, the mate of the ship, and two seamen were killed by the Indians. Robert Haswell later took the *Columbia* as far north as the latitude of Sitka.[19] So many followed in their wake that during the next twenty-five years the Yankee skippers and their bucko mates were known in every bay and cove of the coast of southeastern Alaska.

The Spanish allowed their interest to slumber until the ships of the Americans flitting through the Straits of Magellan and northward along their coasts like white-winged birds aroused their jealousy as they looked out on the Pacific and saw them winging their way north. The Viceroy of Mexico dispatched D. Estevan Martinez in the ship *Princesa*, and Lieutenant Gonzalo Lopez de Haro on the *San Carlos*, on a voyage of discovery in 1788, and they entered Prince William Sound in May. They made surveys in the sound, then went to the Russian settlement at Three Saints, where Delarof, the Russian commander, received them with hospitality. Among other information he told them that he had eight posts under his control, and that he expected to place others farther to the south, possibly one at Nootka. The Spaniards then visited Unalaska, where many courtesies were extended to them by the Russians until they sailed for Mexico on August 18.[20]

The Viceroy received the report of the officers with alarm and at once proceeded to forestall the establishment of a Russian post at Nootka by the placing of a Spanish fort, which was done in 1789. This brought the Spanish into conflict with British interests in which the subsequent events and the controversy to which they gave rise, while not directly pertaining to Alaskan history, were of the greatest importance to the Pacific Coast.

Salvador Fidalgo was sent out the next year to finish the work begun by Martinez, and reached Prince William Sound on May 23. From the results of his surveys we have the names of Valdez Inlet, Gravina Bay, and other places; later he visited Cook Inlet and Three Saints Bay, then returned to Mexico.[21]

Captain Allesandro Malaspina, an Italian navigator in the service of the Spanish Government, with two ships, visited the coast to investigate the possible existence of the Strait of Anian, described by one Moldonado to be in 60° N. Lat. He arrived on the coast near Sitka on June 2, 1791, examined the shore from Mt. Fairweather to Prince William Sound,[22] and decided that the reputed passage did not exist in that latitude.[23]

The Spanish made their last attempt at exploration in those waters in 1792 when Lieutenant Jacinto Camaano in the frigate *Aranzazu* came to the Alexander Archipelago, named Cape Chacon, Cordova Bay, and other points, but did not reach the continental shore.[24] The point farthest north reached by him was about Cape Camaano, which was named for him by Vancouver when he surveyed these waters.

Captain George Vancouver came to the coast in 1792 for the purpose of receiving the surrender of the Spanish fort at Nootka, and to dispose of the last lingering hope of the finding of the northeast passage.[25] He commanded the sloop *Discovery* and was accompanied by the tender *Chatham*. After his work along the lower coast was finished he reached Portland Canal, July 29, 1793, and examined it to the head, then proceeded up Clarence Strait. Near the entrance to the Canal he met the British trading vessels *Butterworth, Prince Lee Boo,* and *Jackall,* all under the orders of Captain Brown, an English trader.[26] He examined the inlets as far as the mouth of the Stikine River but failed to find that stream and the honor fell to the American captain of the *Atahualpa* some years later. At Sumner Strait he narrowly escaped shipwreck in a storm and out of gratitude for reaching a safe harbor he named the refuge Port Protection.

Vancouver wintered at the Sandwich Islands, returned the following year, visited Cook Inlet, Prince William Sound, and Yakutat Bay, then anchored in Port Althorp while his boat parties under Lieutenant Puget[27] continued the explorations past Glacier Bay into Lynn Canal. The ships were then taken down the coast, around Cape Ommaney, and into a harbor from which the boat parties connected the work of the previous year with his recent surveys. He named the harbor as Port Conclusion and left the coast on August 23, narrowly escaping shipwreck in clearing Cape Ommaney. His work was so well done that it was the base for the sailing charts for the region for years after the country became a possession of the United States.[28]

KODIAK ISLAND
From Lisianski's *Voyage*.

KODIAK, OR PAULOFSKI, FOUNDED BY BARANOF, 1792

From Langsdorff's Drawing in 1806.

BARANOF'S BRIGADE OF SEA-OTTER HUNTERS
From Vancouver's *Voyage*.

INDIAN TOTEM AT YAKUTAT

From Malaspina's *Voyage.*

7

The Colony under Baranof

SHELEKOF CHOSE FOR MANAGER OF HIS COLONY ALEXANDER Andreevich Baranof, a merchant of Kargopol, Russia, who was doing a thriving business in trading with the Chukchees on the Anadir River.[1] Baranof at first declined the offer, but misfortune overtook him. His wild customers robbed his caravan, burned his post, and reduced him almost to bankruptcy. Thereupon he accepted the situation.

The choice of a manager was a wise one. The strongly built, active, seemingly tireless man, of less than average size, with an indomitable will, dauntless courage, and a limitless fund of resource in expedient, was just the type of man for a frontier leader and organizer.

He sailed from Okhotsk on the ship *Three Saints*, August 19, 1790. While he was watering his ship at Kosheega Bay, Unalaska Island, it was wrecked. He and his companions reached shore with little other than their lives, and spent the winter amid bitter hardships. One of the Russians, Molof, was sent to Kodiak Island for assistance, but near Unga his party of Aleuts was attacked by natives of the Alaska Peninsula. Five of the company were killed, but Molof escaped to Unga, where he was rescued by Baranof the next year.

The shipwrecked men built underground huts of driftwood, after the manner of the natives, for there was no forest. They boiled sea water to secure the salt, gathered shellfish, fished, hunted, dug roots, adopted every expedient to preserve life till spring. The week before Easter they fasted. A dead whale was then cast up by the sea, and later they killed three sea lions and their starvation was at an end.[2]

Baranof constructed three *bidars* from the skins of the sea lions. Two of these boats were sent to explore and trade along the north side of the Alaska Peninsula, later to rejoin him at Kodiak Island. On the third *bidar* he went, with the remainder of his crew, to Three Saints, about six hundred miles, where he arrived July 27, 1791, and at once took charge, relieving Delaref, who returned to Okhotsk the next year.

At Three Saints the situation was discouraging. The rival companies of Orekhof, of Panof, and of Kisselof were hunting and trading along the islands, pursuing the old tactics of the trade. The Lebedef-Lastochkin Company held the Pribilof Islands and all of Cook Inlet except the post of Alexandrovsk at the lower part. In Prince William Sound, and to the southeast from that place, the English, French, Spanish, and Americans were sailing, trading with goods of a better quality and of a lower cost than those brought across Asia by caravan. Competition was keen, and the conditions adverse. Ships were few, and stores of trading goods were scanty. Baranof wrote to Shelekof for shipbuilding material, for authority to purchase trading goods from foreign vessels, and for a well-informed priest.[3] He found that he must move the chief factory to a bay at the northeast part of the island, known as Pauls Harbor, so called for the Prince Imperial. It is now known as Kodiak.[4]

In the spring of 1792 Baranof made a visit to Chugach Gulf (Prince William Sound) to cultivate trade relations with the natives of that part. His mission was successful until in the darkness of night, in the shadow of the forest on the beach, his camp was attacked by a party of Kolosh (Thlingits) from Yakutat.[5] Two Russians and ten Aleuts were killed and several others wounded in the battle which ensued, but the Kolosh were driven to their boats, taking with them their dead and wounded. In Prince William Sound Baranof met a Captain Moore, of the East Indian ship *Phoenix,* who gave him much information concerning Sitka, on one of the islands of the southeast coast, and he decided that it was a favorable place to establish a post in the near future. The captain also gave him an Indian servant, a native of Bengal, who served him faithfully for many years. On his return to Kodiak he found the ship *Orel* had arrived from Okhotsk laden with materials for shipbuilding under command of an English shipbuilder named Shields, or Shiltz.[6]

For the building of the new ship a bay on the south side of the Kenai Peninsula, called *Voskresenski,* or Resurrection, had been selected as a suitable site for a shipyard.[7] Here Shields was sent with workmen. The supplies sent by Shelekof must have been meagre, for Baranof wrote: "We have only half a keg of tar, three kegs of pitch, not a pound of steel, not one nail, and very little iron for so large a vessel." A rude sawmill was constructed over a small stream which furnished waterpower. Iron was collected from various sources, but was poor in quality. Baranof tried to extract a supply from ore found in the vicinity but was not successful. For tar he substituted a mixture of spruce gum and whale oil; turpentine was distilled from the pine trees, and paint was manufactured from whale oil and other ingredients.[8]

The first ship to be built in Alaskan waters was completed, launched from the ways in August, 1794, and received the name of the *Phoenix*. It was 73 feet in length, 23 feet beam, 13½ feet deep, and was of a burden of 180 tons, rigged with three masts and had two decks.[9] The sails were made from fragments of canvas gathered from the whole coast from Kamchatka to Kodiak, and were so poor that it was with difficulty that she made the harbor at Kodiak. Over this achievement the rejoicing was great, and it was celebrated with solemn mass and merry feasting; the only sheep in the colony was killed to grace the occasion. "What gluttony!" wrote Baranof.

Further to add to the fleet, two small vessels were built on *Yelovie,* or Spruce Island, near Kodiak, were finished during the next year, and were named the *Delphin* and the *Olga.*[10]

The rival settlement on Cook Inlet increased its strength by a reinforcement which arrived during 1791, under command of Grigor Konavalof, who took command of all the posts of the Lebedef Company, then began to rob and prey on the hunting parties of the Shelekof Company until it looked as if civil war was impending in that far-off corner of the world. Baranof was unwilling to make reprisals, for he knew that his principal, Shelekof, had stock in the other company. At last Konavalof attempted to capture Baranof himself, but the plan miscarried. This could not be ignored. Assuming to have authority to administer justice, Baranof summoned Konavalof to appear before him to answer for his misdeeds. The ruse was successful. Konavalof appeared and was sent to Okhotsk for trial. This action stopped the lawless attacks, but an intense rivalry continued until the Lebedef Company withdrew from the field.[11] Vancouver visited the outposts of the Lebedef Company while on his exploring voyage in 1794, and describes one of them as being near the North Foreland, and the other about eight miles to the southeast of the East Foreland.[12]

At Nuchek, on Prince William Sound, the Lebedef Company hunters established a post called Fort Constantine. In 1795 the Copper River natives attacked the station, captured their leader, Samoilof, whom they tortured to death with as fiendish delight as the Iroquois would have shown, and killed several of the garrison. This disaster, together with the privation of no supplies arriving from Siberia, caused the abandonment of the fort two years later and the dissolution of the company. Part of the men went back to Okhotsk and the others joined the Shelekof Company, who at once took possession of the field.[13] This removed the most powerful Russian rival.

The fur of the sea otter was the lifeblood of the trade. The hunting for these silky, beautiful pelts had been reduced to a science by Baranof. He perfected the methods of the natives and completed an organization which literally swept the seas. The hunters were dressed in waterproof *kamlikas*, or shirts made of the intestines of the sea lions, which were lashed tightly around the hatches, or manholes, of the skin-covered *bidarkas*. Thus protected, they were able to stand any ordinary sea without swamping their boats.

The hunters were Aleuts, who were most skillful gatherers of the sea furs, and whose dexterity with the *bidarkas* was little short of marvelous. Hunting was with them a passion. Golofnin says that when one of them saw the head of a sea otter on the sea he trembled with excitement as a setter dog trembles at the scent of a bird, and he could hardly be made to take his eyes off the coveted prize. In those wonderful little skin boats they searched the seas and when the head of an otter was sighted it was almost equivalent to a death warrant for the animal, for one seldom escaped. All native males over eighteen years and under fifty were subject to call to the hunting brigades each alternate year. The equipment was in later years furnished by the company, and was returned to them at the end of the hunt. The hunters worked on shares, each being entitled to one half of the fur he took while on the voyage.

Each spring the summons went out to the *toyons*[14] of the different villages to assemble the hunters about May 10 (O.S.). There were as many as a thousand men to a brigade in the earlier years. Before leaving Kodiak they were drawn up along the beach, the prow of each *bidarka* resting on the sand. The crew, of two or three men, stood at the side of the boat dressed in their *kamlikas*. On the top of the boat, deftly slipped under the lashings, were the hunting implements, the bows and arrows, or the throwing stick and its arrows, the hunting spear, the broad, double-bladed paddle. The priest, with his choristers, passed down the lines, chanting, blessing the beach upon which they stood, sprinkling each hunter with the holy water. The hunters crossed themselves, took their seats in the hatches of the light skin canoes, and headed for the open sea. As they passed the fort they saluted, then from the cannon belched forth a farewell salvo as the *bidarkas* skimmed over the water under the powerful strokes of the broad paddles. The hundreds of light, graceful craft dancing on the waves among the green isles at Kodiak made a stirring sight.[15]

The Aleutian in his *bidarka* could make as much as seven miles an hour, and with the *kamlika* tied fast around the manhole the craft was almost proof against the wash of the sea as long as the strength of the paddler held out. The hunters went out as far as thirty to forty versts in search of their quarry. If a storm arose they lashed two or three of the boats together and thus rode in safety till they made a port. They made journeys as far as to Sitka and return in a season, a distance of nearly twelve hundred miles by the route they followed, and the Aleut and his boat were as inseparable as the Indian and his horse.

When in the Kolosh country, in later years, the hunters were escorted by an armed ship and camped under the protection of her guns at night. On the ship sentinels were posted, and no one was allowed to approach at night. The guns were loaded with ball or with grapeshot, and boarding nets were stretched along the bulwarks.

As the hunting party moved along the coast offshore, the hunters were divided into parties of six or eight *bidarkas*. When one of the hunters in a party sighted the head of a sea otter lifted from the water to take a breath of air, he cast an arrow at it and shouted. As it disappeared beneath the water he took his stand where it went down and held his paddle in the air. The other hunters formed a circle about him and waited for the reappearance of the animal, which, for want of breath, must rise in from fifteen to twenty minutes. As it appeared from the water the nearest hunter shot an arrow and shouted to frighten it and to prevent its getting a full draught of air. Each time it grew weaker and its stay beneath the water was shorter, until a lucky shot captured it. The man whose arrow was in the prize was the possessor of the skin, and in case of two or more arrows striking it, the rule was that the one nearest the head took the pelt.

When five or six hundred of the light skin canoes were on the hunt the long line extended from shore for miles out to sea. At night they encamped on the shore and they lived chiefly upon the shellfish from the rocks or on the birds shot during the day, with an occasional seal or sea otter. A few dried salmon were carried in the boat to provide against an emergency.

Sea otters were at first found on the land at Bering Island by Steller and his companions, but after a few years of the hunting they changed their habits of life and rarely approached the shore. When storms harassed them for days at a time they became so worn with the continuous strife that they would seek the shelter of the outlying reefs where they could sleep among the kelp beds. As the tempest subsided the Aleuts put out for the outlying reefs of Sannak, or other favorite locations, guiding themselves over the seas through the scud of the turmoil with a sense of direction that seemed almost an instinct. There they made their landing and clubbed the sleeping animals to death, sometimes taking a hundred skins a day.

At the first the hunters believed there was no danger of depletion of the animals. "All the sea otter will be killed only when all the codfish have been caught at Archangel," they said. Yet it was a few years later when there were but two places from Cape Ommaney to Cook Inlet where they could be caught. Then they said, "They have migrated."

The animals already had been almost destroyed along the Aleutian Chain in 1792. They were at that time decreasing in the waters of Cook Inlet and Prince William Sound. New hunting grounds were badly needed to produce the skins required for a profitable business. In 1793 one of the most trusted hunters was sent to Yakutat to inspect that region. His report was favorable, and the next year a fleet of over five hundred *bidarkas* manned by more than a thousand Aleuts was sent to hunt in that vicinity. During their stay in the bay the ship *Chatham*, under command of Lieutenant Puget of Vancouver's expedition, came in, and also the English ship *Jackall*, on which Captain Brown was trading for furs.[16] The Russian hunters went as far as to Cross Sound with good success and more than two thousand skins rewarded their industry.

During the autumn of 1794 reinforcements and supplies arrived from Okhotsk on the *Three Saints* and the *Ekaterina*. There were 150 *promishleniki*, 30 families of colonists or agricultural settlers from the Monarchto Shelekof, and the Archimandrite Joassof with his retinue of priests, who were sent to establish the Church.[17] The winter passed unhappily for all. Conditions in the new settlement were not at all to the taste of the clergy, and their protestations in their letters to Russia are bitter and vehement against Baranof, while at Three Saints they fomented discord among their fellow colonists.[18] So many of a nonproducing class in a settlement already struggling for existence in a country so far removed from a base of supply was an irksome burden, and the problem of supporting them was a serious matter. The bigotry of the churchmen was antagonistic to the ideas of Baranof. The agricultural settlers were of the exile class; they had been dissatisfied under their previous surroundings and were doubly so in their present environment, fault-finding, rebellious, mutinous. The naval officers sent to the colony as navigators joined in the mutinies. "Even under my very eyes they had their secret councils, and when I went away in the winter it came near causing disastrous consequences," writes Baranof.[19]

The next year the priests went out to convert the natives to the Greek faith, and they claim to have baptized twelve thousand converts before a church was completed at Kodiak. The clergy accuse Baranof of delaying their work, but the record shows that he gave fifteen hundred rubles from his own purse toward the construction of the building.[20] Father Juvenal was sent to Iliamna Lake to teach the people of that village. He went in a *bidarka* with an Aleut, crossed by way of the Barren Islands to Cook Inlet, then across Cook Inlet, a long and arduous journey in so frail a craft. The principal men of the tribe practiced polygamy, which the father felt obliged to censure and forbid. The chiefs, with the usual liberality of the wild tribes, offered to give him as many wives as he desired, but when he refused their generosity and still insisted on their putting away the additional spouses they became offended and beat him to death with ivory clubs.[21]

The instructions of Shelekof with reference to the agricultural colony were that it should be at Cape St. Elias, but Baranof considered that Yakutat was preferable. Why either should have been chosen is unexplained, unless it be that it was intended as much for a hunting base as for a farming community. Kodiak is far better adapted for the purpose of agriculture. It is more than likely that it was a move on the way toward the great plan to push the posts to the southeast.

In 1795 an attempt was made to establish the Yakutat Colony. Manager Polomoshno was sent with a ship laden with colonists and material, but he deliberately went to Nuchek instead, wasted the summer in inaction, then returned to Kodiak.[22] This is but one instance of the insubordination of the naval officers who were sent to navigate the ships of the company—others were frequent. They were filled with the egotism of their service and despised the merchant class to which Baranof belonged. Baranof went on another ship, tarried at Yakutat for a time, waiting for Polomoshno, then went to Sitka to reconnoitre for a suitable site for the post he hoped to establish there.[23]

The station at Yakutat was founded in 1796, two separate buildings being constructed, one for the hunters, the other for the colonists and their families, and the whole was named New Russia. By this the Russian posts were advanced four hundred miles to the east along the mainland. The settlement was left in charge of Polomoshno.

8

The Founding of New Archangel

To increase the take of the sea-otter skins that made the chief profit for the stockholders, and to carry out the policy of Shelekof, preparations for placing the post at Sitka were urged as rapidly as possible. Kuskof,[1] the most trusted of the lieutenants of Baranof, was sent to Nuchek to hold the trade of the Chugach Gulf. Talin was sent to make surveys of Sitka Harbor. Other preliminary work was done, and by the spring of 1799 the manager felt he was able to take the step. The undertaking was so great for his limited resources that he would have been glad to relinquish the work to a successor, and he had sent his resignation to Shelekof in the hope that he might be relieved, but it was not accepted, so he went on with the preparations.[2]

In April he gathered his forces. More than a thousand Aleuts and Kadyaks, in a fleet of 550 *bidarkas,* went under convoy of the *Ekaterina,* hunting as they passed along the coast.[3] Talin was sent in the *Orel* direct to Sitka, while Baranof went by way of Yakutat in his favorite cutter *Olga.* All were to rendezvous at Sitka Harbor.

At New Russia, Baranof found the settlers in a miserable condition between disease and dissension. Scurvy had attacked them during the winter; several had died, while the traders and farmers continually quarreled. He adjusted matters as well as possible and proceeded to Sitka, where he arrived July 7, 1799, found the *Orel* already at anchor. The *Ekaterina* with the convoy of hunters came soon after. Vasili Medvyednikof, one of his party leaders, had chosen a location which Baranof confirmed, although he preferred the site on which the later settlement was placed, but which was occupied by the village of the Sitkas. The place selected was on a harbor about six miles north of the present Sitka, a part of Katleanski Bay, sometimes called *Starry Gavan,* or Old Harbor. It may be seen from the ships passing to Sitka, at the distance of a mile or more to the left of the ship channel.

Skayeutlelt was chief of the Sitkas, or at least one of them. Baranof paid great attention to him and with presents and cajolery purchased the ground for a fort. On the 15th the work of building began. Thirty Russians and a detachment of Aleuts were retained to carry on the work.

Lieutenant Talin, one of the naval officers, in command of the *Orel (Eagle)*, refused to take orders from the manager, whom he considered as only a merchant and not equal to himself in rank and threatened to hang Baranof to the yard-arm if he came on board his ship. He then sailed to Yakutat, took the furs from that station, as well as Polomoshno and some of his men, sailed to Prince William Sound, and there his ship was thrown on the rocks and became a total wreck. Five men, including Polomoshno, were drowned, while the furs lost amounted to over twenty-two thousand rubles.[4]

The larger part of the detachment of Aleut hunters was sent back to Kodiak, hunting along the shore as they went. Two days after their departure, while encamped on the strait north of Sitka, they ate black mussels, which they found on shore. Many were taken violently ill and within two hours more than a hundred died. From this occurrence the strait became known as *Pogibshe*, meaning pernicious, and the name has passed to us as Peril Strait.

The Aleuts remaining at Sitka hunted and fished for the maintenance of the workers. Ten Russians were required for guard duty, so the work progressed slowly. When completed, the post consisted of a two-story barracks building, with outbuildings, enclosed by a stockade reinforced by block-houses at the ends. This advanced the settlements another two hundred miles to the southward.

Trading ships, both English and American, frequented the harbor. The American ship *Caroline*, under Captain Cleveland, had been in the harbor on March 30, and in two days purchased three hundred sea-otter skins at two yards of broadcloth for each skin.[5] The English held a large share of the trade through the excellence of their goods, while the Americans competed by the sale of arms, ammunition, and especially rum, in large quantities.[6] When Baranof protested against their engaging in this dangerous traffic they replied that they came ten thousand miles to get fur and would trade any kind of goods to secure it. During the summer Baranof saw over two thousand sea-otter skins bought in the harbor by the trading ships.[7]

The winter came before the buildings were completed, and the shelters were poor. Storms of rain and snow beat down. Scurvy attacked the garrison, and the time passed most unhappily for all. With spring the herring ran in the harbor, and the fresh provisions restored health. The hunters took 45 sea lions and 250 seals in the bay. To quote the words of Baranof: "We swam in abundance."[8]

The Sitkas at first seemed friendly, but later became insolent and irritating, showing their hostility on many occasions.[9] Baranof's constant watchfulness prevented surprise, and his courage kept them in check till spring, when he returned to Kodiak, leaving Medvyednikof in charge of the post, which he named New Archangel,[10] warning him to be constantly on his guard against the hostility of the natives, and to avoid carefully all causes of offense.

At Kodiak affairs had been going very badly during the absence of Baranof. The priests and the insubordinate lieutenants of the Navy had been making the most of the opportunity to foment dissension and to undermine his authority.

Wrecks of his ships followed one on the other with appalling frequency. Soon after the loss of the *Orel,* the wreckage of a vessel had been found along the west shore of Kodiak Island, among the salvage of which were goods which could only have come from the *Phoenix,* which was long overdue from Okhotsk. Searching parties were sent out, but nothing was found that indicated the time or manner of the disaster. The fate of the ship is one of the unsolved mysteries of the sea.

A little later the *St. Michael* was lost near Bolscheretsk, and the *St. Alexander* was wrecked on her way to Okhotsk with a cargo of fur. Years had elapsed since the arrival of a supply of goods; the warehouses were lacking in trade articles but full of furs.[11] To pay the Aleut hunters, parties were sent out to kill bright-plumaged birds from which parkas were made by the native women and which were used to pay the men of the hunting brigades.

The situation was critical when the ship *Enterprise* from New York, one of Astor's trading vessels, came into the port laden with goods. The authority of Baranof did not extend to the purchase of foreign merchandise, but it was a case of last resort, so he bought the cargo and paid for it in furs with such profitable results that he continued the traffic during the whole of his management of the colonies.[12]

An encouragement for the sorely tried manager was the arrival of Mr. Banner, an employee of the new company, who came in a *bidarka* from Unalaska, six hundred miles, with dispatches telling of the formation of the Russian American Company and of its powers and privileges.[13]

9

The Organization of the Russian American Company

AT ONCE UPON HIS RETURN TO RUSSIA, SHELEKOF DEVOTED himself to securing rights to the fur trade of the whole of the Russian possessions in America. His son-in-law, Nicholas P. Rezanof, who was high in court circles, later joined with him to promote this enterprise. The Shelekof-Golikof Company had succeeded in crowding out or absorbing the most of the smaller interests before the death of Shelekof in 1795, and the only strong competitor was the Muilnikof Company. In 1798 these two firms combined in what was known as the United American Company.[1]

In 1799 a charter was given to the new company organized under the name of the Russian American Company, by the Emperor Paul. Rezanof prosecuted the plans of his father-in-law with even a greater breadth of vision than the originator of the great scheme, and the privileges, given Under Highest Protection, included all sources of profit by sea or land in letters patent.

Paul had at first been antagonistic to the monopoly's being granted, but the ability of Rezanof overcame the opposition and finally secured the privileges.

The capital of the organization was 724,000 rubles, divided into 724 shares of 1,000 rubles each.

The terms of the charter forbade all other companies' encroaching on the territory granted, which comprised the whole of the Russian possessions in America, together with the Kurile Islands and other islands situated in the northeastern ocean. The company was to "use and profit by everything which has been or shall be discovered"; to use the timber; to purchase, at cost price, powder and lead from the Government magazine at Nerchinsk, and the right to all this for the term of twenty years.

The process was much the same as that adopted by the trusts in the United States in recent years. All the small companies or traders were required to list their holdings within a certain time and to receive stock in the company at such rating as was offered to them, within a certain time.

A thousand shares of additional stock was authorized and soon was subscribed. The office of the company was at first in Irkutsk, but was transferred to St. Petersburg in 1800.

The management of the company was vested in a board of directors in St. Petersburg, and in a chief manager in the colonies. The chief manager was to decide all local matters, and from his decision the only appeal was to the directory in St. Petersburg.

The charter bears the date as follows: "Given in St. Petersburg in the year from the birth of Christ 1799, the 27th of December, in the reign of our Sovereign the Fourth." A memorandum attached says: "Be it So. July 8th, 1799 in Peterburg."[2]

Thus, after a lapse of thirteen years from the time he left the island of Kodiak, in the far eastern ocean, the dream of Shelekof's life had come true so far as the privileges of the trade were concerned. The extending of the empire southward to the sunny shores of California was in the future, and many obstacles lay in the way.

10

The Destruction of Old Sitka

A BITTER HOSTILITY AROSE AGAINST THE RUSSIANS AT THE new settlement called *Novo Arkangelsk,* or New Archangel, to us known as Old Sitka. It was caused partly by the custom of the Russian traders of taking the native women, as they had done among the defenseless Aleuts.[1] The Kolosh were a different people; they had not been beaten into submission. They had the best of firearms, furnished by the traders of the other nations whose ships frequented the sounds among the islands, and their country was adapted to their methods of warfare. The Hoonahs, the Chilkats, the Kakes, and others of the *kwans* of the Thlingit people taunted the Sitkas with being the slaves of the Russians. There was also an antagonism engendered by the superior skill of the Aleuts, who in their skin boats took so many more of the valuable sea-otter skins in which were the chief profits of the fur trade. They considered these skins were their legitimate booty, and that the hunters for the Russians were intruders. It was believed by the Russians that the enmity was connived at by the English and American traders who wished to drive out the intruders on what they considered their trading grounds.

The Sitka *kwan* of the Thlingits held the territory immediately surrounding the new post. Hardy, independent, and warlike, when aroused they were implacable enemies, and, bound together by the totemic brotherhood that existed among them, they were formidable foes. The tribes from Vancouver Island north to Cross Sound are the fiercest and bloodiest of all the native peoples of the west coast of North America. These were of the people the Russians called Kolosh. The country that they inhabit is covered to the water's edge with a dense forest; the waterways are intricate and difficult to follow. From the heads of the inlets are portages leading to other inlets which open miles away, to reach which entails a far journey in large boats. On land an ambuscade is offered at every turn, so that pursuit is difficult almost to the point of impossibility.

Khlebnikof tells us that there were in the fort, twenty-nine Russians, three Englishmen who were left by the commander of a ship, two hundred Aleuts, and some Kodiak women who were married to the Russians and Aleuts. From these, in May of 1802, Medvyednikof sent out ninety *bidarkas* manned with Aleuts and accompanied by Urbanof and two other Russians to hunt sea otter in Frederick Sound. After this, other men, five Russians, the three Englishmen, and eight Aleuts, went out to hunt seal and sea lions, leaving only twenty-one men, Russians, with some sickly Aleuts and some Aleut women.

Medvyednikof placed too much confidence in the friendship of the Thlingits, notwithstanding the warning of Baranof, and also that some Aleuts had been killed by them during the previous year. The chief fortification consisted of a two-story barracks building, with two blockhouses and a stockade, in the upper story of which was a cannon commanding the approach.

On the Sunday of the 20th of June, 1802, after midday, Medvyednikof sent some men to catch fish. Others were looking after the traps in the creek, and some of the women went to the forest for berries. The Indian women who had been living with the Russians had doubtlessly informed their countrymen of the conditions and of the favorable time for the attack, and they had gathered in great numbers in the surrounding forest.

A horde of savages, painted like demons, wearing masks of wood carved to the semblance of heads of animals, and armed with guns and spears, quietly emerged from the forest and were climbing over the stockade before an alarm was made. On an adjacent knoll stood Skayeutlelt directing the attack, while Katlean, young and active, was in the midst of the fray. From behind a projecting point of the bay came a fleet of war canoes with hundreds of brawny warriors driving their paddles frantically to be in before the finish. The Russians defended themselves as best they could with muskets and the small cannon. In a short time the buildings were fired. The women in their terror crowded upstairs and got over a trap door which gave way and precipitated many of them into the midst of the enemy, who seized and carried them away to their canoes with shouts of triumph. Those who attempted to escape were caught on the spears of the yelling butchers and were held up to the view of the defenders. The struggle was short and disastrous to the Russians.[2]

The women and children who were captured were held as slaves. A few Russians and Aleuts who were in the woods escaped to the English and American boats which were lying in the sound. The ship *Alert,* of Boston, and the British ship *Unicorn,* under Captain Barber, rescued some of the survivors. Later some Kolosh chiefs came on board the ship and were held as hostages until other captives were brought in and surrendered.

Medvyednikof, Tumakof, and Shashin were killed. Plotnikof was in the woods for eight days and escaped to a ship. Baturin was hunting in a *bidarka,* and with five Aleuts hid in the woods till they reached a trading vessel. Kochetof, a Creole, and Erlevski were wounded, captured, and tortured by cutting off fingers, noses, and other members of their bodies. The former soon died, but the latter endured the misery for a whole day before death relieved him.

Captain Ebbetts, with one of Astor's boats, was in the harbor and rescued some of the prisoners. He is said to have fired on some of the Kolosh canoes and destroyed them and their inmates.[3]

Captain Barber on the British trading ship *Unicorn* is said to have secured many of the sea-otter skins, of which there were twenty-seven hundred in the magazines and which were taken out by the Kolosh as plunder. He also took on board all the captives, and sailed to Kodiak, where he delivered three Russians, five Aleuts, and eighteen women and children, the survivors of the massacre, and demanded fifty thousand rubles as a ransom from Baranof. Mr. Baranof protested against the extortion, but finally paid ten thousand rubles for the release.[4]

The party of hunters that had been sent out under Urbanof went to Bobrovoi, or Sea Otter Bay, took thirteen hundred skins, and were returning by Kenovski (Kootznahoo?), Chatham Strait,[5] and on the night of June 20 encamped for the night. They took no unusual precaution, for they had heard of no hostility from the Indians. The Kolosh had evidently been watching for them, and in the night attacked without warning and massacred the entire party with the exception of Urbanof and seven Aleuts who escaped in the forest. The marauders broke up the *bidarkas*, and with the plunder of skins set out for their villages in triumph, having suffered no loss from the timid victims.

Urbanof and the seven Aleuts returned after the Kolosh left, made *bidarkas* from the fragments on the shore, and traveling by night reached Sitka and found only the smoking ruins, so they continued to Yakutat, where fifteen other Aleuts presented themselves a few days later, having escaped the massacre by different means.

In these two massacres over two hundred men were lost, and out of the whole garrison of Old Sitka there were saved only forty-two souls, including the women and children. The two attacks evidently were parts of the same widespread plot, which probably included all the different tribes from the west coast of Prince of Wales Island to Hoonah, and possibly to Chilkat. Khlebnikof says of this, that it "is difficult to imagine how they kept the agreement to exterminate the Russians a secret. But the reason is in general with the custom of these people, in deliberating on matters of war they put in council only those of mature years and experience, and carefully hide the situation from young people and the women."[6]

In April of this year, Kuskof, the lieutenant of Baranof, in charge of Yakutat post, set out with more than 450 *bidarkas* for a hunting trip down the coast. He had received some hints of the intention of the Kolosh, but as the Yakutats were seemingly friendly he held the rumors to be false. He was evidently somewhat on his guard, for at a place they called Akoi, about forty miles below Yakutat, they met a large number of armed Thlingits who attempted to provoke a quarrel and beat the Aleuts. Kuskof endeavored to preserve peace, till on the 22nd of May, in open day, the enemy attacked him, and were repulsed with a loss of ten men. The Aleut loss was one killed and four wounded. Kuskof then retreated in his boats across the small bay and fortified a place for further defense. A truce was had, and hostages exchanged, then Kuskof returned to Yakutat for arms and ammunition.

Leaving on June 6, he went south again, and at Cross

Sound met a friendly old Sitkan whom he knew, who warned them to be cautious, that the Kolosh were waiting to attack again, also gave him information about Sitka. Kuskof then sent six *bidarkas* by night to reconnoitre. They returned with the news that Sitka was in ashes and the people massacred. One *bidarka* with its crew was destroyed by the Thlingits on the way.

The Aleuts were panic-stricken, wailed over the loss of their relatives and friends, and Kuskof retreated to Yakutat, where he prepared for defense.

Kuskof, in the course of his stay in after years, found that the chiefs of the Queen Charlotte Islands, Stikine, Kake, and some other places met at Kootznahoo, where they formed a binding agreement to destroy the Russian forts.[7] Then they invited the Sitkas to join, and threatened that if they did not assist that they too would be killed. The chief of the Kanegas agreed to provide all the necessary powder and balls. Later the Chilkats and Yakutats joined. The plan was to strike at all the different places at the same time, and the northern attack was only prevented by the unexpected resistance of Kuskof and his hunting party.

These were grievous misfortunes for the colonies, and the chief manager was filled with discouragement. An attack of rheumatism added to his mental misery and confined him to his room, chafing under the enforced restraint, for he felt he must recover the lost ground at whatever cost, but the question was how, in his present crippled condition.

Late in the year the ship *Elizabeth* arrived, laden with men, provisions, and trading goods, a welcome addition in every way to the depleted establishment. In command was a skillful navigator, Lieutenant Khvostof, of the Imperial Navy, and his assistant was Lieutenant Davidof. News came also of the completion of the organization of the new company, and of the plans for the enlarging of the business. In May of the next year tidings came that Baranof was made a shareholder, that he was given the honor of the gold medal of the order of St. Vladimir, and that the execution of the company's plans in America was entrusted to him.[8]

The *Elizabeth* was dispatched to Okhotsk with a cargo of fur valued at 1,200,000 rubles, in which there were over 17,000 sea-otter skins, and which was one of the largest shipments sent from the colonies. Baranof was thankful for a navigator whom he could entrust with the important mission of conveying the results of his labors during these long years.[9]

Then followed the preparation for the retaking of Sitka from the Kolosh. To reconnoitre the ground Baranof took the little cutter *Olga* and sailed to the sound, then returned by the way of Yakutat, to which Kuskof had been assigned to replace the ill-fated Polomoshno, and ordered two small vessels built for use the next year. In the midst of his labors came an appointment as Collegiate Counsellor, which honor being conferred made him the equal of rank with the insolent naval officers who had snubbed him to show their superiority over a merchant. He was deeply affected by the distinction conferred and the reward given. Then tears filled his eyes, says his biographer, and he exclaimed: "I am rewarded, but Sitka is lost."[10]

11

Battle at Sitka and Re-establishment of the Post

WHEN THE SUMMER OF 1804 CAME THE NATIVES OF KODIAK and the Aleuts were called to assist on the expedition to take Sitka from the Kolosh. The number of the hunters was sadly diminished, but Baranof mustered 300 *bidarkas*, manned by 800 men, and also equipped 2 small ships on which sailed 120 Russians. The *bidarka* fleet was under the charge of a tried leader, Demianenkof, and Baranof followed later with the *Ekaterina* and the *Alexander*.[1] At Yakutat the two little vessels, the *Yermak* and the *Rostislaf*, which had been built by Kuskof, were added to the fleet.[2]

The *Ekaterina* and the *Alexander* were sent to Sitka. Baranof took the *Yermak,* in which he overtook the hunting party under convoy of the *Rostislaf,* at Cross Sound, for after the disaster of the loss of Urbanof's brigade no hunting party went out except under convoy of an armed ship. All entered the straits with a fair wind. No sooner were they in the maze of channels between the islands than the wind fell. A dense fog closed down on them, and they were caught in the tide rips which run through those passages like a maelstrom, and they were whirled here and there in imminent danger of ship-wreck. The strait was finally cleared in safety except for the loss of a few *bidarkas,* and they hunted through to Lynn Canal, then back by way of Chatham Strait and Peril Strait, to Sitka, and anchored in *Krestof Bay* (Cross Harbor). They arrived on September 19 and found the *Ekaterina,* the *Alexander,* and the *Neva* lying at anchor.[3]

Fortune, so often adverse to Baranof, favored him in this event. In St. Petersburg the company had projected a new venture in the way of sending ships by sea around the world from the Baltic, thus avoiding the long journey across Siberia by caravan. Two vessels, the *Nadeshda,* under Captain Krusenstern, and the *Neva,* commanded by Captain Lisianski, left Kronstadt, Russia, August 7, 1803, on the first Russian expedition to circumnavigate the earth, and the *Neva* reached

Kodiak July 13 of the next year. The *Nadeshda* went to Japan, having on board Rezanof, the Imperial Ambassador to Japan, and his suite, on a diplomatic mission to that kingdom.[4]

Lisianski found at Kodiak a message from Baranof, asking his assistance in recovering the post at Sitka, and at once set sail for that port, where he arrived on August 20 and waited the arrival of Baranof and his force. During his stay in the harbor an American ship under Captain O'Keen arrived and commenced trading with the natives. The captain, on a trip ashore, was attacked by the Kolosh, and Lieutenant Lisianski sent an armed launch to his assistance. The Kolosh escaped by carrying their canoe over a shoal into another bay where it was impossible for the launch to follow. Lisianski says: "Their skill as marksmen was apparent from the shattered condition of Captain O'Keen's launch, as well as from the collar of his coat, through which a bullet had passed."[5]

Meantime the natives of Kodiak and the Aleutians were arriving in their *bidarkas* and camping on the shore under the protection of the guns of the ships. Lisianski described their camp: "A bidarka, or boat, is turned up sideways, and at a distance of four or five feet, two sticks, one opposite the head and the other to the stern, are driven into the ground, on the tops of which a cross stick is fastened. The oars are then laid from the boat to the cross stick, and covered with sealskins, which are always at hand for the purpose. Before every tent a fire is made."[6]

Baranof consulted with Lisianski on the attack on the native stronghold. The Kolosh had placed a fortified post on the ground occupied by the present town of Sitka, and in so doing had chosen a spot of rare beauty. A low-lying peninsula juts out into the waters of the sound. In front, and protecting it from the sea, are more than a hundred evergreen forest-covered islands dotting the blue waters of the sea with emerald settings, through which the view stretches away to the broad Pacific. At the north of the sound is an extinct volcano, Mt. Edgecumbe, a truncated cone almost as faultless in its outline as Fujiyama; and to the east and south are encircling mountains barring all winds from those directions. Indenting these forest-clad slopes are bays and inlets reaching out like a network into the land as do the fjords of Norway.

The main Kolosh fortification was near the mouth of
Indian River, in the bounds of the present park, where upon
careful search may be found faint traces which still exist of
the redoubt. It is described as "An irregular square, its longest side looking toward the sea. It was constructed of wood,
so thick and strong that the shot from my guns could not
penetrate it at a short distance of a cable's length," says
Lisianski. It had a door, and two large gates, in the sides
toward the woods. Within were fourteen houses, or *barabaras,* as they are called by the natives.[7] Their settlement was
around the hill, or *kekoor,* upon which the building of the
Agricultural Department is now situated. This hill is often
called the Castle Hill, or the Baranof Hill, because the residence of the chief manager occupied it for so many years.
The Thlingits also say that there was a fort on this hill when
the Russians came, and it was abandoned for the stronger
one at the mouth of the river.

On September 28 the Russians moved their ships toward
the site of Sitka, the *Neva* being towed by upward of one
hundred *bidarkas.* The Kolosh were dancing their war dances,
and their shamans were invoking the aid of God on their
arms as the boats drew near the shore. The next day Baranof
landed, took possession of the hill where the settlement of
the Kolosh was located, and placed several cannon there.[8]
Negotiations were then opened for the surrender of the fortification near the river with the intention of avoiding further
hostilities, which was rejected by the Kolosh, and an attack
was ordered. The canoes on the beach were destroyed, the
woods were searched, and caches of food were discovered
and destroyed by the Aleuts. One hundred and fifty men were
landed with fieldpieces, and an attack was made to take the
fort by storm, but the defense was so strong that it was repulsed with the loss of ten killed and twenty-six wounded,
Baranof himself being among the number of the wounded.

The ships were then moved nearer the shore and the fire
of the cannon directed against the fort. An Indian canoe
loaded with powder to supply the defenders attempted to
reach them through the Russian lines, was struck by a cannon
shot and blown up. On the 3rd of October the Kolosh hoisted
a white flag, and later some hostages were given by them
while negotiations were opened for the surrender of the

fortification. This continued until the 6th; then, seeing no preparation for surrender, the Russians opened fire again. During the night the Kolosh abandoned the fort and retreated over the mountains to the northeast point of Baranof Island, from which point they crossed to Chichagof Island. The next day the Russians found only two old women and a little boy, who had been left behind, but inside the fort were the bodies of thirty Kolosh who had been killed during the battle, and the bodies of five children were also found who had been killed to prevent their cries making known the retreat. Everything of value was removed and the stronghold was destroyed by fire.[9]

Work was at once begun on the new settlement. Timber was cut in the forest, which stood thick and heavy almost to the water's edge. A storehouse and other buildings were erected, and the whole was enclosed in a stockade during the winter.

The lost ground had been regained. The farthest Russian outpost had been re-established, was named New Archangel, and the fort was called Redoubt Archangel Michael. Baranof composed an ode, called the Song of Baranof, proclaiming the work of the Russians in the New World, which was sung at the dedication, and at the establishing of every post afterward placed in America by the Russians this ode was made a part of the ceremonies.[10]

Печ Дарланг.　　　　　　　　　　　　　　　　　　Рис. Смирновъ.

Николай Резановъ

NICHOLAS P. REZANOF

Son-in-law of Shelekof, and one of the organizers of the Russian
American Company.

12

Rezanof and His Policies

IN THE SPRING OF 1805 THERE WERE EIGHT COMPLETED structures in Sitka. The ground had been cleared for fifteen kitchen gardens, while the livestock that had been brought on the ships to the new settlement were thriving in their new surroundings.

The Kolosh kept aloof from the post during the winter and built a fort at Kootznahoo, also one on Peril Strait near the opening into Chatham Strait. The *Neva* returned with the hostages. The Sitkas were invited to New Archangel, where they were entertained with feasting and were given presents, to which they responded with much dancing. A treaty was concluded with part of the tribe, but many remained hostile and refused all dealings with the Russians.

Lisianski made a survey of the region adjacent to Sitka, prepared a chart of the harbor, took time to make an ascent of Mt. Edgecumbe, the first of record, then set sail for Russia, September 1, with a valuable cargo of furs, going by way of the Cape of Good Hope.[1]

Rezanof, the Chamberlain of the Emperor, who had been the envoy to Japan, had also supreme control over the affairs of the Russian American Company in the colonies. He was to visit all the posts of the company and was to advise and direct the future management of the business. He left the *Nadeshda* at Petropaulovsk, took passage for the colonies on the *Maria,* visited the Seal Islands, where he found conditions prevailing that compelled him to order the killing discontinued to prevent further depletion of the herds.[2] He then went to Kodiak, established a school and founded a library with books brought from St. Petersburg. He placed Mrs. Banner, wife of the manager, in charge of a class of girls who were to study housekeeping.

Rezanof called in the monks, reprimanded them for their lack of attention to their duties, urged that they use their greatest endeavors to cultivate the lands and educate the youth. He placed Father Nektar in charge of the general schoolwork for boys, and Father Herman was assigned twenty boys for instruction in general farm work.

Father Herman selected a site on Spruce Island, built a chapel, and for many years carried on his work at what is known as Uzinkie, where he died in 1837. From there Rezanof went to Sitka, where he found the conditions crude, the quarters rough and primitive, and the fare of the poorest. He says: "We all fared poorly, but worse than all lives the founder of this place, in a miserable hut, so damp that the floor is always wet, and during the heavy rains the place leaks like a sieve."

They lived in perpetual fear of the Kolosh, for he writes home to Russia: "Our cannon are always loaded, and not only are sentries with loaded guns posted everywhere, but arms of all kinds constitute the principal furniture of the rooms." The lesson taught by the destruction of Old Sitka had not been forgotten.[3]

With the addition of the members of the suite of Rezanof the supplies were not sufficient for the demand. The American ship *Juno* came into the harbor laden with salt beef, sugar, molasses, flour, etc., and Rezanof bought ship and cargo for sixty-eight thousand piastres, Spanish, or about the same amount in dollars. Of food for the Aleuts there was yet a shortage, so Khvostof was sent to Kodiak for a cargo of *yukali* and whale fat.

On Khvostof's return he brought the disheartening news that the brig *Elizabeth* was wrecked and most of her cargo lost; that six *bidars* loaded with furs sank in a storm with the loss of their cargo and crews; that New Russia (Yakutat Fort) had been destroyed by the Kolosh, and that the old and trusted leader, Demianenkof, and nearly two hundred *bidarkas* with their hunters had been lost in a storm.[4]

At Yakutat the inhabitants had relaxed their vigilance, and in the heedlessness of their fancied security they were massacred with the exception of a few Chugaches and Aleuts, who escaped to Nuchek, and some women and children, who were captured and held as slaves.[5] In this manner the Kolosh partly revenged themselves for their defeat at Sitka.

The brigade of hunters under the leadership of Demianenkof had left Sitka for Yakutat, and as they went up the coast they heard rumors of the destruction of the settlement at New Russia. They left Akoi, forty miles below, at night for greater security in traveling, and after ten hours of steady paddling they reached the site of the ruined post. Horrified by the evidences of the fate of their countrymen yet to be seen among the ruins, and exhausted by their long journey, the hunters were panic-stricken. A council was had, and all but the occupants of thirty *bidarkas* decided to set out on the sea for Kayak Island, a hundred miles to the west. A storm arose while they were on their way, and the wearied travelers were thrown on the ice-bound, inhospitable shore in front of the Malaspina Glacier, where every man perished, including the leader, Demianenkof. The men who were too exhausted to proceed and preferred the chance of death at the hands of the Kolosh to the dangers of the sea were the only ones saved of the finest brigade of hunters in the service of the company.[6]

The Kolosh were elated at their success in the destruction of the post at New Russia and determined to follow it up by attacks on the forts at the westward. They went in eight great war canoes to the mouth of the Copper River, where six of the boats remained while two canoe loads went under the leadership of their chief, Fedor, to spy out the land. Fedor went to the commander at Nuchek, Ouvaroff, under pretense that he wished to trade. A Chugach native told Ouvaroff of the coming of the war canoes to the Copper River, so Fedor was at once placed in confinement, while the Chugaches attacked his men and killed some of them; the survivors escaped to their countrymen at the mouth of the river, then all put to sea. A storm was raging, which swamped all the canoes, and the war party was destroyed in the same manner as were Demianenkof's[7] hunters.

Through all these outbreaks and massacres there were Sitka Kolosh who were friendly to the Russians, and at the invitation of one of these, Dr. Langsdorff, the physician who accompanied Rezanof, and Captain DeWolf, the master of the *Juno,* were invited to visit the Kolosh stronghold on Peril Straits. The visitors were entertained with barbaric hospitality at the fort, which was situated on a point commanding the strait; it was built of heavy logs and was inhabited by about fourteen hundred people.[8]

Rezanof through personal contact appreciated the difficulties and understood the magnitude of the undertakings with which Baranof was contending. He was in full sympathy with the policy of expansion along the coast to the southeast, as outlined by Shelekof, and had high hopes for trade with California, as well as for colonizing the coast with a chain of posts, even to California.

In his stay, during the winter, he became fully acquainted with the character of the men with whom the chief manager had to contend, not only in the mutinous and turbulent *promishleniki,* but in the lieutenants of the Imperial Navy who were sent out to command the ships. Some of these sank into drunken rioting and from on board their ships fired cannon shots all the night as a manner of relieving their weariness at having to spend the time in the dullness of a frontier port. Others scarcely moved from their quarters, and were steeped in vodka from one week to the next. They refused to obey orders, delayed the progress of the work, and promoted demoralization.

During the winter the provisions became low. The Aleuts were afraid to hunt or fish on account of the danger from roving war parties. Scurvy attacked the garrison, and all were reduced to a miserable condition. Rezanof decided to go to California for a cargo of foodstuffs, and he also wished to inspect the coast for possible locations for future posts, for he was a staunch supporter of the policy of expansion of Russian dominion to the southward.[9] He sailed in February, 1806, attempted to enter the Columbia River but was not able to cross the bar. The ship drifted north to Willapa, where Rezanof sent Dr. Langsdorff in a *bidarka* to reconnoitre the entrance. The weather was bad, and some of his crew were sick with scurvy, so he was compelled to hasten southward. He entered the Golden Gate, anchored in San Francisco Bay, and was entertained by the Spanish commandant at the Presidio, which, with the Mission, constituted all there was of Yerba Buena at that time. The laws of the province were unfavorable to the trade with foreigners, but Rezanof's diplomacy overcame all obstacles, and from the padres at the Mission a cargo of wheat, groats, peas, beans, and meat products was procured and paid for in Russian goods. On June 8 he reached Sitka on his return voyage.

At Yerba Buena he met the charming daughter of the commandant, Doña Concepcion de Arguello, and fell captive to her charms. Their courtship has been the subject of many romances of both California and Alaska. She is mentioned in his letters, and to her his success in securing his cargo is largely due. His work was now done in the colonies, and he crossed the Pacific to Okhotsk. From there he traveled overland through Siberia during the winter, presumably to ask the permission of the Emperor to wed the fair Californian. The hardships of the journey were too great for his strength, and he died at Krasnoyarsk, Siberia, March 1, 1807.[10]

Rezanof was ambitious, brilliant, and energetic. It is unfortunate that his career was cut short so early in life, preventing the carrying out his plans. His great mistake was his bitterness toward Japan, on account of the failure of his embassy to promote trade between the two nations. He sought revenge by sending Khvostof and Davidof with two ships to harry the coast of the lower Kurile Islands, and to destroy the Japanese villages situated there.[11]

13

Trade Extension and Shipbuilding

BARANOF HAD ACCOMPLISHED HIS PURPOSE IN RE-ESTAB-lishing the post at Sitka, so next he turned to the task of preventing the American traders' taking the furs he wished to gather for his company. To remove the opposition, and to add to his slender stock of goods, which was yet to a great extent brought across Siberia by caravan, he bought all the cargoes that he could make of use. He also made agreements with Yankee shipmasters under which they took Aleut hunters, with their *bidarkas,* to hunt for sea otter along the coast as far south as Cedros Island, Lower California. The skins so taken were to be shared equally between the shipowner and the Russian American Company. The first of these contracts was made with an American, Captain O'Cain, or O'Keen, in 1803, who took twenty *bidarkas,* manned by Aleuts under the leadership of Shutzof, a trusted hunter in the service of the company. O'Keen hunted as far south as San Quentin, Lower California, and returned in March of the following year with twenty-two hundred sea-otter skins.[1] This venture was so successful that several ships were equipped with hunters on the same terms during the later year, much to the disquieting of the Spanish governors of California, for they plied their trade in the very Bay of San Francisco, and as far south as San Diego, off which port the *Mercury* hunted in 1808, and returned to Sitka with more than two thousand skins. Ten ships between 1805 and 1812 took over twenty-two thousand skins in those southern waters.[2]

Captain O'Keen returned to Sitka in August, 1806, on the ship *Eclipse.* Baranof, always seeking to extend his trade, entrusted a cargo of furs valued at three hundred thousand rubles to the captain for sale in Japan. The Japanese refused the right to trade, or even to land, in Japan. The venture was a financial failure, and the ship was wrecked on Sannak Island on her return voyage.

Considering Sitka now to be safe from attack, Baranof left Kuskof in charge and returned to Kodiak.[3] Some of the captives taken by the Kolosh at New Russia were still in the hands of the savages, so he devoted his efforts to their rescue. Among the unfortunates were the wife and child of the commander of the post, Larionof. Through an American, Captain Campbell, the release of an Aleut and his wife was secured. The following year Bulagin, one of the company's navigators, was sent in the *Kadiak* to try to liberate the others. Bulagin sailed into the harbor under a foreign flag, enticed a chief on board and held him as a prisoner until the remaining captives were delivered on board the ship.[4]

The Kolosh at Sitka considered the absence of the chief manager an auspicious time for an attack on the fort, so they gathered from every village from Stikine to Hoonah until more than four hundred war canoes with more than two thousand warriors were collected in Sitka Sound at the herring fishing season. They encamped along the shore, taking the roe and preparing it for food, and with savage faces peering from the woods night and day they watched for a sign of weakness that would give an opening for an attack. The Aleut hunters were driven home from Chatham Strait. Not a Russian dared to venture beyond the stockaded wall; not an Aleut went out to fish. Thus they remained for months. But Kuskof was worthy of the trust of the manager. He maintained the strictest vigilance without relaxation for an instant. The Kolosh women who lived with the Russian hunters were permitted to come and go unhindered. He knew that they would acquaint their countrymen with conditions inside the fort. The waiting wearied the besiegers, for their virtues did not include limitless patience. Then, through the women, Kuskof opened negotiations with a Chilkat chief, fomenting dissension between the factions, and finally the hosts of dark warriors melted away and scattered to their homes.[5]

To provide for the needs of the colonial commerce the building of ships was vigorously continued. The tender *Avoss* was the first, followed by the brig *Sitka* in 1807, the *Otkrietie* during 1808, and the schooner *Chirikof* in 1809.[6] The last one of these vessels was constructed under the supervision of an American named Lincoln, and the shipyard was in

the protected cove in front of the present post-office building, on a part of land later used as a parade ground by the
marines, which is now the public square.

There was need of the building of ships, for wrecks were
of frequent occurrence, the *Avoss*[7] being lost in the Bay of
Islands on her return from Japan, and the *St. Nicholas* on
the rocks on the western coast of what is now Washington,
near Destruction Island.

The *promishleniki* of the company were a varied, turbulent body of men, gathered from all parts of the vast Russian
Empire. Exiles for political reasons, convicts sent to Siberia
for punishment, fur hunters of the frontier, all passed on to
the new colonies, for the company was continually sending
out new men to take the place of those lost in the precarious
business of fur gathering on these uncharted, rock-bound
shores of the stormy northern seas. In some instances this
turbulence was promoted and encouraged by the intrigues
of the naval officers in their efforts to discredit the work of
the chief manager. Numerous conspiracies were formed at
different times, the most serious of these being that of Naplavkof, a Polish exile, and in it a number of men were implicated.
Their plan was to kill the manager, seize arms and stores,
take as many women as suited their desires, and sail for the
south seas in the *Otkrietie* with a cargo of furs. The furs
would be a currency convertible into everything they desired
as they touched at southern ports, and they would sail the
world over as did Benyowski. Their meetings were held with
the greatest secrecy, but when the final meeting was held
to determine the details of time and place there were two men
who separately went to Baranof and informed him of the
plot. He gave one of them a keg of brandy to promote the
recklessness of the conspirators. Then, at the time when they
were in the height of their deliberations, his men broke into
the room. Naplavkof was just receiving the signatures of
his accomplices to the binding oaths. He thrust the incrim-
inating papers into the stove, seized his weapons, and resisted
desperately, but was overpowered and bound while the papers
were rescued to be used as evidence. The chief conspirators
were sent to Okhotsk for trial, in 1809, and there the case
remained for many years, the defendants alleging cruelty
on the part of Baranof as a defense. They were finally sen-

SITKA IN 1805

This is the first picture ever made of Sitka.

From Lisianski's *Voyage.*

tenced in 1817, and Baranof was exonerated from the offenses charged.[8]

The aggressions of the American traders and the dangers from the Kolosh caused the Russian Government to dispatch the sloop-of-war, *Diana,* under Captain Vasili M. Golofnin, for Sitka, where she arrived in 1810, the first Russian war vessel to visit the colony.[9] During the stay of Captain Golofnin at Sitka the American ship *Enterprise,* owned by John Jacob Astor, the great fur merchant of New York, came to port with a cargo of goods selected by Mr. Astor personally as being specially fitted for the trade. In the ship's papers Golofnin professed to find evidence of a conspiracy on the part of Astor to seize the Russian colony, and he opposed the purchase of the goods by Baranof. The chief manager, however, did not take the same view as the captain, but purchased the cargo and also sent furs on the ship for trade in China.[10] Neither the danger from the Kolosh, nor the alleged plotting of the American merchant could long keep Golofnin in this part of the world, so he loaded a cargo of fur from the warehouses at Sitka and set sail for Kamchatka in August.

This trade was a part of the plan of the chief manager to extend his commerce to all the countries bordering on the Pacific. He endeavored to promote the coming of ships from New York, and when Wilson P. Hunt, in the ship *Beaver,* arrived at Sitka the next year he bought the cargo and made arrangements for later shipments to be made. Hunt sailed to the Pribilof Islands to get the sealskins in which payment for the goods was made, then went to China. The sale of Astoria to the North West Company and the War of 1812 prevented further carrying out of the agreement by future consignments.[11]

The complaints against Baranof, and his continued requests for relief by the appointment of a successor, caused the sending of Collegiate Assessor Ivan Gavrilovich Koch, who was to act as an assistant to the chief manager, with the intention that he was in the future to assume the command. Koch reached Kamchatka, where he took passage on the company's ship *Maria,* but he was taken ill and died at Petropaulovsk in 1811.[12]

14

Ross Colony

THE POLICY OF THE RUSSIANS FROM THE DAYS OF SHELEKOF was to extend their settlements to the southeast, even as far as to New Albion. Settlements at Nootka, at the mouth of the Columbia, and even in northern California were discussed by Baranof and Rezanof. The need for breadstuffs in the colonies made an added necessity. The raising of grains on the Alaskan coast had not been successful. The *promishleniki* were averse to farming; the Aleuts were hunters and fishermen by birth and training; and the climate was not favorable to the ripening of cereals. A little barley was raised at Kodiak; several hundred head of cattle were kept on the same island; cows were kept at Sitka, at Unalaska, and on Cook Inlet; but the employees of the company were fur gatherers and not farmers. So Baranof wished to place a settlement on the southern coast to supply the foodstuffs for the northern colonies, gather the furs of that part of the coast, and to provide a port for the ships employed in hunting in the southern waters.

Two ships were sent in 1808 to make surveys of the coast from Washington to California. They sailed separately and were to rendezvous at Grays Harbor, then to proceed in company. The *St. Nicholas* was wrecked on the coast near Destruction Island. The crew were captured by the Indians, who held them prisoners until an American trader found some of them on the Strait of Juan de Fuca, ransomed them from their captors, and returned them to Sitka.[1] Kuskof was in charge of the other ship, the *Kadiak*. He went to the rendezvous, then, not being joined by his consort, sailed south as far as to Bodega Bay, in California, which was called Rumiantzof by the Russians. He had a successful voyage and made a report on return that it was unoccupied by Europeans throughout the region north of San Francisco and that it was specially adapted to agriculture and grazing. The next year he was sent in the *Chirikof* to Bodega Bay, where he purchased land of the natives, then returned to Sitka.[2]

Preparations for the colony were at once made. The best men for agriculture were selected, tools and equipment chosen, and Kuskof was sent on the *Chirikof* with 95 Russians, a *bidarka* fleet of 40 boats manned by 80 Aleuts, and all necessary materials for the new settlement. The site was chosen about 8 miles above the Russian River, in Sonoma County, California. Buildings were erected, and it was dedicated on September 10, 1812 (N. S.), with appropriate ceremonies, as Fort Ross. It was on a tableland about a square mile in extent, bounded on the side next the sea by a bluff nearly 70 feet in height. The stockade was built of redwood, was about 250 by 300 feet in size, and was in form of a quadrangle, with blockhouses at the angles, in which cannon were mounted. Within the stockade were the Commandant's quarters, officers' quarters, barracks, chapel, storehouses, and offices. Near at hand on the plateau outside were the farm buildings, cattle yards, a tannery, workshops, and the village where the Aleuts and Kodiak men attached to the station lived. On the beach was the wharf, buildings for the protection of the lumber and the *bidarkas*, and a Russian bathhouse.[3]

At Bodega Bay a wharf and a warehouse were also maintained, as the anchorage at Ross was not safe for ships at all times.

A station was kept at the Farallones from 1812 to 1840, where for several years from one thousand to fifteen hundred fur seals were taken each year. After 1818 the catch of seals had decreased so there were not more than from two to three hundred a year. From that time only one Russian and a few Aleuts were left to collect eggs of gulls and to kill sea lions and gulls for provisions for Ross and Sitka[4]

Surveys were made of the interior rivers, the first conducted on the Sacramento and its tributaries by any nation, says Captain Golofnin in his account of his voyage there in later years.[5]

Food supplies of grain, fruit, and livestock were produced. Beef and grain were sent to the northern stations, but farming was not generally very profitable. Grapes were planted, peach trees were brought from Chile, and gardening of all kinds was carried on. During the year of greatest abundance, 1826, the agricultural products were of the value of 29,904 rubles.

Many articles were manufactured by the mechanics of the colony and sold to the Californians, including tiles, pitch, leather, rowboats, etc. Barrels and kegs were made for curing of beef, and two hundred poods of salt beef were shipped to Sitka in 1829.[6]

The sea-otter hunting yielded about a thousand skins from 1812 to 1817; after that time the catch was small, for the animals had been practically exterminated along the coast above San Francisco Bay. The brig that had been kept for hunting was sent to Sitka, and agriculture was the chief industry from that time onward.[7]

Shipbuilding was carried on at Ross, under charge of Grudinin, who had worked with Lincoln at Sitka. The timber used was the California live oak. The galiot *Rumiantzof* was built in 1816-1818; the brig *Volga* in 1821-22; and the *Kiachta* in 1823-24.[8]

The Californians were opposed to the settlement's being made, and protests against its continuance were presented at different times on the ground of its being an encroachment on their territory. Russia felt strong enough to disregard the claim and continued her occupation.[9]

The Russian interests in Ross Colony were sold in 1841, to Mr. Sutter, a Swiss, for thirty thousand piastres. Sir George Simpson tells us that the last of the colonists of Fort Ross sailed on the brig *Constantine* from Whalers Harbor, just above the entrance to San Francisco Bay, for Sitka, Dec. 30, 1841.[10]

15

The Closing Years of Baranof's Management

THE YEAR 1813 OPENED WITH ONE OF THE SHIPWRECKS which occurred with such appalling frequency during the early years of the colonies. One stormy day in January a Kolosh canoe came into Sitka in which were some Russian sailors, half dead from exposure and hardship, who were from the ship *Neva* that had struck on the rocks off Cape Edgecumbe and had broken up in the surf on January 9. The remaining survivors of the crew and passengers were encamped on the beach near the scene of the disaster, in dire need of assistance, which was sent them at once.

The *Neva* had left Okhotsk the previous year and had met with misfortune from the very beginning of the voyage. Contrary winds delayed her reaching Sitka for months, and finally, battered by storms and short of provisions, she went on the rocks at the very entrance of the harbor with a loss of forty-one persons, including the commander of the ship, and of Collegiate Adviser Bornovolokof, who had been sent to relieve Baranof as chief manager.[1]

On this ship came the news of the loss of the brig *Alexander*, with a cargo of furs which included 8,000 sea otter, of a value of $250,000, on one of the Kurile Islands.[2]

The loss of two ships was a severe reverse to the manager. To repair its effects he bought two American ships that came into port to escape capture by the English, the *Atahualpa* and the *Lady*. The first of these, renamed the *Bering,* was sent to the Seal Islands for furs, thence to Okhotsk and from that place to the Sandwich Islands, where she was wrecked and her cargo fell into the hands of the Kanakas. The other was called the *Ilmen* and was sent to California on a trading voyage which was at first very successful, but later while hunting along the coast lost the ship's doctor, an American named Elliott, some Russians, and thirty Aleuts, who were captured by the Spanish and held as prisoners. An attempt to extend trade to Manila, through an American agent named

Davis who went to that port on the *Isabella,* also ended in failure. Baranof seemed to be losing the good fortune that had accompanied him in his earlier years.

Undismayed by his misfortunes, Baranof made one more attempt to extend the Russian dominion to the southward. He had long wished to gain a foothold on the Sandwich Islands, for he appreciated with a keen foresight the value of those islands at the crossroads of the Pacific. There is no doubt that he was advised by the company to use means to secure them, although there seems to be no record remaining containing the evidence. A doctor named Sheffer had remained from the ship *Suvarof* when Captain Lazaref of that ship sailed from Sitka in violation of the orders of Baranof.[3] Sheffer was a Collegiate Assessor in the company's employ, and was sent by Baranof to the Sandwich Islands in 1815 to negotiate with King Kamehameha with relation to the goods lost from the *Bering,* to open up a wider trade in the products of the islands, and it would seem likely he was instructed to seek a foothold on one of the islands. Sheffer was at first successful in his mission, secured trade concessions, a tract of land for agricultural purposes, and orders for the restoration of any goods remaining from the cargo of the *Bering.* He also secured from the subchief, Tomara, the right to the sandalwood trade of one of the islands. He then erected buildings and cultivated a plantation.[4]

Kamehameha became distrustful of the establishment of Sheffer, considering it to be too much in the nature of a fortification. The English and American residents encouraged the jealous feeling of the king. Sheffer was compelled to leave hurriedly in an American ship for Canton, and the dream of a Russian colony in the Sandwich Islands ended in a loss of about two hundred thousand rubles to the Russian American Company.[5] The letters in the archives of the company as preserved in Washington, D. C., indicate that a hope was cherished by the company management in St. Petersburg for several years that the islands might yet be acquired, but no further settlement was attempted.[6]

The region to the north of the Arctic Circle was yet an unknown land, and the Russian Chancellor, Count Rumiantzof, equipped the ship *Rurik* in 1815 for a voyage through Bering Strait into the Arctic for new explorations, especially

to see if the long-sought passage from the Pacific to the
Atlantic lay in that part of the continent. The expedition
was under the command of Lieutenant Otto von Kotzebue,
of the Russian Navy. Kotzebue sailed through Bering Strait,
examined the American shore to the northeast, and on August 1, 1816, he entered what is now known as Kotzebue
Sound. To the east stretched, as far as the eye could reach,
a wide expanse of sea, and his hopes rose high that at last the
hoped-for passage to the Atlantic was discovered, but he was
doomed to disappointment, for it was but an arm of the
ocean that soon terminated in the shallows of the upper
sound. He made surveys, discovered the famous ice cliffs on
Escholtz Bay, then went to the Sandwich Islands for the
winter. Further exploration during the next year was prevented by an accident that compelled his return to Russia.[7]

The chief manager was growing old. For twenty-seven
years he had been in this far country, and the three score
years and ten allotted to man had passed. Since the failure
of his plans in the Sandwich Islands he had been broken in
health and spirits. In November of 1817 the ship *Kutusof*
came into Sitka in command of Captain Leontii Hagemeister,
who waited until January and then notified Baranof that he
was commissioned to relieve him of his office. Baranof had
long been looking for a successor, but the manner of his
coming cut the old man to the heart. Decrepit in body and
depressed in spirit, he rose from a sick bed to begin the
task of transferring the company property to Kyril Khlebnikof, a commissioner for the purpose, who accompanied
Hagemeister.[8]

The new manager made many changes in the details of
the business, among them being the payment of salaries to
the hunters instead of giving them a share in the furs secured
by them. The *kayours,* who had been practically slaves who
worked for their food and clothing, were to have pay for
their services. There was organized a classification according
to length and efficiency of service, and promotions for merit.

Several exploring expeditions were sent out, and by one of
them under a leader named Korsakof the fort at Nushagak
called Alexandrovsk was built.[9]

A third French expedition visited the country in April
of 1818, in command of Camille de Roquefeuil, in the ship

Bordelais, in search of furs.[10] He made a contract with the company for twenty-nine *bidarkas* and the Kodiak men to man them, and sailed to Prince of Wales Island to hunt for sea otter. While he was at anchor in a bay on the west side of the island, with the hunters encamped on the shore, the Kaiganas made an attack on them, killed twenty and narrowly missed killing Roquefeuil himself, who escaped by swimming out to one of his ship's boats. He was so much discouraged by his ill-fortune that he went to Sitka, paid for the lost men as stipulated with the company at two hundred piastres each, and sailed away from the scene of his misfortune in disgust.

Baranof was seventy-two years of age when he completed his transfer of the property. He had been away from his home for twenty-eight years. The old bonds were broken, and his wife had been dead for years. He debated whether to return to Russia or to build a home at the Ozerskoe Redoubt and spend his last days in the land he had learned to love.[11] Captain Golofnin, who was making another voyage to the colonies in the *Kamchatka,* persuaded him to go to St. Petersburg on the return of the *Kutusof,* telling him that the company needed his advice and experience and would be glad to have him there.[12] This decided his course, and he took passage on that ship after seeing his daughter Irene, a Creole, married to Lieutenant Yanovski, one of the officers of the *Kutusof.* After an affecting farewell to his friends at Sitka, both Russian and native, for many of the Kolosh came to bid him adieu, he sailed November 27, 1818.[13]

Hagemeister left Yanovski in charge of the office at Sitka and took command of the vessel.[14] The *Kutusof* entered the harbor of Batavia on March 7, 1819, and remained in that port for thirty-six days. Baranof took lodgings on shore, and the stay in the tropical climate was too severe for his feeble frame. When the ship sailed he was carried on board. On April 16 he died, and the following day was buried at sea, opposite Princes Island, in the water of the Indian Ocean.[15]

Yanovski made an inspection of the posts of the company, going to Kodiak, Unalaska, and to the Pribilof Islands in a sailing ship, accompanied by his wife. At the islands he reports the condition of the seal herd as being badly depleted and he advised a *zapooska,* or cessation of killing for a period of some years in order to permit the recuperation of the rookeries.

The mission of Captain Golofnin to the colonies was to make a review of their condition and to report on the advisability of the renewal of the company's privileges for another period of twenty years. While his recommendations were not entirely favorable to the company, the Government granted a renewal two years after the expiration of the old charter, and in the meantime on September 15, 1820, Matvei Ivanovich Muravief assumed the duties of the office of chief manager.

16

The Second Charter, 1821-1842

THE FIRST CHARTER OF THE RUSSIAN AMERICAN COMPANY expired in 1819, and the efforts to have it renewed were so successful that on September 13, 1821, a new charter was granted, conferring the same privileges for the period of twenty years from that date. It included the use and enjoyment of all that had been discovered or might be discovered, to make new discoveries, to make new settlements and to construct works of defense. The company was to maintain churches and schools, and to protect the rights of the Creoles and natives as well as those of the employees and shareholders. The chief manager must be selected from the naval service, be of no lower rank than a captain of the second class, and the assistant manager must also be a naval officer. The board of directors, four in number, was to be selected from the shareholders.[1] The capital in money, notes, and furs was, in 1820, the sum of 4,147,950 rubles in scrip.[2]

There was little or no gold or silver in the colonies. A paper currency was used, and the paper ruble was valued at about twenty cents.[3] Payment to the merchants who came to the colonies in their ships had to a great extent been made in sealskins and other furs, the vessel going to the Pribilof Islands to receive the skins in some cases. After 1818 payments were made in drafts on St. Petersburg.[4]

The Russian Government issued a ukase in 1821 restricting the commerce of the coast to Russian subjects and forbidding all foreign vessels to come within one hundred Italian miles of the coast unless in case of dire distress. Both the United States and Great Britain protested against this action. The Russian sloops-of-war *Kreissler* and *Ladoga* arrived to enforce the order. Finally, April 5-17, 1824, a treaty was made between the United States and Russia providing that: "The ships of the two powers, or which belong to their citizens or subjects, respectively, may mutually frequent, without any hindrance whatever, the interior seas, gulfs, harbors, and creeks upon said coasts, for the purpose of fishing and trading with the natives of the country."

The treaty was to be for the term of ten years from the date thereof, and by it the lower extreme of the Russian possessions was fixed at 54°40′ N. Lat.

A treaty was also concluded during 1825 between Russia and Great Britain, agreeing upon the boundary line between Russian America and Canada. The description of the line was the same as was later used in the treaty between the United States and Russia in 1867. A little more care taken in specifying the details would have saved a wearisome negotiation which ran through many years. Under this treaty the vessels of Great Britain were to enjoy the same privileges as those of the United States for the period of ten years.[6]

The Russian American Company protested that the treaties were a direct infringement on their rights under their charter, in that they gave to the United States and Great Britain rights of trade that belong exclusively to them.

The natives of the Alexander Archipelago maintained a hostile attitude and generally refused to trade with the Russians.[7] Small parties from the settlements were at all times in danger of their lives. When Roquefeuil was at Sitka the Indians killed two Russians in sight of the fort. They had not been allowed to inhabit their old village after the occupation of New Archangel by the Russians, until in 1821, when Muravief invited them to return and rebuild their homes on the old site. The Kolosh accepted, returned, built the village called the "Ranche" and have remained there to the present.[8]

Shipwrecks of colonial boats were less frequent, owing to surveys which gave better charts and the navigators in the service who were more skillful. During the period of the second charter, most of the disasters were of smaller coasting craft on their annual voyages to the ports of the outlying districts. The *Karluk* was lost in 1830 on the north side of Kodiak Island. The next year the *Sivutch* was wrecked on Atka Island. In 1837 the *Chilkat* sank just off Edgecumbe.

To repair the losses and to serve the increasing commerce with new regions new ships were built at Sitka. In 1827, the schooner *Unalaska;* in 1828, the *Bobr,* the *Sivutch,* the *Karluk,* and the *Aleut* were put off the ways at the Russian chief factory. In 1830, the *Kvichpak* was launched.

Ships were also built at Okhotsk and Kamchatka, between 1829 and 1832. The schooner *Aktzia*, the brig *Polypheme*, and the sloop *Sitka*, were built and equipped.[9]

To increase the production of furs the company extended its operations and explorations farther to the northward and toward the interior of the country. In 1821 two boats, the brig *Golofnin*, under Lieutenant Etolin, and the cutter *Baranof*, under Lieutenant Kromchenko, were sent to explore and trade along the shores of Bering Sea. Kromchenko went to Nunivak Island, then to Norton Sound, and discovered and named Golofnin Sound. Etolin sailed to the Nushagak, entered the Kuskokwim, where he traded with the natives, then went to Nunivak Island, made some new discoveries, and named Cape Vancouver.[10] During the same year Captain Mikhail N. Vasilief made a voyage as far north as Cape Lisburne on the Arctic coast.

Captain-Lieutenant Peter Egorovich Chistiakof was made chief manager on October 14, 1825, and continued the northern surveys. In 1828 Captain Lutke sailed along the northern shore of the Alaskan Peninsula and mapped Port Heiden, Port Moller, and other places. The following year Vasilief was sent to the Nushagak, which he ascended to the lakes, then returned to the redoubt and went to the Kuskokwim.[11] In 1830 Kolmakof traded for furs in the Kuskokwim Valley with good success.

In England the interest in Arctic exploration had been aroused, and in 1826 Captain Frederick William Beechey, R. N., entered Kotzebue Sound in H. M. S. *Blossom*, expecting to meet Sir John Franklin, who was to come from the Mackenzie River to this point. During his stay he surveyed and named Hotham Inlet, and charted the coast as far north as Point Barrow, which he discovered and named. Franklin came no farther west than Return Reef on the Arctic shore, then returned to the Mackenzie. Beechey remained at Kotzebue until October, went south for the winter, returned the following summer, then not meeting Franklin he gave up the quest and went to England.[12]

The eminent explorer and scientist, Baron Wrangell, took charge of the colonies in 1830. He had already earned fame on an expedition in the Arctic Ocean and brought to his work a trained mind.

The sea otter which had been the great source of wealth in the earlier days of the colony had decreased until the *bidarka* brigades that went out each year from Kodiak and Sitka took but a few hundred instead of gathering two thousand or more as in 1795.

The resource next in importance was the seal herd of the Pribilof, or Seal, Islands, and the condition of this was little better. From the time of the discovery of the group in 1786 to the securing of control by the Russian American Company in 1799 the islands were exploited by several companies, each taking all the skins they could gather and dry. After this date there was no competition in the killing, but there was likewise no economy in the methods. Thousands of skins spoiled after being taken, and hundreds of breeding bulls were killed for their skins. Cows perished in the drives to the killing grounds. The whole system was wasteful. In 1805 Mr. Rezanof visited the islands and found the herds in such a depleted and deplorable condition that he ordered the killing stopped, but after his death the demand of the Directory at St. Petersburg for profits compelled the resumption of the taking of skins. In 1819 Yanovski visited the islands and advised new methods and a cessation of slaughter, but not until 1822 was any action taken. Then for a few years a lesser number was taken, but in 1828 the manager was ordered to kill forty thousand, and with his utmost efforts was able to get only twenty-eight thousand, on account of the depleted condition of the herds. Wrangell presented the matter in such a convincing manner that in 1834 the kill was restricted to five thousand male seals on St. Paul and a closed season was declared on St. George for two years.[13] Wrangell introduced new methods in the fur taking in every department and placed new posts to the northward.

Ivan Lukeen was sent to the Kuskokwim in 1831, where he established an *odinochka*, or one man post, at the place where in later years the redoubt Kolmakof was built, and it was called Lukeen's Fort.[14] Etolin cruised and traded in the region above the Yukon, or Kvichpak, and in 1833 Tebenkof was sent to the Aphoon mouth of the Yukon in the sloop *Urup*, and on St. Michael Island he built a fort which he named Redoubt Michaelovsk, the St. Michael of today.[15] From Michaelovsk, during 1834, the Creole, Glazunof, was sent to explore to the eastward, crossed to the Anvik River, traversed the upper part of that stream, during the following season went down to the Yukon, and then to the Kuskokwim.[16]

The Hudson's Bay Company, chartered on May 2, 1670, under the name, "The Governor and Company of Adventurers of England trading into Hudson Bay," had controlled the greater part of the fur trade of Canada for many years. It was incorporated by the enterprising cavaliers of the court of Charles the Second, and the first governor was Prince Rupert. Their posts had been gradually extended westward from Hudson Bay until they reached the Pacific, and, after being firmly established at Fort Vancouver on the Columbia River, their trade was extended northward along the coast. In 1831 they built a post at Nass River, which empties into the Observation Inlet of Portland Canal. The same year one of their ships traded at Cordova Bay, in Prince of Wales Island, and at the same time two American ships were lying there engaged in barter with the Kaiganas, but were compelled to withdraw from the competition on account of the superior quality of the British goods. The English goods were the best to be had, and the four-point Mackinaw blanket of the Hudson's Bay Company was known to every frontiersman and Indian from California to the Arctic Ocean as a standard.

The ten-year period of the trade agreement of the United States expired in 1834 and was not renewed. The American boats had ceased trading with the natives because of their inability to compete successfully with the opposition of the two great companies. Wrangell reported April 28, 1834: "Merchants from the United States did not visit the straits during the past winter and our only rival is the Hudson's Bay Company."[17]

Between the two companies the competition became very keen. Every subterfuge and trick of the frontier trade was put in practice to secure the native business. The mainland, back of the strip of coast held by the Russians, was rich in fur, especially that of the beaver and land otter, and of these the output was estimated at ten thousand skins.

The Hudson's Bay Company sent their traders into the headwaters of the Stikine as far as Dease Lake in 1834 under

J. McLeod. In 1838 Robert Campbell reached the "Terror Bridge" on the Second North Fork of the Stikine, and there met Chief Shakes of Wrangell, who was there trading with Russian goods. Shakes was so hostile that Campbell's party was probably saved from massacre only by the friendship of a remarkable woman, the chieftainess of the Nahonnies. On July 25, 1840, from the top of the mountains Campbell saw the river he named the Pelly, "after our home governor, Sir H. Pelly."[18]

The difficulties of the overland route were so many that the Hudson's Bay Company reconnoitred the mouth of the Stikine for an entrance with boats, in order to establish a post above the Russian boundary.

To prevent an English settlement on the Stikine the chief manager of the Russian American Company sent Lieutenant Zarembo in the brig *Chichagof* to establish a fort at the mouth of the river on Wrangell Island. This was accomplished in 1833.

The British brig *Dryad,* in charge of Chief Trader Peter Skene Ogden of the Hudson's Bay Company, with eight officers, sixty-four servants of the company, and a cargo of materials and merchandise for the new post, arrived off the Stikine, June 18, 1834 (N. S.). A Russian officer went on board and notified them that their landing would be opposed. Ogden sent a messenger to Sitka to appeal to the decision of the chief manager. Wrangell was absent. Etolin, the assistant manager, was firm in his support of Zarembo, sending a six-oared boat as a reinforcement for him and also sending instructions to the commander of the *Chilkat,* then trading in Lynn Canal, to report at the Stikine. Ogden was desirous of establishing the new post. Competition for fur was keen between the companies. The watershed of a noble river like the Stikine with its sources far back in the Rocky Mountains was a prize worth contending for, but open war with the Russian Bear was not to his taste, so he retired to Fort Vancouver.

Zarembo continued building the redoubt, completed it, named it St. Dionysius, and hoisted the flag on August 26, 1834, with an appropriate salute from the Russian cannon. It was situated near the north end of Wrangell Island, on the site of the present town of Wrangell.

Chief Factor John McLoughlin of the Hudson's Bay Company estimated that the loss to his company in the expedition was £22,150, 10s., 11d., sterling, for which a claim was presented through the British ambassador to the Russian Government.[19] After much correspondence the representatives of the two greatest of the world's fur companies met in Hamburg, and on February 6, 1839, an agreement was made by which the Hudson's Bay Company waived the damages in consideration of a lease being made to them by the Russian American Company of the coast line from Portland Canal to Cape Spencer for ten years at an annual rental of two thousand land-otter skins. The agreement also covered the delivery of a certain quantity of grain and meats to the Russians from the farms of Nisqually and Vancouver each year. The lease was renewed for another term of nine years in 1849, and, with certain restrictions on coal, timber, fish, and ice, was later extended to the time of the transfer of the leased territory to the United States. The hold of the Russian on his possessions in America was slipping.

Redoubt St. Dionysius was transferred to the Hudson's Bay Company in accordance with this agreement, on June 1, 1840. The Russian flag was lowered, the British ensign hoisted, and the name of Fort Stikine was given by Sir James Douglas, who took possession for his company.[20]

Fort Taku (Taco) was built on Taku Harbor, about twenty-five miles below the present town of Juneau, soon after the transfer. Governor Simpson mentions it in 1841 as, "Only a year old, yet very complete, with good houses, lofty pickets, and strong bastions," but it was abandoned two years later.[21]

Trading trips were made by the Russians while negotiations were pending, from Cape Fox to Chilkat Inlet, and surveys of the important points were part of the work done. Kuznetzof reconnoitred the Taku Inlet and River in 1834. Wrangell Strait was surveyed and named the following year, and the Stikine surveyed and sounded as far as the British boundary. The Chilkat River and the upper part of Lynn Canal were surveyed the next year by Captain Linderberg.[22]

Wrangell was succeeded by Captain Kupreanof in 1835, and went to Russia via Mexico, crossing overland to Vera Cruz.

Kupreanof's attention was attracted to a remote part of his territory. The inhabitants of Cape Prince of Wales, occupying the village known to them as Kinegan, were the most aggressive and turbulent of the Eskimo peoples. Their geographic position gave them an advantage in trade between Asia and America, and across Bering Strait they carried goods in their skin *bidars*, acting as middlemen between the Asiatic Chukchees and the Eskimoan tribes of the American coast. The establishment of the Russians at Michaelovsk interferred with their business, and they organized an expedition to destroy it. At Norton Bay was a Russian trader, Kurepanof, with a small party. They attacked and killed some of the men, but the trader escaped to Michaelovsk and gave the alarm, thus frustrating the chance of a surprise.[23] The Eskimos then retreated to their homes.

The English improved the interim prior to the settlement of the Stikine case by sending out an expedition to the coast to make observations. The commander was Sir Edward Belcher, who sailed in the ship *Sulphur* in 1836. He was a guest of Kupreanof at a ball given in the Baranof Castle, which was then just completed, and Lady Kupreanof, who accompanied her husband across Siberia to reach Sitka, presided over the festivities.[24]

To connect the surveys of Beechey with the explorations of Sir John Franklin from the east, and to gain trade information along the Arctic coasts, the Hudson's Bay Company sent Thomas Simpson. He left the mouth of the Mackenzie River July 9, 1837, proceeded in a boat to the westward and along shore to Point Barrow, then returned by way of the Mackenzie. To this expedition we owe the names of Point Beechey, Colville River, and other places on our charts.[25]

Aroused by this activity of their rival, in 1838 the Russian American Company sent Alexander Kashevarof in the brig *Polypheme* to prosecute investigations in the Arctic regions. He reached Cape Lisburne with his ship, but from that point was compelled to use skin *bidars* because of ice conditions. His farthest point attained was about thirty miles east of Point Barrow. Into the Yukon for extension of trade during the same year the Creole, Malakof, was sent, and at the confluence of the Nulato with the Yukon he established a post, which was afterward called Nulato.[26]

The management of the company passed into the hands
of Captain Adolph Etolin, June 1, 1840. He had been many
years in the service of the company, having arrived in the
colonies in 1817, and rose to the rank of assistant manager
under Wrangell. Many of the servants under this regime
continued in the employ for long periods, among them being
Zarembo, who was rewarded in 1844 for twenty-five years
of service; Krukof, who was rewarded and pensioned in
1821 after forty years with the fur companies; Kuskof, who
came with Baranof in 1790 and remained until 1821, and
others.

These years were the ones of the most interest and the
greatest devlopment of Russian America. The dominions
were at the widest they reached. The buildings at the chief
factory were the best in the history of the settlement, and
the schools were prospering. The dealings with the Kolosh
were the most satisfactory. It might be called the Golden
Age of the Colonies.

Etolin cultivated friendly relations with the Kolosh, employed them in the service of the company as workmen and
as sailors, and he instituted a fair at Sitka, modeled after the
plan of the great Russian fur fair at Nizhni Novgorod, to
which they brought their furs each year.[27] To this fair gathered all the tribesmen of southeastern Alaska from Portland
Canal to Yakutat, with their peltry: beaver, otter, mink,
marten, all the denizens of that northern forest, and Etolin
played the host to his savage visitors, who spent the proceeds
of their traffic in potlatches in the "Ranche."

In the shipyards and machine shops the mechanics were
busily employed in the building of new steam vessels and the
repair of old ones. The first steam vessel constructed on the
western coast of North America was the product of the yards
at Sitka before 1840, when the *Muir,* a tug of eight horsepower, was equipped there, engines, boilers, all complete.
This was followed by the *Nikolai I* of sixty horsepower, but
the boilers were brought from Boston. During the years from
1839 to 1841 there were built in Sitka, the steamer *Nikolai I,*
the brig *Promissel* of seventy-five tons, and the *Muir,* and
others followed to the last years of the Russian regime.[28]

During 1842 Lieutenant Zagoskin was sent to extend the
trade still farther into the Yukon Valley, for rumors had

reached the company that their rival had plans for invading that field. Zagoskin went from Michaelovsk to a river he calls Unagaklit (Unalakleet), where he established a post at a point convenient to the portage to the Yukon. Traveling with dog teams, he reached Nulato January 15, endeavored to ascend the Koyukuk, called by him the Kuyuk, but was unable to proceed far and returned to Nulato, where he built a *bidar,* and in the beginning of June went up the Yukon one hundred Italian miles, according to his journal, which would be about to the mouth of the Nowikakat River. He then returned, went down the Yukon as far as Ikogmute, crossed to the Kuskokwim, and then went to Kolmakof Redoubt.[29]

To ascertain the value of the interior valleys two expeditions were sent in 1843 to explore the region between the Susitna River and the Copper River, and to endeavor to reach Plaveshnoi Lake, which was supposed to be the source of the streams flowing into both these rivers. The Copper River expedition was under the *praporschik* Gregorief, and succeeded in reaching the lake. Gregorief's report states that he followed the river Tishlina, or Tlishlitna, and that for a distance of 1250 versts he found no special obstruction.[30]

The Hudson's Bay Company found the Kolosh, or Thlingits, around Fort Stikine to be an intractable and turbulent lot of neighbors. Soon after their occupation of the fort the post doctor and his assistant were captured and held for ransom. On another occasion the aqueduct that supplied the water was cut, but fortunately an influential chief was in the fort who was held as a hostage till the damage was repaired. Within two years after their occupation, during an altercation between the employees, John McLoughlin, Jr., the Commandant of the post, was killed. He was a son of Dr. John McLoughlin, chief factor at Fort Vancouver. Urbain Heroux is supposed to be the murderer and he was taken to Sitka and left among the Russians as a punishment. Upon McLoughlin's death being known to the surrounding tribes they assembled to the number of over two thousand men, planning to capture the place while it was in a state of insubordination and without a leader. Governor Simpson of the company was on a visit to Sitka at the time. On his return in the steamer he was accompanied by a Russian ship and

arrived opportunely at the height of the disturbance. The
presence of two armed ships dispelled all hope of capturing
the fort.[31]

As the disturbance arose during a drunken debauch it
resulted in an agreement between Etolin and Governor
Simpson, in 1842, by which they, for their respective companies, proposed to cease the sale of liquor at their posts in
the territory north of 50°.

In 1841 the Russians made another retreat. A sale was
effected to Captain John A. Sutter of the fort buildings at
Ross, California, for the sum of thirty thousand dollars, and
the Russian people of that colony took ship for Sitka.[32]

17

The Third Charter

THE THIRD CHARTER OF THE RUSSIAN AMERICAN COM-
pany was dated October 10, 1844, but was related back to the
expiration of the previous privilege. The terms were similar
to those of the previous instrument, with additions concerning the employees and natives.

The company had abandoned the policy of expansion of
trade and the acquisition of territory as pursued under the
rule of Baranof, when he sent ships to Manila and to China,
extended his post to Russian River in California, and attempted to gain a foothold on the Sandwich Islands.

They were also pursuing a different policy in regard to
the fur-bearing animals in their territory. The experience of
the first part of the century, during which the Directory at
St. Petersburg drove the manager to search every available
source for seal and sea otter with the result that the hunting
grounds were depleted, bore its fruit in a policy of conservation which was begun by Baron Wrangel and was continued
by his successors.

The Government was also more mindful of the rights of
its subjects than it had been during the previous periods of the
company's existence. It prescribed regulations for both
Russian and native which were calculated to secure more
equitable treatment and greater respect for their persons
and property.

The employees were "actually in the Government
service" and "enjoy the right of being promoted to ranks
and wearing the uniform of the Ministry of Finance," while
the company had been granted the privilege of a distinctive
flag.[1]

There were no courts of law, but the chief manager had
the power to decide minor offenses and to report the decision
to the general administration, while criminal cases were referred to a special commission appointed by him, which, in
case of their inability to agree, might refer the proceedings

to the nearest court of justice in Russia. The rights and privileges of the natives and of the Creoles were provided for.

The Creoles were the children of Russian fathers and the native women.[2] They had the rights of tradesmen. Many of them were educated by the company, and in this case were required to serve in the company's pay for not less than fifteen years.

The natives were divided into two classes: the settled natives, or those subject to the Russian control, as the Kodiaks, the Aleuts, the Chugach, Kenaitze, etc., and the wild tribes, over whom the company exercised little control.

The local business was conducted in assignats, or scrip, issued by the company, the same as had been done in previous years. The Kolosh used tanned deerskins as currency, and they also had much of the *hiaqua*, or small seashells, used by the Indians on Puget Sound as money *(dentalium)*, which was called by them *tzukli*, and which was valued at about thirty rubles per hundred in trade in 1825.

Ice was sold in California, being cut both at Sitka and at Kodiak, a company incorporated in San Francisco under the name of the American Russian Company, known as the Ice Company, handling the business. Two sawmills cut timber for local use and for export. Sawmills were introduced in the colonies at an early date. Baranof constructed a crude mill at Resurrection Bay, near Seward, for use in building the *Phoenix*. Rezanof ordered the machinery for one at Sitka in 1806. About 1848 a mill was placed in Sawmill Creek on the Kirenski River. Two flouring mills, one at Sitka, the other at the Ozerskoe Redoubt, ground the grain brought from Chile or California. A tannery prepared leather of various kinds and tanned the *lavtaks* for the *bidarkas*, using cattle hides from California and sea lion skins from the coast.[3]

A well-equipped brass and iron foundry, with a machine shop in connection, occupied the space to the east of the church, and here the engines for the boats were built. The workmen were Russians and Creoles. Every master had a number of Creole boys as apprentices, many of whom made good workmen for they had quick perception and a natural inclination for mechanical pursuits. Bells were cast, the first at Kodiak in 1793, under the direction of Baranof, of a weight of 183 pounds; and plowshares and spades were made and shipped to the California market. Some of the mission bells of the Franciscan Missions of California were cast at Sitka.

Hospitals were maintained at Sitka and Kodiak. Of the one at Sitka, Sir George Simpson says: "The institution in question would be no disgrace to England." In the Kodiak hospital were ten beds.

The period of the greatest building activity of the colonies was during these years. The Cathedral of St. Michael was built 1847-1849; Baranof Castle, between 1836 and 1837; the clubhouse, living quarters for the officers of the company, about 1840; the Countinghouse, used by the U. S. as a Governor's Office and a Customhouse, in 1857; the dam in the Kirenski River, in 1847.

A terrible visitation of smallpox swept the country between 1836 and 1840, coming from the southeast and passing on to the north into the Arctic, which killed thousands of natives. The progress of the scourge may be traced among the Mandans of Dakota and in the valley of the Willamette as well as in Russian America. In 1862 the scourge again came, but because of the efficient regulations enforced by the company only a few died, the natives under the Russian control being vaccinated. During Etolin's administration twelve hundred were vaccinated at Sitka, and under Furuhelm vaccine was distributed at every station.[4]

Venereal disease was very prevalent for a time and caused the management much trouble, but was finally eradicated at all the western points, and at Sitka was practically suppressed before the close of the Russian regime.[5]

Captain Michael Dmitrievich Tebenkof took charge in 1845, and being specially interested in hydrography he collected the charts of Alaskan waters, made new surveys, and published an atlas under the title of *The Northwest Coast of America from Bering Strait to Cape Corrientos and the Aleutian Islands, etc.*, the first edition of which was published at Sitka (Tikh Pt. 2, p. 248). A Creole named Tarentief engraved the plates, while the maps were prepared by a Creole captain named Kadin.

The impression has been that the company discouraged the finding of minerals and that Baranof put to the knout a hunter who brought to Sitka gold-bearing quartz. This is highly improbable, for Baranof tried to smelt iron, attempted to reach the native copper on Copper River, and at one time wrote to Russia asking for a man skilled in mining,[6] while in 1848 the company sent a mining engineer named Doroshin to the colonies, who discovered limestone, marble, graphite, coal, and gold. In 1855 a vein of coal was opened at Port Graham, and a shipment was sent to San Francisco, which did not prove profitable, but the coal continued to be used for the steamers of the company.

Although the Russian American Company had been granted the right under their charter to take and use every form of resource on the land or water, they either neglected or had not the capacity to utilize one prolific source of profit on the sea, and it fell to the hardy, venturesome, enterprising Yankee seamen to take the prize offered in the whaling of the Pacific and Arctic. When Bering sailed north into the unknown northern seas he found the waters swarming with seal, walrus, and whale. Other Russian navigators record that the schools of whale played about their ships at night, spraying the decks with water from their gambols, while the blows of their tails on the water sounded like cannon shots.

The New England whalers invaded the Pacific in the early part of the nineteenth century, and by 1835 they had reached the prolific waters adjacent to Kodiak Island, Captain Barzillar Folger, a Nantucket whaler, of the ship *Ganges*, being the first to cruise there. These whaling grounds soon became the most important in the Pacific and were known as the Northwest Right Whaling Grounds.[7]

The right whale was at that time the coveted prize of the deep-sea whalers. It is the one that carried the commodity much desired at that time, the balaena, or whalebone, of commerce. It became of the value of about seven dollars a pound at a later time, and was used for whips and corset-stays. From this whale came both bone and oil. The other varieties that yielded no bone were not sought. As soon as the right whale was swept from the ocean, the ships moved over to the coast of Kamchatka, where they found the Arctic right whale, the bowhead, at the edge of the ice pack, for it lingers along the Arctic ice field as it advances and retreats each year.

From 1835 to 1869 the whaling grounds above 50° N.

Cathedral of St. Michael in Sitka

BARANOF CASTLE

It was built in 1837 to replace original building erected by Baranof. Official residence of chief managers of the Russian American Company from the time of Kupreanof. From 1867-1877 was the headquarters of U. S. troops. Destroyed by fire in 1894. The site is now occupied by the U. S. Department of Agriculture building.

Photograph by LaRoche, 1892.

Interior View of the Cathedral of St. Michael

THE MADONNA OF THE CATHEDRAL OF
ST. MICHAEL

Lat. in the Pacific produced 60 per cent of the oil secured by the American fleet, amounting to 3,994,327 barrels, and the principal localities were discovered by Americans and were controlled by them, but few foreign ships being engaged there. The sea was full of ships; from the lookout of a whaler one could count seventy or eighty sails, like white wings over the ocean, and from many of them the black smoke rose like a cloud, indicating they had struck whales and were boiling their oil pots. No less than 292 whaling ships cruised in those waters in 1846.

The whalers struck the ice pack off Cape Navarin, on the coast of Siberia, where the bowhead whale was found; hung along the pack as it drifted northward until their casks were filled with oil and the holds stowed with whalebone. In 1847 Captain Royce of the bark *Superior* passed through Bering Strait into the Arctic Ocean and in the full glory of an Arctic night struck his first whale at midnight, for the perpetual light in that latitude enabled them to work night and day. Within the next three years 250 ships took cargoes in the Arctic. In 1853 about 250 ships passed through Bering Strait, whaling, but not all were successful, for in 1854, 30 ships returned without a drop of oil. The first whalers passed to the east of Point Barrow in 1854 and returned in September of the same year.

Some of these American whalers were as evil a lot of pirates as ever sailed with Morgan along the Spanish Main or harried the coast of Louisiana under Lafitte. The ships sailed from some New England town as New Bedford or Nantucket, touched on the coast of Africa and "black-birded" for negro slaves which they sold in the South, bought Jamaica rum and headed around Cape Horn for the Arctic, where they traded the rum for whale oil, whalebone, and furs, of the Eskimos. Some crews were as sturdy and honest seamen as sailed from any port, but when a ship's crew went short they shipped whatever came to hand in Rio or in the Sandwich Islands, and the material from which to choose was the worst in the Western World. In later years the crimps of the sailors' boardinghouses of New Bedford and Nantucket thrived by supplying seamen for these cruises. The scenes of *Moby Dick* are true to the life of the time.

The Russian American Company noted the coming of

the whalers, for they scoured the seas, landed on the western islands, boiled oil on shore and disturbed the sea-otter hunting, robbed the native villages of their supplies, burned the stocks of driftwood which had been collected at great exertion along the stormy shores, and even destroyed property of the company. The company protested to their Government against these acts, but the protest, when referred to the United States, received scant courtesy or attention, so the company decided to enter the business and derive a share of the profit. A corporation, the Russian-Finland Whaling Company, was organized in St. Petersburg in 1850, sent out the ship *Suomi* in 1852-3, and took 1500 barrels of oil and 21,400 pounds of whalebone in one voyage. A second ship, the *Turko,* was equipped in 1852, and took only one whale on the first cruise. The Crimean War interfered with further operations, for, although the English and Russian Governments agreed to respect the rights of the frontier settlements of the two great fur-trading companies on the shores of the Pacific, the ships on the open seas were not included, and the three Russian whalers, the *Suomi,* the *Turko,* and the *Aiyan,* were withdrawn, and the venture was discontinued.[8]

The two companies, the Russian American Company and the Hudson's Bay Company, were keenly competing for the trade of the interior of the country along the rivers flowing into the Pacific and the Arctic. Adventurous explorers from England were seeking to lift the veil of mystery which hung over the northern ocean and which has shrouded a great portion of it to the present day. Seeking for new fur-producing territory, the Hudson's Bay Company traders penetrated farther and farther into the unknown wilds of the Northwest. In 1844 John Bell explored the Porcupine River, which falls into the Yukon at the Arctic Circle. Three years later Alexander Murray crossed the portage from Lapierre House, on the Peel River, descended the Porcupine River to the Yukon, and there established Fort Yukon, about three miles above the mouth of the Porcupine, in July of 1847. Murray was a Scotsman, as might be guessed from his name, born in Argyllshire, Scotland, 1818. His story of his journey and accomplishment of its purpose, as told in his *Journal of the Yukon,* is an interesting one,[9] illustrated by sketches made with a "few steel pens now going on their *third year,* and filed down to stumps." Among them are the only drawings extant of the old buildings of the Hudson's Bay Company at Fort Yukon. He well knew that he was in Russian territory, and that he had not the right to erect a post or to conduct trade, for he says, "We are over the edge, and that by a 'long chalk,' which I call six degrees of longitude across the Russian boundary." And again, "We lived on good terms with the natives and feared nothing, except to see two boat loads of Russians heave round the point."[10]

The Yukon at that time was supposed to empty into the Arctic Ocean, but Murray surmised the true course, for he says, when referring to the Russians, "The river they ascend from the coast must as far as I can judge, fall into Norton Sound."

He brought some potatoes for planting, and remarks, "May God grant us a genial summer say I, though it should be only for the 'taters,' for I would fight with the pigs for them."

He found among the natives rumors of the Russians' having visited the upper Yukon before his arrival, but this must have been erroneous, for there seems to be no record to substantiate it among the Russian archives.

Robert Campbell went from Fort Selkirk to Fort Yukon in 1851, and completed the exploration of that part of the river, but the identity of the river Kwichpak of the Russians and the Yukon had not been established, for the gap between the mouth of the Nowikakat, the farthest point attained by Zagoskin, and Fort Yukon, had not been passed. Campbell went up the Porcupine, over the portage to the Mackenzie, thence up to Fort Simpson.

About 1861 the Russian trading expeditions reached Nukluklayet at the mouth of the Tanana. Soon after that the fur traders from Fort Yukon were sent to the same place to gather furs for the Hudson's Bay Company, thus carrying the fur war to the Yukon Valley, and in 1863 the Russian, Simon Lukeen, made the continuous journey to Fort Yukon from St. Michael, the first adventurer to accomplish that feat.[11]

In an attempt to explore the Copper River the Russian Serebrennikof visited Plavezhna Lake, on one of the western tributaries, then returned to the Copper River, where he was attacked in the night by the natives and his party destroyed. The cause of the massacre is supposed to have been the mistreatment of the natives by his men. His journal was afterward delivered to the Russians by the natives, in which it appears that the last observation was taken at 62°48'43" N. Lat.[12]

The most romantic of the many interesting stories of the mysterious North is that of the brave Sir John Franklin, one of the finest characters who came to that wilderness, whose name among the Eskimo means "the man who does not molest our women," and whom one writer has called the Sir Galahad of explorers. He left England in 1845 to attempt the long-sought northwest passage from the Atlantic to the Pacific. Three years having passed in which no tidings were received, the British Government and Lady Franklin labored with untiring energy to send out expeditions to his relief. Some of these came to the Pacific. The *Plover,* under Captain Moore, reached Kotzebue Sound, July 15, 1849, where she was joined by H. M. S. *Herald,* and in the sound on the same quest was the yacht *Nancy Dawson,* equipped by the private enterprise of Robert Sheddon. The commander of the *Plover* sent Lieutenants Pullen and Hooper to search the coast east from Point Barrow to the Mackenzie, which they accomplished and then made their way overland to Hudson's Bay. Captain Richard Collinson, in H. M. S. *Enterprise,* accompanied by Captain Robert McClure in H. M. S. *Investigator,* came in 1850 on the same mission. McClure passed Point Barrow, went as far east as Prince of Wales Strait, passed two winters locked in the ice in Mercy Bay, then abandoned his ship and with his crew made his way to Beechey Island, where he took a ship for England, having made the northwest passage on foot over the ice. Collinson returned by Bering Strait, left Lieutenant Barnard and Surgeon Adams of his command to investigate the interior of the country, then returned to the Arctic, where he spent three winters before giving up the search.

Lieutenant Barnard went up the Yukon as far as Nulato, where he remained until February, 1852, when, in an attack on the post made by the Nulato Indians, he was murdered, together with the Russian Commandant, Derabin, and several others.

The story of the tragic fate of Sir John was not finally told until Captain McClintock in 1859 found the last relics of the unfortunate party.[13]

Chief Manager Rosenberg and his successor, Rudakof, failed to understand the Thlingit and neglected to cultivate his friendship as Etolin had done. The good feeling established by Etolin between the Russians and the Kolosh was disturbed by different events. Feuds raged among the different *kwans*. The Sitkas, under the gates of the fort, preserved their primitive customs and practiced witchcraft with all the attendant atrocities which accompany that weird belief. At the slightest provocation they would swarm out of their houses, their faces blackened with war paint, wearing hideous masks made in images of wild beasts, and shout defiance at their neighbors over the stockade.

In consequence of an ancient feud forty Stikine Indians were killed at a potlatch in Sitka, where they had gone on a visit. In 1852 the Stikines made an attack on the Ozerskoe Redoubt and the Hot Springs. The inmates escaped with their lives but had to make their way by land to Sitka, a difficult journey, from which they arrived more nearly dead than alive, after more than thirty miles of trackless wilderness, along bristling cliffs, through thickets of devil's clubs and over rugged mountains around the fjord of Silver Bay.[14] In 1855 the ill-feeling against the Russians culminated in an attack of the town at Sitka. A sentinel caught an Indian stealing some articles, and proceeded to punish him. The tribesmen in war paint and armed with muskets made an attack on the stockade at the point occupied by the Koloshian church, through the outer doors of which they forced an entrance, and fired from the doors and windows of that building on the town and fort. The cannon of the batteries and the rifles of the Siberian Battalion were turned against them and in a battle of two hours' duration the Kolosh were defeated with a loss of sixty killed and wounded, while the Russians had two killed and nineteen wounded. This was the last serious difficulty between the Russians and the Kolosh.[15]

Meanwhile the Chilkats, at the head of Lynn Canal, had been jealous of the Hudson's Bay post at Fort Selkirk, for they considered that the trade of the interior belonged to them exclusively, having controlled it for years through the ownership of the trail over the Dyea and Chilkat Passes. These trails were called grease trails, probably because over them was taken the oolachan oil which was a staple article of barter. In 1851 a war party from the coast attacked Selkirk, burned the buildings, but did not harm the inmates, who escaped with the loss of their property. The post was not rebuilt.

The Hudson's Bay Company was not exempt from difficulties with the Thlingits on the coast, for in August of 1862 the steamer *Labouchere* was attacked at Hoonah. The main deck was taken and held for several hours, and a serious condition prevailed, for the captain and mate were held as prisoners. A truce was finally concluded and the quarrel settled without loss of life on either side.[16]

From California, during the gold-mining days of the early fifties, came ships to be repaired on the ways at Sitka. To that country were shipped whole cargoes of goods from the warehouses, and a profitable trade in ice, fish, and lumber was promoted in California, Mexico, and the Hawaiian Islands.

On the Fraser River gold was discovered in 1858. Thousands of prospectors thronged up the Fraser River, passed through the mountain passes to the Caribou country, and in 1861 "Buck" Choquette discovered gold on the upper waters of the Stikine. Many others followed, and on the Stikine a small steamer called the *Flying Dutchman* was run by Captain William Moore, which went as far as Glenora and Telegraph Creek.[17] But the Fraser River diggings proved the richer field, and the Stikine was deserted until other discoveries in later years again brought the crowds of gold seekers to this gateway.

The difficulties of laying the Atlantic Cable seemed so unsurmountable that the Western Union Telegraph Company conceived the idea of a line by the way of Bering Strait and overland across Siberia. Ships were purchased in 1865. Parties of men were sent to British Columbia, to Siberia, and to Alaska, involving a vast amount of expense, amounting, it is estimated, to as much as two or three millions of dollars. The successful completion of the laying of the submarine cable by Cyrus Field caused the abandonment of the project at an immense financial loss, but a knowledge of the country was gained which was invaluable.[18]

The occupation of the Russians in their possessions in America was drawing toward a close. In Sitka, the chief factory, the citizens lived a busy and uneventful life. The usual serenity of the village was disturbed only by the arrival of ships from far-off Russia, the Fatherland, or by some great church festival. Ships from home were few and far between. From 1804 to 1849 there were only forty-one arrivals; after this they came more often, between 1849 and 1852 there were fourteen, an unusually large number.

The fear of the Kolosh was constantly before the people of the colony. In Baranof's time it was very real. He had few men, and his guns were inferior to those sold by the Americans and British to the Indians. The massacre at Old Sitka was fresh in their minds when Rezanof came. He said in a letter of Nov. 6, 1805, "The great brutality shown by the Americans has taught us extreme caution. Our guns are always loaded, everywhere are sentinels with loaded guns, and in the rooms of each of us are weapons which constitute the larger part of the furniture. All night from the coming of dark, signals are with war discipline and we every minute are ready to receive our dear guests, who profit by the darkness of night and the rainy weather to make their attack. . . . "

Baranof had no soldiery. He purchased safety with his meagre force by unceasing vigilance. He is accused of drunkenness. He was never intoxicated long enough to forget. Lutke says of him in *Voyage of the Seniavine,* "Nothing was overlooked in all that was to be prepared, was the rule of Baranof; the soul of this remarkable man guards, it appears, even now over the establishment, by him founded."

The watchfulness taught by Baranof was vanishing from the people. They began to clamor for soldiers. The outbreak of 1855 roused their fears to the breaking point. In 1857 in the annual report of the chief manager appears the following, "The ship Czarevich . . . was sent to the Amoor for cargo . . . and a command of the Siberian Line Batallion."

In the *Doklad Komitita,* in 1863, is stated, "In New Archangel are found 147 soldiers of the Siberian Line batallion and 39 Crown seamen." It continues, "Strengthen means to defend New Archangel from the attacks of the Kolosh, this sword of Damocles eternally threatens Sitka."

The officers of the Imperial Navy were in command, but

they lacked the eternal watchfulness that Lutke records. They did not inherit the spirit of Baranof when they took up the reins of government that fell from his dying hands. Russia was loosing her grasp on her colonies in America.

There were few women in the colonies, other than Aleuts or Thlingits, until the time of the third charter. Natalia Shelekof came with her husband in 1784 to Three Saints Harbor. She was the first Russian woman to come to the Russian settlements, and she returned to Russia with her husband. The women of the thirty families of exiles nearly all perished from disease, or were destroyed by the Thlingits at Yakutat. Mrs. Larionof, the wife of the manager at Unalaska, was probably the next woman of the better classes to come, and she remained till after the death of her husband, then went to Russia with her daughter on the ship with Captain DeWolf in 1806. The next woman of whom there is a record was Mrs. Banner, wife of the manager of the Kodiak District. Lady Wrangell was the first cultured woman at Sitka.

Lutke, Russian commander of a round-the-world ship, says, "The house of the Chief Manager remains a general meeting place in free hours. By established custom, all the officers are gathered to it, and on holidays they dine.

"The establishment of the present manager presents in itself in this relation an epoch; the first cultured lady in the presence of the wife of Baron von Wrangell, enlightening this desert place."

Lady Kupreanof accompanied her husband across Siberia to be with him at Sitka. Lady Etolin also enlivened the manager's mansion, and she taught in the girl's school.

In 1860 the census of the colonies showed 208 Russian women, and 576 men.

Russian hospitality is famous the world over, and at Sitka the people upheld the traditions of the race. Dinners and festivals of all kinds were frequent, and weddings were elaborate affairs with a ceremony an hour and a half in length. Easter was the greatest of the many holidays. All dressed gaily, attended church, where they stood throughout the entire ceremony; then all went about the town, carrying gilded eggs, hard-boiled, which they presented to their friends, greeting them with the salutation, "Christ is risen."

The schools were provided for with liberality. The first one was placed at Three Saints in 1785 by Shelekof; the priests Juvenal and Herman continued the work at Kodiak; Rezanof placed a school at Paulofski, Kodiak Island, in 1805, and also established a girls' school at that place, over which Mrs. Banner, the wife of the district manager, presided until her death. At Sitka a school was begun in 1805, and in 1820 Mouravief assigned a naval officer to the work; in 1833 Etolin organized it in a more thorough manner, transferred the girls' school from Kodiak and placed Lady Etolin in charge of it. At one time there were five schools at Sitka, in one of which navigation was taught. Others were held in Kodiak, Amlia, Unalaska, and Nushagak. When the Russian Government withdrew from the territory the schools were closed.

The shipping in the harbor presented a busy scene, from ten to fifteen vessels often being in the roadstead lading or unlading cargo. Ships for exploring voyages, others for gathering furs in Bering Sea or in the Arctic, some preparing for the long journey to Kronstadt, to St. Petersburg, or for crossing the Pacific to Okhotsk, were anchored in the bay. Before the sailing the chief manager went on board for inspection; the officers and men dressed in their finest uniforms; every appointment was seen to be in perfect order. On the deck was a priest to bless the ship before she departed on her voyage; he sprinkled the flag with holy water, and the company partook of a collation. The harbor tug took the ship slowly out through the passage between the spruce-clad islands. There was a parting salute from the shore batteries; then the sails were spread to the ocean breeze. The people of New Archangel went back to their beating and sorting of furs, the work of the mills, to the homely tasks of the village, and the sentries kept their ceaseless vigil along the stockade.

Aged employees of the Russian American Company, who had served their active life in the colonies, were provided with a small pension. They were classed as colonial citizens, and received from 30 to 240 rubles, silver, a year for each family. In 1841 there were 20, with families. In 1860 the number had increased to 240 persons. (*Doklad Komitita*, p. 77.)

The company prospered during the last period of its existence, under the better regulations which had been observed on the hunting grounds. The conservation of animals in a quarter of a century of the management of the Seal Islands, and in the sea-otter hunting, had just begun to bear fruit. From 1842 to 1860 there had been taken but an average of 964 skins of the sea otter for each year, and they observed a system of hunting a locality but one year of a certain number and rotated them so that each had an opportunity to recuperate.

The correspondence of the company shows that they had only begun to consider the increase of the catch after 1860.

The sealing on the Pribilof Islands had also been conducted in accord with the same policy and but 17,820 skins a year on an average were taken during the period. Other furs were taken in moderation, the annual average being: beaver 8,475, otter 3,360, fox 3,890, white fox (pestzof) 2,290, marten 1,390, mink 130, wolf 5. They expected during the next period to reap the fruits of their foresight and moderation. On the Czarevich in 1867 was shipped a cargo valued at over two million rubles. The company looked forward to a harvest of fur in the coming years and hoped for a renewal of their lease until the very time of the purchase by the United States.

Captain P. N. Golovin[19] was sent by the Russian Government to make a survey of the colonies, and his report, when rendered, was favorable to a renewal of their privileges, but a controversy arose in St. Petersburg over some of the acts of the company with reference to their treatment of the natives. A Creole captain named Kashevarof, who lived in St. Petersburg, but who had sailed for many years in the employ of the company, wrote an answer to the report of Captain Golovin, and exposed certain abuses. This called out a reply from the company and the controversy became so heated that Baron Wrangell was called upon to state as to the truth of the accusations of Kashevarof. He substantiated them, at least in a measure. This prevented the issuance of the charter, as there was already considerable opposition to the granting of such special privileges. Prince Dmitri Maksoutoff was appointed to the charge of the colonies on behalf of the Government, and the matter was held in abeyance.

The Russian American Company was second in the fur trade of the world only to the Hudson's Bay Company, the great English corporation that held control of nearly all of

Canada's fur resources. Its trade rights held part of eastern Siberia, the Kurile Islands, the eastern Amoor region, the Komandorski Islands, and the colonies in America. Literally millions of beautiful pelts of the northern fur bearers passed through the warerooms of the company. Its fleet combed the waters of the northern Pacific, passed into the Arctic, collecting the catch of the native peoples, while its round-the-world ships conveyed the precious cargo to China and to Russia. Its richest prize was the sea otter. Its greatest source of supply was on the Seal Islands of the Bering Sea, in the fur seals that thronged the breeding places of those islands by millions, and whose skins were to be had for the taking. It employed the Aleuts to kill and take the pelts.

During the time the company had the lease of the colonies it shipped out nearly 4,000,000 skins, and of these more than 140,000 were of the sea otter, and over 2,500,000 of seal.[20]

During the last thirty years of its occupation it conserved fur animals by establishing periods of rest, called *zapuski*, in different places for certain of the animals, and restricted the catch on such as appeared to be in need of conservation. It also transferred foxes to islands which had been denuded of fur animals.

The Hudson's Bay Company wished to get control of the country and the fur. They haggled over the lease of the southeastern part and alleged that the Russians did not sufficiently protect them against outside traders. They projected a holding company in the nature of a vast fur monopoly, which was intended to absorb both the Hudson's Bay Company and the Russian American Company, which would control the fur trade of the world, but the attempt failed.[21] The Russian Government appears to have been opposed to the land's falling into the hands of Great Britain.

To retain the land with its sparse population was an expense in time of peace and a menace in time of war, for both men and ships would be required for its protection.

The sale to the United States seems to have been considered as early as during the administration of President Polk.[22] Sumner, in his speech in defense of the purchase, says: "The Russian government was sounded on the subject during the administration of Mr. Buchanan, and the amount of $5,000,000 was suggested at that time." It was stated in

Congress, July 1, 1868, that five million dollars had been twice offered and refused. There was a friendly feeling between Russia and the United States during the time of the Civil War. The influence of the Pacific States was favorable to the acquisition because of their appreciation of the value of the fisheries, and a memorial was addressed to Congress by the Legislature of the Territory of Washington to that effect in 1866. There was also a strong influence exerted on the part of prominent fur merchants of San Francisco in favor of the purchase.

At the foundation of the matter was the fact that the Russians had been loosening their grasp on their possessions in America for nearly thirty years. The first step was the lease of the *lisiere* of the coast from Portland Canal to Cape Spencer to the Hudson's Bay Company in 1840. Next was the sale of Ross, in California. Then followed the failure to expel the Hudson's Bay Company from Fort Yukon when they placed that post in the Russian territory and there maintained it. Russia was averse to surrendering it to Great Britain, for she had been against them in the Crimean War, and had crowded them hard on their American borders. As a result of these influences the United States received the territory now known as Alaska.

The treaty was concluded by Wm. H. Seward, Secretary of State, on March 30, 1867, under which for the sum of $7,200,000 the Russian possessions in America were transferred to the United States.[23] The treaty was ratified on May 26 of that year and the boundaries under it were the same as those of the treaty with Great Britain in 1825. The ratification was hotly opposed by some members of Congress, but Senator Sumner of Massachusetts championed the purchase in a speech that was an epitome of the existing knowledge of the territory, and the press gave it such publicity that the attention of the public was more drawn to the country than it was again for more than thirty years. Eminent men differed on the wisdom of the purchase and of the value of the territory, some holding it to be worthless, others marveling that it had been possible to purchase it at such an insignificant price.

PART TWO
1867 - 1937

18

The Transfer to the United States

ON THE EVENING OF A QUIET, MISTY DAY, OCTOBER 18, 1867, three ships of the United States, the *Ossipee*, the *Resaca*, and the *Jamestown*, lay in the harbor of Sitka. Through the streets of the quaint old Russian town blue-coated soldiery marched to the slopes of the Baranof Hill where they were drawn up in front of the residence of the chief manager. Russian troops formed alongside. The Imperial flag of Russia lifted lazily in the light ocean breeze. At 3:30 p. m., to the accompaniment of a salute from the artillery of both nations, the Russian ensign was lowered. It fouled in the halyards. A marine was sent aloft to release it. He tore it loose and flung it down on the heads of the Russian soldiers. Then the Stars and Stripes were raised to the booming of the cannon, and Alexei Pestchouroff, the Commissioner of the Czar, spoke a few words of transfer. General Rousseau, for the United States, signified his acceptance. The land we call Alaska passed to the dominion of Uncle Sam, and became a part of our country.[1]

The young and beautiful Princess Maksoutoff, the wife of the last chief manager of the Russian American Company, is said to have wept as the flag of her country was lowered and the land in which they had labored and loved passed from the rule of the Fatherland.[2]

The United States troops were quartered in the Russian barracks. The Commandant occupied Baranof Castle as his headquarters. The other buildings were taken as Government property, except the church and other private property. The archives of the company were sent to Washington to be deposited in the State Department.[3]

Jewish merchants from San Francisco were present to purchase the vast stocks of goods contained in the magazines of the chief factory of the company, but a wealthy war contractor of New England, H. M. Hutchinson, by his diplomacy gained the attention of Prince Maksoutoff, who acted for the

Russian American Company in selling the goods, and to him was transferred the whole of the merchandise of all kinds, for the sum of $155,000, according to the *Alaska Herald* of San Francisco. It consisted of every description of merchandise incidental to an important frontier post, including sheepskin coats, brass cannon, barrels of rum, casks of wine, Russia leather, sheet copper, lead, tea, drygoods, and hundreds of other articles, of which to San Francisco alone there was shipped to the value of over $250,000.[4] The sale also covered ships in the harbor, the *Politofski*, well known on the coast for many years, the *Menshikoff*, and others.

Captain Gustave Niebaum, in the employ of the company, is said, through some advance information, to have secured possession of a large quantity of sealskins and manipulated them in a manner that caused him to become a member of the company soon after formed and known as Hutchinson, Kohl & Company. This company took over all the goods, furs, and ships of the partners. An example of the profit realized by the purchase is shown by the transfer of the *Politofski* from the Russian American Company to Hutchinson for the sum of four thousand dollars while the ship was taken over by Hutchinson, Kohl & Co. within six months after for the sum of ten thousand dollars.

Most of the Russians who had the means of transportation departed for the Fatherland by the first available ships.[5] Those who remained were promised rights of citizenship.[6]

By the purchase of the territory the United States gained control of about 375,000,000 acres of land for an average price of less than two cents per acre. With it went forests containing billions of feet of lumber, fishing banks and streams with millions of dollars in value of the finest fish, mineral veins containing millions in value of copper, gold, lead, silver, coal, and other minerals, thousands of fur-bearing animals, and the different groups of native inhabitants, numbering over thirty thousand souls, distributed over the land in the various sections.

The Hydahs, Tsimphiens, and Thlingits, all called Kolosh by the Russians, inhabiting the southeastern part, were similar in habits and customs, but spoke different languages. They were a maritime people, living largely by the products of the sea. They wove beautiful baskets. They carved canoes con-

SITKA ABOUT 1860

From Tikhménef's *Historical Sketch.*

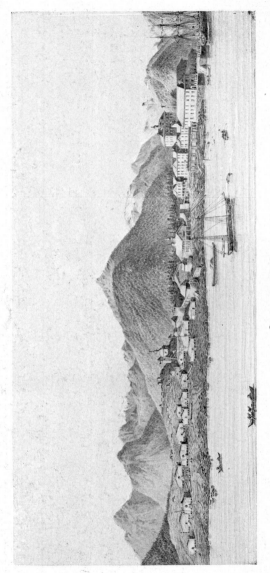

SITKA IN 1869
From Alaska Coast Pilot, 1869.

The Governor's Walk, Sitka

"THE RANCHE," OR INDIAN TOWN, OF SITKA

structed of a single log that were marvels of workmanship and beauty of design. In front of their houses they erected totemic emblems, or carved them on the posts of their dwellings, indicating by them the family of the owner of the house. They are a brave and warlike people, inured to hardship, independent in spirit, and they numbered about six thousand souls according to the Russian records.

The Aleuts, the mild, inoffensive, intelligent people of the western islands, lived on the long chain that reaches out toward the coast of Asia. They likewise subsisted mainly by the products of the sea, and their boats, like those of the Eskimo, were of a skin covering over a framework of wood. They were, most of all the native peoples, influenced by the domination of the Russian.

The Eskimos, living from Kodiak Island along the western shores and north to Point Barrow, thence east to the Canadian boundary, were hunters of the sea, subsisting by the whale, walrus, seal, and fish, with the caribou, or wild reindeer, and the animals and birds of the land. The southern villages were the most in contact with the Russians, and Unalakleet was the farthest north trading post among them. No census of their number had been made, but they probably numbered some thousands more in 1867 than at the present.

In the valleys of the interior were the Athapascan Indian tribes, hunters and fishermen, who made their way on the rivers in birchbark canoes, while in winter they traveled with their dog teams. Their cabins by the streams were at the best fishing places, for they depended largely on the salmon that makes its way for more than two thousand miles up the Yukon.

With many of the Eskimos of the North and the Indians of the interior the Russians had never come in contact. In the colonies in 1860 there were 9,568 who were counted as having embraced Christianity and who had been baptized into the Greek Church.[7]

Sitka was the first and the only post occupied by the military during 1867, and it was the headquarters of the District.[8] Later there were posts established at Wrangell, Tongass, Kenai, and Kodiak, the total military force comprising about five hundred men at one time.

According to reports of various officers, some of them

in the military service, it would appear that the stationing of troops in Alaska was a mistake, and that the needs would have been far better served by one or two light, swift boats.[9] Sitka is on an island, and without transportation the soldiers were like prisoners in confinement. Without boats they were powerless as to aggression against the surrounding villages. The thousand inlets and passages between the islands were retreats in which the Thlingits might hide without fear of pursuit.

Into Sitka flocked a motley crowd of adventurers. Saloons and houses of prostitution opened for the first time in the land. Traders, speculators, politicians, gamblers, and harlots made their advent. On the one and only street of the village the front-foot values rose to dizzy heights.

William Sumner Dodge had been appointed under date of August 15, 1867, as:

Special Agent of the Treasury Department, to act as Collector of Customs for the District of Country lately ceded by the Russian Government to the United States.

His instructions were:

You will locate your office at the port known as Sitka or New Archangel, which will be the only port within the territory at which a report and entry can be made or goods unloaded.[10]

One of his early reports states:

The great need of the country is the organization of a civil government with a general code of legislation. It is full of wealth and under proper encouragement bands of hardy adventurers, the pioneers of our civilization, will rapidly develop its resources and in a few years repay ten-fold the cost of the purchase besides extending well towards the coast of Asia the Genius of Republican Institutions.[11]

In Congress the purchase roused the bitterest opposition. Senator Sumner supported it in a speech that shows a breadth of research that to this day stands as an epitome of information about the territory prior to that date.[12]

A member of Congress in a speech characterized the purchase in the following language:

Mr. Chairman, that Alaska was created for some purpose I have just as little doubt as I have had since the Rebellion, of the necessity for the infernal regions. . . . The use and necessity for such a place as the infernal regions we now fully comprehend, but in relation to Alaska our information is so limited that conjecture can assign no use for it unless it was to demonstrate the folly to which those in authority are capable in the acquisition of useless territory.[13]

ALASKAN AND INDIAN BASKETRY WORK
Attu, Chernofski, Unalaskan, Thlingit, and Eskimo.

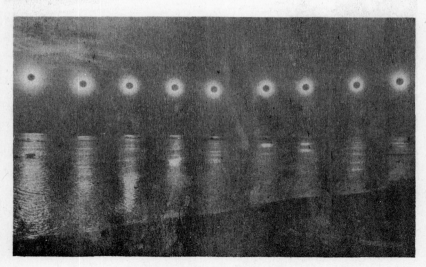

THE MIDNIGHT SUN IN ALASKA

THLINGIT GRAVE TOTEM AT WRANGELL, ALASKA

In this way was the land known as the Russian Possessions in America, or, as our maps placed it, Russian America, acquired, transferred, and taken possession of. A century and a half of discovery and occupation by the Russians had closed, and a new era was opening.

The territory became divided into two sections, the eastern portion, comprising the panhandle, or strip of coast below Mt. St. Elias, and for awhile the southern coast as far as Cook Inlet and Kodiak Island was under the jurisdiction of the Army of the United States. After about two years the military forces withdrew from Fort Kenai and Kodiak. The region westward from Yakutat Bay went under the rule of the fur traders, almost as completely as it was during the regime of the Russian American Company.

19

The Military Occupation

SITKA WAS THE CENTER OF THE EASTERN DIVISION OF Alaska and the autumn of 1867 was a busy time in the northern frontier port. The mob of fortune-seeking adventurers had not departed. The Russian people destined for the homeland had not yet been able to embark. The soldiers of the United States were quartered in the old barracks, while the Russian troops were billeted in the few houses of the village. A motley crowd, Americans, Russians, Germans, Jews, Finlanders, Aleuts, and Thlingits filled the streets.

The Russian ship *Czarevich*, the brig *Constantine*, the brig *Olga*, the bark *Menshikoff*, and the steamers *Politofski* and *Constantine* lay in the harbor and were purchased and documented as American vessels. The *Fideliter*, a steamer of doubtful origin, was listed as Russian, but became the subject of a libel suit by the Government.

A flock of schooners flitted along the passages between the islands bent on contraband trade or carrying army supplies and bartering for furs. The *Louisa Downs*, the *Nor'wester*, the *Gen. Harney*, the *Sweepstakes*, the *Pioneer*, and the *Nanaimo Packet* became more or less famous or notorious as time went on.

The steamer *John L. Stephens* came from San Francisco. The British steamer *Otter*, of the Hudson's Bay Company, ran between Victoria and Fort Wrangell.

The fur trade and the liquor traffic were profitable and enticing prizes in the half-organized region. The military had no jurisdiction of those matters. The Collector had no boats to follow the intruders. He was practically defied. He writes on January 16, 1868, that the *Otter* sailed from Victoria, November 18, 1867, and had not reported, and intimates that she must be trading in the passages. An Austrian had established himself on Kasaan Bay, had allied himself with one of the most powerful native families, and owned the *Pioneer*. The Collector says of him, "Baranoviz is an old smuggler, and last March he violated the English Colonial law of Customs ... at Metlakatla, when he had cleared for Sitka." The next year he states, "Within three weeks four vessels have boldly crossed the mouth of the harbor in plain sight, ... and yet I am powerless."

The revenue cutters *Reliance* and *Lincoln* cruised in those waters but accomplished little as at least one of them was a sailing ship and the smugglers openly boasted that they could run away from it.[1]

The congestion in the village was relieved slightly in December of 1867 by the sailing of the *Tzaritza*, with 168 passengers bound for Russia. In January the *Cyane* carried 69 soldiers of the Russian garrison to Novgorod, Asia, and in December, 1868, 300 more of the Russian people set out for their homes in Russia by the *Winged Arrow*.

The floating population, attracted by the hopes of gain, gradually departed. The ships for San Francisco were laden with tons of sheathing metal, sheet lead, cordage, hoop and bar iron, bells, brass cannon, anchors; thousands of yards of linen, *mitkal* (calico) and other cloth, casks of cranberries, bales of furs, every description of merchandise from the warehouses of the company. From the Seal Islands came barrels of seal oil, 10,600 gallons in one shipment; thousands of skins from the fur seal, and other furs.

Between October 18, 1867 and August 27, 1869, 71 vessels entered at the port, coming from Asia and from the Sandwich Islands, from San Francisco and from Victoria, B. C. Out from the port cleared 67 ships with an aggregate tonnage of 22,346 tons, and the trade was over $400,000, not including the coastwise trade.[2]

The beginnings of the postal service in Alaska are shrouded in mystery. A Government publication states that the post offices at Sitka and Wrangell were established in October, 1885, yet it is undoubted that in 1879 Collector M. D. Ball was acting as postmaster at Sitka.[3] Mail was brought from San Francisco by the monthly steamer, while communications with Unalaska and other western points was through the same city, involving between three and four thousand miles of transportation.

Of aids to navigation there were none. The Russians had kept a light or beacon on Baranof Castle. Of it the Collector says, on November 10, 1867: "On the top of the house is a tower, or balcony, the sides of which are windowed, and in which there is a spacious stand with three sets of arms, each set supporting four shallow, square cups in which seal oil was poured." A reflector three feet in diameter projected the light to a distance of about six miles at sea. He asked that permission be given to procure oil, and to secure the services of a soldier on special detail to attend the light. On January 14, 1868, the matter was referred to the Lighthouse Board, with the result that on November 11, 1868, permission was given, and under it the first light in Alaska under American occupation was established.[4]

In May of 1867, Assistant George Davidson, of the U. S. Coast and Geodetic Survey, was detailed to proceed on the revenue cutter *Lincoln* for a survey of the southern coast of Alaska, as far west as Unalaska. This was completed by November of that year.[5] Two years later he was returned to the North for further work, and from the result of these investigations, as well as from other sources he compiled the interesting and valuable *Coast Pilot of Alaska*, which was published in 1869, and which was not only an invaluable aid to navigation, but is to this time an original source of historical data.[6]

Excepting military rules prevailing at the garrison, no laws, civil or criminal, were provided for the territory in the beginning. In July, 1868, the laws of the United States relating to customs, commerce, and navigation were extended, the territory was designated as a Customs District. The port of entry was to be at or near the town of Sitka, or New Archangel.[7]

For some years a most unhappy condition prevailed. Murder, attack with dangerous weapons, theft, and other outrages were not prohibited, and they prevailed unchecked.[8]

A discharged soldier, W. A. Bird, shot and killed Lieutenant L. C. Cowan, U. S. Revenue Service. The military took him in charge. "He is still in custody," is the last record to be found.[9] There was neither civil nor military authority to take charge of Lieutenant Cowan's effects. The Collector of Customs and the Commander of the revenue cutter at the station disposed of them.

The Greek Catholic church at Sitka was plundered of its decorations and its service, the covers of the Bible being torn off and carried away as part of the spoil. Four men were arrested by the military, and investigation was made by a Board. The only record of the result is a statement made by Vincent Colyer to the effect that the thieves were drummed out of the service of the United States Army and sent to the States on the transport *Newbern*.[10]

The citizens attempted to form a provisional government for the town. They called a meeting, framed a charter, elected a mayor and council, drew up city ordinances, and opened a school. All depended upon public subscription for financial support. The first mayor was W. S. Dodge, the Collector of Customs. There was no law under which to levy taxes. The roughnecks opposed any restraint. By 1872 or 1873 the organization dissolved for want of funds.[11]

Intoxicating liquors were prohibited under United States statutes relating to Indian country, but no adequate provision was made for enforcement of the law. For many years the revenue laws provided for licensing the sale of intoxicants, while the customs revenue officers were supposed to prevent the importation and sale. From British territory liquors and other goods were smuggled in large quantities. The profits were so great and the enticements so alluring that even officers of the post indulged in the trade in contraband.[12] A villainous concoction called "hooch" originated at this time, being distilled in the various villages.[13]

The jurisdiction of crimes was later given to the court at Portland, Oregon, twelve hundred miles distant, where criminals were transported for trial. There was no code of procedure till 1884 under which white men could be convicted, but Indians were convicted and hanged in some cases.

The Indians, usually peaceful and well disposed, were resentful under ill-treatment, and proud and jealous of what they considered their rights. When under the influence of hooch they were simply incarnate devils among themselves. The women seemed to have the best of it often, for when drunken, they retained their skill with the knife to which they were trained by skinning animals, and many were the gashes the army surgeons were called upon to repair.

Colcheka was a Chilkat chief, one of the proudest of the most arrogant *kwan* of the Thlingits, whose home was at the head of the Lynn Canal. On New Year's Day he was visiting at Sitka, and was the guest of the commanding officer, at the headquarters in the castle. He is rumored to have been treated to various refreshments by the Commander, and when he left was greatly exhilarated by his experiences. As he crossed the parade ground he did not follow prescribed paths and in consequence was kicked by the sentry. Filled with rage, he wrested the gun from the soldier and carried it in triumph to the "Ranche," as the native village was called.

The guard was called to arrest the offender, but after a lively skirmish among the Indian houses they were compelled to retreat. The next day a parley was had; Colcheka surrendered, was placed in the guardhouse for a time, then released.

When the trouble started, an order was made that no Indians should be allowed to leave the village. This was rescinded upon Colcheka's surrender, but through some error the sentries were not notified. A canoe with a party of natives started out to get wood, were fired on by the sentries, and two men, a Kake and a Chilkat, were killed.

The tribal law of the Thlingit is "a life for a life" as was the old Mosaic code. This may be commuted to indemnity payment; otherwise there must be blood atonement. The family of the murdered Kake demanded the payment of blankets or the alternative of a victim, which was contemptuously refused by the Commandant.

Two prospectors, Ludwig Mager and William Walker, went along the shores of Chatham Strait searching for gold. On these the family of the dead Kake took their revenge and justified themselves in the eyes of their kinsmen by exacting the blood atonement.

When this came to the ears of General Davis he called on Captain Meade of the U. S. S. *Saginaw*, then at Sitka, to assist in punishing the guilty Kakes. On the *Saginaw* an armed force proceeded to Kake Island. The Indians fled to the forest on the approach of the ship. The *Saginaw* thereupon bombarded and destroyed Old Kake Village of sixteen houses, Old Tom's Village, five miles southwest of Old Kake Village, and an unnamed village.

This closed the Kake War, as it was sometimes called, but the question of the guilty parties was not settled; the resentment of the Indians was not quenched, and it smouldered for

many years. Whether or not other lone prospectors helped
to pay the price of revenge is not known, but the echoes of
those shots of the sentries and of the warship may be heard in
that region to the present day.[14]

The Chilkat native who was killed lived at Lynn Canal.
His tribesmen waited until they caught a trader named
Louthan at their village with his schooner, trading. They
captured him and made him pay the blood money, in blankets,
before he was released.[15]

A man named Parker killed two Indians at Sitka, at
different times. In each case a military board investigated the
matter, returned the decision that "the act was not justifi-
able," then discharged the murderer for lack of jurisdiction
over the offense.[16]

A fort was established at Wrangell. Christmas Day, 1869,
a drunken Stikine Indian named Lowan bit a finger off the
hand of the post laundress. A lieutenant with a file of soldiers
went to arrest the offender, and in the melee that ensued
Lowan was killed and his brother was shot through the shoul-
der. A tumult arose in the village. The Stikines mustered
their old Hudson's Bay muskets and went out to retaliate.
Leon Smith, the post trader, partner of William King Lear,
post sutler, went to the village to endeavor to quiet the insur-
rection and was shot to death by a medicine man named
Scutdoo.

The surrender of Scutdoo was demanded, meeting with
immediate defiance, while the Thlingits assembled under the
leadership of their chiefs, Shustaks, Shakes, and Toyatte; the
women were sent to the forest beyond the reach of danger.

The cannon of the fort were trained on the village, and
solid shot crashed through the walls of the old tribal houses.
The Indians climbed the hill back of the town in order to
shoot down into the stockade but were soon dislodged, by
cannon fire from that vantage point. All night long cannon
shot smashed into the village. With morning, shells began to
be thrown among the buildings. That was a new terror to
which the Stikines yielded, and they brought Scutdoo to the
fort, where he was tried by court-martial. On the 29th he
was hanged in full sight of the assembled natives and the
garrison.

The Thlingits were cowed, but the memory was an unhappy legacy that confronted the inhabitants who remained after the departure of the troops.[17]

Secretary Seward, who negotiated the purchase of the territory in 1869, visited the land which he had added to the domain of the nation. He was entertained by General Davis at headquarters in Sitka, then journeyed to Lynn Canal and was feasted with barbaric hospitality at the Chilkat village of Klukwan by Chief Klokutch. To the chief he presented, among other gifts, a blanket woven in special emblems for the occasion, and this blanket remained one of the most prized possessions of the owner until his death. Here Seward met Professor George Davidson, who was engaged in surveys for the Coast and Geodetic Survey, and together they voyaged to Puget Sound.[18]

Congress and the people of the United States seemed to have forgotten Alaska. It might almost have been said to be a part of the "Land that God Forgot." All who remembered it, except the few who had faith and raised their voices in its behalf, engaged in decrying its worth and lamenting its purchase. There were those who had a vision of the future. In a speech at Sitka on July 4, 1868, Collector Dodge said: "Commerce has new fields in which to operate; the honest and hardy miners here have a broad expanse of territory to explore and develop." But the mining laws were not extended to the territory and it was not possible to file a legal claim. The only newspaper of the territory, the Sitka *Times,* says: "Hundreds of fresh-water rivers come leaping down the mountains into the sea, and into these in summer the salmon run; and so thickly that they often blacken the water." These were the glimpses that they had of the nearly two billion dollars in value that the fisheries and mines of Alaska have poured into the channels of commerce. Some of the officers of the garrisons tried to better the conditions, but their hands were tied. There were traders who were fair to the natives; but the smuggler and hooch-peddler, Stevens, could do more damage than all the rest could mend.

Beginning with 1858 on the bars of the Fraser River in British Columbia, following up the stream to the Caribou, then over the divide to the Omineeca, finally coming in from the east up the Dease River and locating the placers of the Cassiar, were thousands of prospectors. The Cassiar was discovered by McCullough and Thibert in 1872, on the waters of the Arctic slope, in British Columbia.[19]

The following year McCullough, Thibert, and two partners named Tifair and Loozon, who had joined them, returned to their discovery by way of the Stikine. Captain William Moore with his three sons and a few others who had heard of the strike followed after. They landed at the old army wharf at Wrangell, hired Indians with their canoes to put them on the ice of the Stikine, then struggled up the river through the deep snows, "necking" their sleds, as the old-timers call it. They dodged the deathtraps where the swift current cut through the ice under its covering, and slept on beds of spruce branches laid on the snow, building their fires on layers of closely laid logs in front of a rude shelter of boughs.

At Wrangell, when they passed, were but three men. They were William King Lear, a little, weazened, war-hardened veteran who had been the post sutler and who stayed behind when the soldiery vacated the barracks in 1870; Charles Brown, an Indian trader; and the Deputy Collector of Customs in charge of the port.[20]

Along the Stikine were a few men, "Buck" Choquette, Miller, Casey, and others, some known as Sixty-one Men, having come to the country in that year. They had remained to trap and mine.

In 1875 there were more than fifteen hundred men in the gold camp about Dease Lake, while the output of the mines for the two years previous was more than two million dollars.[21]

The British steamer *Otter* of the Hudson's Bay Company, the American steamer *California*, the American steamer *Gussie Telfair*, and a fleet of smaller craft plied the waters of the ocean passages, loaded with passengers and freight. On the Stikine River, running between Wrangell and Glenora, were the steamers *Glenora, Hope, Gem, Gertrude,* and others.[22]

When the season's work was done the miners came back down the river with their buckskin pokes filled with the yellow dust. Then Wrangell boomed and roared. Stores, saloons, and hurdy-gurdies multiplied. The coast from Sitka to Port Simpson was raked to get Indian girls for the dance halls. Each autumn the young men, filled with life and vigor, came down to the coast to purchase joy with their newly found riches. Some stayed in Wrangell; others went to Sitka where they had Indian sweethearts, while many journeyed to Victoria or San Francisco. That is the way of the miner for gold the world over.

The ubiquitous prospector, undaunted by the lack of laws, wandered everywhere. The first gold found in Alaska is supposed to have been about forty thousand dollars taken from the Windham Bay or Schucks Basin region where placers were worked in the seventies.[23]

Soldiers from the garrison at Sitka threaded the canyons of the mountains on Baranof Island. Croppings of quartz ledges were discovered that assayed rich in gold. The first mining company known to exist was the Alaska Gold and Silver Mining Company, which mined on Silver Bay at what was called the Stewart Ledge. From this mine the first clean-up was over eighteen hundred dollars, according to Captain Beardslee, commander of the *Jamestown*.[24]

With characteristic American enterprise the people of Sitka wished to keep abreast of the events of the time. A newspaper was established, *The Alaska Times*. Vol. 1, No. 1, was issued April 23, 1869. It was issued until Oct. 1, 1870. It was followed by the Sitka *Post*, Oct. 20, 1876, to Feb. 5, 1877.

The military occupation was drawing to a close. On April 10, 1877, orders were signed providing for the withdrawal of the troops, and for a revenue cutter to be stationed at Sitka.[25]

20

The White Whalers

THROUGH THE 19TH CENTURY THE AMERICANS WERE IN command of nearly the whole of the whaling in the Pacific and Arctic Oceans. Up to 1884 the fleet sailed from the New England ports; after that they began to shift to San Francisco, which became important in the trade.

The Civil War was a severe blow to the American whaling industry, through the operations of the Confederate privateers. The financial depression of 1857 had made profits doubtful. Forty ships were sold to the Government, many of which were used in the famous stone fleets sunk off the harbors of Charleston and Savannah in connection with the blockade of those ports in 1861.

The *Shenandoah* pursued the whaling ships to the very portals of Bering Strait in 1865. A steamer, she made the sailing ships an easy prey, as they had only their sails and were at her mercy. When she captured a ship she set it on fire as a beacon for others. In that distant region everyone reaches out to his neighbor for he knows not when he may have need to call for help. The other whalers, seeing the smoke, believed it to be a signal of distress and came flying to the rescue, only to fall into the hands of the enemy and be sent up in pillars of fire in their turn.

This privateer captured thirty-eight ships, bonded four of them to carry the crews home, and burned the others.[1] The fine ships, with their cargoes of whale oil, made a blaze that shone for miles over the northern ocean. But this disaster did not long deter the bold mariners of the North, and the fleet returned each year, though in lessened numbers, to follow the bowhead to the limit of the Arctic ice pack.

As the ships advanced the whales retreated along the edge of the pack until they were between the great field of ice that lies to the north of Point Hope, and the shore. This opening is but a narrow lane at the best, for the ice field lies just over the horizon at the most favorable time and may start back with the first onshore breeze. They were invading the Land of the Midnight Sun.

There were forty-one ships in this narrow passage, busily engaged in killing and "cutting in" whales in August, 1871. On the 7th some of the ships were at Wainwright Inlet. On the 11th a sudden onshore wind brought the ice in, penning the ships close to the land. On the 15th the ice crushed closer although grounded, almost forcing the ships ashore. On the 25th an offshore wind drove the ice to sea, and the Eskimos begged the seamen to go south, for they said the next time the ice came in it would stay. The friendly warning was unheeded, and the taking of whales went on.

On the 29th a southwest wind sprang up and brought the ice so quickly that some of the ships were caught in the pack. On the 2nd of September the brig *Comet* was crushed, and her crew barely escaped to the other ships. The ice packed tighter. On the 7th the bark *Roman* was caught between two immense floes, and the crew fled, barely saving their lives, taking nothing from the ship. The next day the *Awashonks* met a similar fate.

A council of masters was held and it was decided to abandon the ships and make their way down the coast to seven ships lying below Icy Cape, where they had gone on the warning of the Eskimos. The morning of the 14th of September the ships were left to their fate, with flags set, union down, and 1219 persons, some of them women and children, families of the officers, went down the coast to where the ships were standing below the Blossom Shoals. The castaways were distributed among the ships and after a fair voyage reached Honolulu on October 24, or soon after.[2]

The whaling trade was one of danger at the best. Nearly every year one or more ships were lost in the ice or by storm in the northern sea. Four were lost in 1872. In 1873 none were lost, though six did not take a whale, but the good fortune was reversed in 1876 when twelve were lost or crushed in the ice. Most of the crews escaped, a few perished, and more than fifty men were dependent on the Eskimos for their surviving the winter.[3] The next year the fleet went east of Point Barrow, returning early in September.[4]

Through all the years of the whaling, when a ship failed to make her take of whales, it was the custom to kill walrus to fill the oil tanks and also to get the ivory tusks, weighing about five pounds to the pair. The ship *Onward* took one thousand in 1874; the *Mercury* killed two thousand in 1877. The whole kill from 1870 to 1880 is estimated at one hundred thousand animals.[5] The result was almost to exterminate the animals in the Pacific, causing suffering and death among the Eskimos because of the taking of their food supplies in whale and walrus, thus throwing them onto the caribou and seal, which were insufficient. The caribou were nearly exterminated, and the natives perished from famine and consequent pestilence.[6]

The "Golden Age" of the whaling industry was from 1835, when Captain Folger of the bark *Ganges* struck the first right whale on the Kodiak grounds, to 1855, when the bowhead was being taken in the greatest numbers on the northern waters. In 1846 there went out from the whaling ports of the United States no less than 678 ships and barks, 35 brigs, and 22 schooners, in the whaling trade. The greater part of these went into the Arctic. The investment was of a value of $21,-075,000.[7] From that time until 1910 the fleet declined until there were only seven vessels, one of which was wrecked. A few years after this, Arctic whaling from the ships ceased entirely.

Steam vessels began to be used in 1880, the first being an American ship from New Bedford. As the fleet went farther north among the ice floes more power boats were used, until, before the industry was abandoned, most of them were steamers.

At the height of the industry the ships were mainly outfitted in the New England States, New Bedford and Nantucket being famous whaling ports. In 1884 it began to shift to San Francisco, and in the latter days of the Alaska fleet most of them were from that port.[8]

The rendezvous of the white whalers for many years was at Port Clarence, where they met their tenders loaded with supplies for their cruise past Point Barrow to the mouth of the Mackenzie to winter at Herschel Island. These were the last they would get for from two to three years, and all bone and oil taken thus far was sent back to San Francisco. It was a busy scene when the ships came dropping into the harbor, like white-winged birds of passage, as soon as the ice opened in the latter part of June. They followed the bow-head up the coast from Cape Navarin, keeping close to the pack, sometimes getting caught in it, and many a fine bark has been ground to kindling wood along these shores. Some of the toughest, hardiest men in the world manned these ships, ruled by "bucko" mates who mauled them into submission by sheer prowess of fists, or by the aid of a belaying pin if need be. The salty old skipper who commanded could drive a tack with the prow of his ship, and he feared nothing that swam the seas. It was men like these who furnished the in-spiration for some of the characters in *Moby Dick*. Those were the days of mutinies, of fights with flensing knives and keen-edged blubber spades, in which at times the natives of the neighboring coasts took an active part.[9]

In 1889 the fleet went east of Barrow to the mouth of the Mackenzie River. An old whaler, Joe Tuckfield, had dis-covered that the monster cetaceans rolled in herds in the warm waters that the river poured into the Arctic, so the next year nine whaling ships accompanied by the U. S. reve-nue cutter *Thetis* made their way to Herschel Island, where the whale men remained to cut in whales for the bone and oil. Vessels coming into these waters usually remained from two to three years on the cruise.[10]

The autumn of 1897 one of the too-frequent disasters that attend the whaling in the Arctic waters overtook the steam whaler *Navarch* just above Icy Cape, and nearly half her crew were lost trying to reach the shore. Later in the season the news came out of the North that eight ships were caught by the ice in the vicinity of Point Barrow and were in need of relief. On November 15 Secretary Gage of the Treasury Department ordered the R. C. S. cutter *Bear* to sail for the Arctic and land an expedition of officers from his ship to make the journey to Barrow, to render assistance to the men.[11]

Lieutenant D. H. Jarvis with a party was landed at Tanu-nuk, on Nelson Island, between the Kuskokwim and the Yukon Rivers, on December 16, from which point he made his way northward by dog team to Cape Prince of Wales where he secured the reindeer of the mission of that place and the services of Mr. W. T. Lopp, missionary-teacher, with his Eskimo herders, to drive them to Barrow. He went on, reaching Barrow on March 29, 1898.[12]

Mr. Lopp with six herders, driving the reindeer, left Wales February 3, with 448 reindeer, and he arrived at Barrow, 700 miles distant, on March 30, with 382 deer, which were delivered to Captain Jarvis. He then returned with his herders to Cape Prince of Wales by dogsled, having made the longest journey in the shortest time, with a herd of reindeer, that has ever been recorded.[13]

Captain Jarvis stayed at Barrow, took charge of the situation, and remained until the next August, when the ships took the crews of the wrecked vessels south.[14]

Soon after this the whale became so scarce that the balaena rose to the price of about seven dollars per pound. Then a substitute was discovered which took the place of that article in manufactures. The petroleum products had supplanted the whale oil for many uses, so whaling declined in the Arctic and soon practically ceased, except the few taken by natives and others in shore or flaw whaling from the ice.[15]

21

The Land of Furs

A VAST, STRANGE, ALMOST UNKNOWN LAND LAY TO THE
west of Prince William Sound. Eight hundred miles to
Unalaska, it was another eight hundred nautical miles to
Attu at the end of the Aleutians. From Unalaska it was a
thousand miles north to St. Michael, at the mouth of the
Yukon, and from there to the north lay nearly a thousand
miles of coast line before Point Barrow was in sight. This
stretch commanded river valleys reaching afar inland, holding
thousands of square miles in their drainage. Unalaska was
the center and chief factory of this region.

Over the valleys and islands hung the romance of fur.
Even the waters teemed with the animals that yielded the
soft, beautiful pelts that enchanted the eye and ravished the
touch of the most abandoned wanderer, as well as that of the
beauty wrapped in silk and sable. On the Pribilof Islands
millions of fur seals hauled and brought forth their young.
Along the Aleutian Islands the sea otter, the richest of the sea
fur-bearers tossed their little ones and played in glad abandon.
In the valleys of the Yukon and the Kuskokwim were fox,
beaver, and marten. Even on the bleak shores of the Arctic
were the soft-pelted white and blue foxes. All this had been
conserved by the Russians for the past twenty years. No one
had dared to poach on these preserves while the Russian
American Company held the charter to the rights of its riches.
Now it was suddenly thrown open, as it had been when the
first *promishlenik* sailed his sewed boat from Okhotsk.

Few knew of this misty, northern land that they called
Seward's Folly, and Walrussia, in derision, thereby showing
their ignorance of the unexploited countries, even as some do
today. It was not Alaska; it was Russian America to our
people. Outside of a few translations, all knowledge of it
was contained in Russian books; our libraries held few of
either. Charles Sumner's great speech told much of truth,
yet few read it. There were a few who knew and as soon as

UNALASKA

BERING SEA PATROL HEADQUARTERS

KODIAK FROM THE HARBOR ENTRANCE

the transfer was complete they prepared to reap the harvest. The control of this wonderland was a fief worthy of a prince, and few principalities include such a broad land in their dominion.

As soon as the Bering Sea was clear of ice the schooners, loaded with equipment and supplies for the killing of seals, sailed up to the islands. The first to make a landing was a party outfitted by Parrot & Co. In a few days a schooner put a party ashore for Hutchinson, Kohl & Co. Then a third came with men for Williams & Haven, among them a Captain Morgan who had sailed to the South Seas and killed hundreds of thousands of seals on those rookeries at the edge of the Antarctic ice. This company had bought the salthouses and other buildings of the Russian American Company, and took possession of them. Others came, but these three strong companies held the rookeries and put the others off by means more effective than elegant.[1]

The little group of islands, discovered by Gerassim Pribilof in 1786, low-lying and grass-covered in summer, with rounded hills known by Russian names, and with rocky shores fronted by sandy beaches where the surf pounds incessantly, lies in the waters of Bering Sea. They are known as the Pribilofs, or the Seal Islands, and comprise the greatest fur farm in the world. From the rocky beaches, where all summer long the sleek, silver-colored seals lie, there have been harvested over fifty million dollars in furs since the Russians left them.

At the time of the Cession the seal herd is estimated to have been about two million animals. The wise regulations of Baron Wrangel provided for great care on the rookeries, to kill only the holluschickie, or bachelors, as cattlemen kill only steers, thus leaving the females and enough of breeding males to maintain the herd.[2]

The islands are five in number, St. Paul, St. George, Otter, Walrus, and Sivutch Rock, only two of which are important. St. Paul, the largest, is of about 43 square miles, while St. George, 40 miles to the southeast, is 35.9. A little village of plainly built houses, a church, and a few other buildings marks the center of activities on each island.[3]

When the Cession was completed the Government was content to occupy Sitka, later to establish a few military posts in the vicinity, and the military occupation seems to

have been at the suggestion, or recommendation, of the fur
interests, for: "Alaska was made Indian Country, chiefly
through the efforts of the Alaska Commercial Company,"
says a Government report.[4] The most available asset was
overlooked, except by the fur gatherers who pounced upon
it and in the first year, 1868, took 240,000 skins from the
Pribilof Islands. This was a strong contrast to the average of
17,820 skins taken annually during the last years of the Russian Company's dominion.[5] The next year a special agent
was sent to the islands, and the slaughter was checked. In
1870 a lease was contracted with the Alaska Commercial
Company, a corporation of California, by which the sealing
rights were granted for the period of twenty years.[6]

Each year the fur seals (Callorhinus Alaskanus) come to
the Seal Islands, there to bring forth their young, and to nurse
them until winter sends them out on the ocean for their long
winter swim. The Russians called them kotiks, or little cats.
Now they are called pups, and the mothers are called matkas,
which means the same. The mature bulls, called seekatchie
by the former regime, are the first to arrive from the south in
the spring. They take their stand on the beach, at the same
place each year, to watch for the arrival of their ladies, gather
as many as possible into their harems—for they are Turks in
disposition—watch over them jealously until they are ready
to leave, then, worn down by their long months of fighting
and fasting, they follow the herd southward.[7]

During the interval that the herd occupies the islands the
females do not leave the land until the little ones are born, and
the foundation is laid for the young ones of next year, then
only to get food. On this search they sometimes go to sea
as far as a hundred miles.

The course of the seals on their annual migration was for
many years a mystery, but one which was finally solved. In
the fall they pass through the channels between the islands
of the Aleutian Chain, disappear, till in spring they are
found off the coast of Oregon, then pass north alongshore till
in June they reach the Bering Sea and occupy their island
home again.

From this arose the pelagic sealing, or taking of the seals
at sea. It was found that they passed into the Pacific Ocean,
went south, then east at about the north line of California,

then north. As they passed, the Indians of Washington and British Columbia took a few each year. In 1878, men with sailing schooners began to follow the herd from the Oregon coast to the Seal Islands, killing as they went. The first year but one vessel was in the pursuit. The number increased till in 1894 there were 110 in the fleet, and the take was 121,143 animals, males and females. They then lay off the islands in wait for the mothers as they went to sea for food for the little ones on shore. The decks of the schooners were slippery with the blood and milk of the murdered mothers. Every one taken meant the death of two, *matka* and *kotik*.[8]

The result was rapid destruction of the herd. The Government tried to stop the slaughter, called conferences, passed laws, all to no effect. The laws drove the sealing boats under the Canadian flag where they prospered in spite of the revenue cutters that patrolled the seas. It was the time of Jack London's *Sea Wolf*, and of which Captain Evans, "Fighting Bob," reported, and that Kipling wrote of when he said "There is no law of God or man, runs North of Fifty-three."[9]

In 1890 the North American Commercial Company secured the lease of the islands under which they held them until 1910, by which time the seal herd had decreased to about 125,000 animals and were in imminent danger of extinction. That year the Government took charge of the rookeries and finally negotiated a treaty with Great Britain, Japan, and Russia, by which the pelagic sealing was discontinued, and since that time the entire control is vested in it.[10]

The increase from 125,000 in 1911 to 1,150,913 in 1935 shows the effect of intelligent oversight, and during this time there have been 639,120 skins of bachelor seals taken.[11]

The sea otter was the richest and most valued of the fur-bearers of the North. It had led the Russian *promishleniki* from Siberia along the Aleutian Chain across the Pacific, and it was just as highly prized as it had ever been. The superiority of numbers of the fur seal, and its facility of capture, only, placed it ahead of the sea otter, for the latter was worth more than ten times as much in the market. It was still found from Attu Island, at the western end of the Aleutian Chain, to Portland Canal at the southeast, thanks to the conservation of the Russian American Company.

As there was no charter or contract under which these animals were leased, and as no law controlled their taking under United States rule, it was an open contest between the hunters who should take the prizes, and between the traders as to who should buy them. Under Russian rule no firearms were permitted to be used in the capture. The overhunting of any one section was obviated by alternating the areas during different years. All this was changed, and long-range rifles were trained on any head that showed from shore, the hunter trusting to luck to retrieve the body.

From an average of 964 sea-otter skins from 1842 to 1862, the take was raised to an average of 4,784 between 1881 and 1890.[12] Several companies, the Western Fur & Trading Co., Taylor & Bendel, Schirpser & Co., the Pioneer Fur Co., all engaged in the trade, but the Alaska Commercial Co. held pre-eminence, and in 1883 it purchased 4,375 skins of the whole catch for the year.[13] The others gradually drew out and most of them left the country.

The inevitable result was the destruction of the business and the almost complete extermination of the sea otter. In 1910 the take in the whole of the waters of Alaska was but 29 skins.[14] A treaty was made by which the taking on the high seas was prohibited, this being negotiated at the same time as the sealing convention, and the taking of this fur was made unlawful. It so remains to the present time.[15]

In this land of furs the methods of the Alaska Commercial Company were the same as were those of the great companies of the frontier, as the Hudson's Bay Company, the Russian American Company, and the American Fur Company. They upheld the traditions of the trade, and their policy was shaped on the knowledge of that of their predecessors. They collected the furs with the least possible expense, and adopted measures to control the trade and exclude competition.[16]

A new movement was under way that was going to revolutionize the conditions through all of this wide domain. It was slow in its growth yet inevitably progressing. During the ascendency of the Alaska Commercial Company complaints were made and charges were laid at their doors, but it is probable that the management of the company was as fair and liberal as any company has ever been in the fur trade of the frontiers.[17]

22

The Rule of the Navy

ON JUNE 14, 1877, THE MILITARY FORCES OF THE UNITED States were withdrawn from Sitka, departing on the steamer *California*. Their record during their occupation is nearly a blank page of history, the events being mainly punishments of Indians for quarrels initiated by their own acts. In some ways the land was worse off at their departure than at their coming. If we may believe the testimony of the time, the influence of the soldiery was devoted to debauching the inhabitants, both native and Russian.[1]

Immediately upon the evacuation by the troops the only representatives of Government were the Collector of Customs and his deputies. The monthly steamer from Portland maintained the communication with civilization. A revenue cutter was promised to be stationed in the waters as a protection to the inhabitants; the *Rush*, the *Corwin*, and the *Wolcott* at intervals visited the northern post, but their stay was short as possible and their visits intermittent. If difficulty arose with the Indians their force would not admit of a landing party sufficient to punish any considerable numbers. The assignment to those waters was not sought by revenue commanders.

The Thlingits, aggressive and insolent, thronged the decks of the *California* as she lay at the dock. They intruded into the ballroom of the *Castle* at a party; they tore down the stockade, and rifled the unoccupied buildings. They said: "The United States does not want the country. It belongs to us. We will kill the men and make slaves of the women." The grievances they had harbored but had not dared to express during the stay of the military were rehearsed and revived with new animosity.

There were between five hundred and a thousand Indians in the "Ranche," and this might easily be increased to number eight hundred or a thousand fighting men by drawing on the neighboring villages. The white population was between three and four hundred. The distilling of hooch among the Indians continued unrestrained, adding to the turbulence. A Collector of the Customs, newly appointed, came to Sitka, was so frightened that he returned by the same steamer, and made a report advising that the District be abandoned.[2]

The division of the Thlingits called the Keeksitty, or Kiksadi, under Chief Katlean, was the most turbulent. A white man named Brown and his companion were killed by them at the Hot Springs in 1878. Through the assistance of Annahootz, a friendly chief of the Kokwantan *kwan*, the murderers were arrested.

In one of the big tribal houses of the Keeksitties a council was held. The fighting men fortified themselves with hooch, resolved to rescue the prisoners and to sack the town. Led by Katlean, who was a successor of the old chief of 1802 who led in the destruction of Old Sitka, they advanced toward the entrance to the white quarter where the people of the town had assembled to defend themselves as best they could.

To the discomfiture of the Keeksitties, at the boundary line they met the Kokwantans, under Annahootz, who had decided to fight for the whites. After a few minor encounters, Katlean retreated to gather more recruits from other villages. At this crisis the steamer *California* arrived and took the prisoners to Portland, where they were tried and hanged.[3]

On the *California* many of the women and children went to the States for safety. The citizens who remained sent a written appeal to the Government for protection, but it fell on deaf ears. A petition to the British Government at Victoria was more effective, and Captain A. Holmes A'Court, of H.M.S. *Osprey*, at once sailed for Sitka, arrived there March 1, anchored before the Indian village, cleared his decks for action, and sent word to the citizens, "Where shall I begin?" There were no further demonstrations from the Thlingits.

The *Osprey* lay before the village for three weeks, when the revenue cutter *Wolcott* arrived, but not deeming her force sufficient, Captain A'Court did not leave until the arrival of the U.S.S. *Alaska* on April 3. This ship was re-

ANNAHOOTZ
The Kokwantan chief who saved Sitka in 1878.

MAP OF ALASKA, 1888

lieved by the *Jamestown* on June 14, 1879, and from that time onward, except for short intervals, for more than twenty years a warship was stationed at Sitka.[4]

Captain L. A. Beardslee, commander of the *Jamestown*, was a man equal to the occasion and fitted for the work. He was sent to control a population of about 360 whites and approximately 6,000 Indians. In Sitka were 34 native-born Americans, 79 naturalized citizens, and 247 who had been naturalized by the Treaty of Purchase. Among them were Irish, Italians, Turks, Jews, Austrians, Germans, English, Russians, and Creoles. He was sent without a code of laws. Among the whites he found dissension and anarchy; among the natives, superstition, witchcraft, slavery, shamanism, and blood feuds prevailing.

Many of the population were of the class who seek the frontier because they there escape the regulations and laws which civilized communities place upon their love of license. They had not yet begun to go to the cities and ply the arts of the Black Hand and the racketeer.

Captain Beardslee suggested the solution of the matter by the organization of a provisional government, which was done, but not without much discussion and opposition. An election was held August 1, 1879. A code of laws was drawn up, and a magistrate and board of councilmen were elected. Miners at Silver Bay, in an offensive letter, refused to join, alleging that if a government were organized the warship would leave.[5]

Opposition to the organization was manifest from the inception of the plan. A merchant, Caplin, who dealt largely in blackstrap molasses for the manufacture of hooch, said: "De Captain may go to —— wid his tam Gov'ment; I'll bay no daxes." The movement proceeded, an agreement was secured to stop the sale of molasses, to prevent the distilling and drunkenness. A Jew trader, Sam Goldstein, refused to abide by the rule, as it curtailed his commercial activities. He broke the compact, and the authority was not strong enough to enforce it.

A drunken miner shot his roommate, in consequence of which, being in danger of lynching by the miners, he surrendered to the corporal of the guard, who placed him on the ship in confinement. The city magistrate declined to try him, so after an examination by a mixed board of officers of the ship and citizens he was sent to Portland for trial. The injured man survived five gunshots, and the assailant was discharged from custody by reason of there being no law against such an offense in Alaska.[6]

Thereupon the provisional government dissolved.

Captain Beardslee took up the task of organizing the community and of meeting the problems. He raided the distilleries with an armed force, captured and destroyed thirty-eight stills. He had the Indian village cleaned, the houses numbered, and appointed a force of native police to keep order in the "Ranche." At a cannery, which had been established near by the previous year, distilling was being carried on. He called for volunteers among the Indians, and they proceeded with axes, clubs, and "halibut killers" to smash up forty stills and dump out the liquor.

In December the improvement is noted by the report that "for a community utterly without law, the absence of disorder is wonderful."

In Chilkat, disturbances occurred because of the usual cause of too much hooch, of which it is said, "two or three drinks will transfer a sober man into a murderer." The Indian police were sent to quell the incipient war in which several were killed and Chief Klokutch severely wounded.[7]

At Wrangell a party of Hootznahoo Indians landed at the north end of the town, known as the "Foreign Village," and proceeded to set up their still. The mission Indians, acting under the leadership of Dr. Corleis, undertook to break up the operation, giving rise to a free fight in which two Hootznahoos and three Stikines were killed. The affair lasted several days, and during its course the pioneer missionary, S. Hall Young, narrowly escaped death. He sent for help from Sitka, and in response a boatload of marines arrived at Wrangell. The stills were destroyed, and order was restored.[8]

The organization of the work among the communities being accomplished, the Commander turned to hydrographic work, in surveying unexplored bays and channels, among them being the noted Glacier Bay, best known as the Muir Glacier, discovered in 1879 by the famous geologist and naturalist, John Muir.[9]

Commander Glass followed Beardslee and continued his work. On January 11, 1882, during a temporary absence of the *Wachusetts*, a general drunken debauch began in the "Ranche" in which the abandoned white men joined. The shamans began their invocations, and witchcraft incantations prevailed in the big tribal houses. Fortunately two howitzers and a supply of small arms had been left by the Commander. Major M. P. Berry was appointed to take charge of the organization of the forces available. Katlean and Annahootz were appointed as chiefs of the Indian police. The cell where those accused as witches were confined was broken into. They were released and sent on the ship in the harbor, upon its return, where the Captain protected him and his wife, while the shaman was arrested. His mop of tangled hair—one of the badges of his order—was cut by the ship's barber, and his whiskers were clipped, and he was warned that the next time he would be shaved and scrubbed with a brush.[10]

Other Commanders later stationed there were not so zealous in their official capacity. In April of 1882, the new Commander announced his intention to depart and withdraw his guard from shore. A protest was filed by the Collector of Customs, but the *Wachusetts* sailed for Wrangell after finally leaving a corporal's guard at Sitka. A riot followed. A stone was thrown through the Customhouse door. The shaman's hair was stolen from where it had been nailed to the wall. In a melee that followed, an Indian was shot in the leg by the guard. The arrival of the *Corwin* on the 3rd of June quieted the situation.[11]

The practice of shamanism was from the first, and continued to be for many years, one of the greatest obstacles to the civilization of the natives.[12]

For years the restless prospectors had been searching the mountains for lodes and panning the streams for placer gold. Dick Willoughby entered Glacier Bay on the quest, where his name is commemorated in Willoughby Island. When John Muir passed what is now Juneau in 1879, he is said to have made a favorable report upon that region on his return. The restless ones had been looking with longing eyes for years toward the vast valley of the Yukon.[13]

The way to the Yukon by the Chilkoot had been barred

to the white man by the claims of the Indians, who had for years controlled the best trails, and having improved them they held that they were the owners. The trade of the "Stick" Indians of the interior valleys was also held to be their vested right. It was known as the "Grease Trail," probably because the much-desired oolachan oil, made from the candlefish, was taken over it to be bartered to the natives of the interior. A man named Holt is said to have passed over the trail during the seventies, but there is little more than rumor to prove it.[14] The Indians feared to let miners pass lest they interfere with the trade. They had destroyed Fort Selkirk, of the Hudson's Bay Company, situated at the mouth of the Pelly River on the Yukon, August 21, 1852.[15]

In 1880 negotiations were made by a party of prospectors under the leadership of Edmund Bean, to go over the Chilkoot, or Dyea, Pass, into the Yukon Valley to prospect for gold in the British possessions. Nineteen men signed an agreement not to trade; that no spirituous liquor would be carried; that they would obey the orders of their leader and would behave in an orderly manner.[16] Under the protection of the officers of the warship and under this agreement the party of miners made their way over the pass and down the tributaries of the Yukon River. A trader named Steel, however, followed the miners, violated the trade agreement, and gave rise to later trouble with the Chilkats.[17]

In the decade that had passed, three of the important factors for future development had been established. First, the mining industry was begun, and in 1880 the important discovery of the Silver Bow Basin was made, resulting in the founding of Juneau, first called Harrisburg in honor of Richard T. Harris, one of the discoverers, and the finding of the lodes that constituted the great Treadwell Mine.[18]

When John Muir returned from his famous exploration of Glacier Bay in 1879, he is said to have remarked that the geology near where Juneau was later situated was favorable to the presence of gold.

George E. Pilz, the mining engineer who was working the Stewart Mine in Silver Bay, near Sitka, was not realizing the results he hoped for. He sought for other prospects. He promised rewards to the Indians if they found gold-bearing quartz in place. He hired men and sent them to different localities to prospect, some to Sumdum Bay, some to the Hoonah region, some to the Copper River country, and Richard T. Harris and Joe Juneau to the vicinity of Juneau.

Meantime, Kowee, chief of the Auke *kwan* of the Thlingit people, in 1880 found quartz rock on the watershed of Gold Creek and brought it to Pilz. Pilz sent Harris and Juneau to stake locations, which was done, and the result was Juneau and its great mines.

Next, the fisheries, that have poured over a billion dollars in value into the markets of the United States, made their first advance by the inception of the canning of salmon at two places—Sitka and Klawak—in 1878. The first year's shipment was small—about seven thousand cases—but it was the beginning of a great industry in Alaska that today supplies over one half of the whole production of the world.[19]

The third great movement forward was the beginning of schools and missions. The first mission school was placed at Wrangell in 1877 by the Presbyterian Church. This was followed by the establishing of a school at Sitka, which was the forerunner of the present Sheldon Jackson School, the oldest educational institution in Alaska. It had been a hard and discouraging struggle, but a beginning had been made, and all without assistance from the Government, which should have been the most interested in the territory and its progress. The Government owned the whole domain and its resources, yet did nothing toward the development of them, or even toward the preservation of the lives of the native inhabitants of the land.[20]

Juneau was a wide-open, typical Western mining town of the frontier, but not one that was popular for the gunman, even before the organization of government. The miners "highgraded" the rich pockets in the mines, rolled their blankets around the plunder, then sought the saloons and gambling halls to spend the proceeds in blackjack, or in the dance halls with the Indian girls, but there were few killings.[21]

The closing years of the Navy Rule were marked by an unfortunate event in the destruction of Old Angoon, on Hootznahoo Inlet.

Hootznahoo Inlet, principally known for the hooch a soldier named Doyle taught the natives to make there, is one of the least known and most interesting of the myriads of fascinating coves, bays, and passages of the wonderland of the Alaskan coast. In its recesses are found coal and marble, and there the Russian engineer, Doroshin, found a deposit that he said indicated the presence of diamonds. There was one of the quaintest of the old-time native villages of the region—Old Angoon, or Hootznahoo.

Just below the mouth of the inlet was the oil and guano factory of the Northwest Trading Company at Killisnoo. There had been bitter feeling among the natives of the *kwan* because of the loss of some of their people on the schooner *San Diego,* in the employ of a white man. Under the Indian law, something like our employer's liability statutes, the owner was held liable for the payment of indemnity. He refused the payment.

On the night of October 22 a whale gun burst on board the launch of the oil and guano company operating in the inlet, killing an Indian. This added another claim of indemnity, so the Indians attacked the launch and held the crew as prisoners for hostages, to secure the payments.

Commander Merriman, of the U.S.S. *Adams,* at Sitka, put a howitzer and a gatling gun aboard the *Favorite,* and in company with the *Corwin,* carrying a force of one hundred marines and sailors, sailed to Angoon, released the prisoners, fined the Indians four hundred blankets, and in default of payment shelled the town and destroyed it.[22]

23

The Pioneers of the Yukon

AT FORT YUKON IN 1867 THE HUDSON'S BAY COMPANY still kept the post that was established by Murray in 1847. Captain Charles F. Raymond, U. S. A., was detailed to ascertain if it was in the territory ceded by Russia to the United States, and he embarked on July 4, 1869, on the little steamer *Youkon* at St. Michael, to carry out his orders. The *Youkon* had been brought up from San Francisco on the deck of the brig *Commodore*, for use in the fur trade, and this was her first voyage.[1]

As the little steamer passed up the river, belching fire and smoke, the Indians along the bank in their fishing camps fled for their lives and hid in the forest. They thought that a demon had come to their land to devour them. On board were the traders on their way with goods with which to open posts on the river.[2]

Raymond arrived at Fort Yukon, July 31, found that the post was on American territory, and notified Mr. John Wilson, the officer in charge, that he must withdraw with his goods beyond the national boundary.

Ferdinand Westdahl, the chief trader, placed a post at the abandoned station, with Moses Mercier as trader, while the steamer returned down the river, establishing posts at Fort Adams and Anvik.[3]

A great, unknown valley like the Yukon is a lodestone to frontiersmen and prospectors. It was to them as Kentucky was to Daniel Boone. Those of the Fraser River and Caribou had long looked toward the north where they believed that the "Run of Gold" would be traced. In the summer of 1873 two parties of trappers and prospectors arrived at Fort Yukon, coming by way of the Rat River Portage and the Porcupine River from the Mackenzie. Arthur Harper and his party arrived first, followed in about two weeks by L. N. McQuesten and his companions. Harper went up the Yukon to the White River, while McQuesten wintered on Beaver Creek, below Fort Yukon. In the spring all went to St. Michael on the barge of the Alaska Commercial Company, where Mayo, Hart, and McQuesten bought goods from the company to open trading posts; Harper, Finch, and McKniff purchased outfits for prospecting, while Nicholson and Gutter (Gesler?) went to San Francisco.

The 10th of July the steamer left St. Michael with four barges of goods for the Indian trade, each carrying ten tons. One barge was left at Anvik, one at Nulato, and one at Tanana *(Nukluklayet)*. The fourth was taken to about six miles below where Dawson, Y. T., now stands, where McQuesten established what he named Fort Reliance and spent the winter, trading. The next year Harper and McKniff went to work for the company. McKniff went to Fort Yukon, while Harper and Mayo were at Fort Reliance.[4]

For years few came to the Yukon, except a few traders to the lower river for the company, as Fredericks, the Belkoffs, Kamkoff, and others. After the first party over the pass in 1880 to the headwaters, a few returned in 1881, but the first to the American side were twelve men in 1882, among them Joe Ladue, G. F. Spangenberg, and others.[5] The Scheiffelin party, from Tombstone, Arizona, came up the river this year on a small steamer called the *New Racket* that they brought from San Francisco, as far as the mouth of the Tanana and wintered at Nukluklayet.[6]

George Marks and three companions came down the river in 1883, stopped on the Stewart River, found some gold on the bars, and wintered at Tanana, or Nukluklayet. The next year he crossed the portage to the Kuskokwim and went up that stream 250 miles, lost his outfit, and returned to Kolmakoff.[7]

Nearly all of the early prospectors on the river struck gold at some point; Harper took out five hundred dollars near the mouth of the White River in 1873-4. The first really paying diggings were on the Stewart River, and there many of the men who came over the pass stopped to mine.[8] Boswell, Densmore, and others were there in 1885.[9] Sixteen men wintered at Fort Reliance the winter of 1885-6, among them Poplin, Boswell, Fraser, Powell, Hess, Franklin, and Ladue.[10]

Franklin found pay on Franklin Gulch in 1886, on the

LEROY NAPOLEON McQUESTON

FORT YUKON, ALASKA

CIRCLE CITY, ALASKA
The oldest town in the Yukon Valley.

Fortymile, and the next year the stampede to these diggings began—the first good creek mines on the American Yukon.[11] About 200 men came over the divide this year, and about $250,000 in gold was taken out during the season. In 1891 Miller Creek was discovered by Miller and was named for him.[12] McQuesten outfitted Pitka and Sonesko, two Indians, who prospected Birch Creek, found gold, and the result was the establishing of Circle City.[13] In this manner was the far north country pioneered and the way opened for the great gold stampede to the Klondike of 1897-8.

These early pioneers were men of sterling qualities, and fine types of American frontiersmen. McQuesten, Mayo, Harper, and others are outstanding for honesty, fearless faith in the country, and fellowship for their brother pioneers.

The Government began to take a slight interest in the Yukon. In 1883 Frederick Schwatka, of the U. S. Army, was detailed to make a reconnaissance of the river. He went over the Dyea, or Chilkoot Pass, termed by him the Perrier Pass, traversed the river on a raft, made a running survey of the stream, and went to San Francisco on the schooner *Leo*.[14]

Another invasion of the unknown regions was made in 1885, when Lieutenant H. T. Allen went up the Copper River, toward which longing eyes had been cast for nearly a hundred years for the copper deposits, and into which Serebrennikof had gone to meet his death at the hands of the Indians. He accomplished his mission faithfully, making one of the most notable expeditions of the North, and the Indians, instead of treating him as they did Serebrennikof, fed him out of their scanty stores, and helped him on his way. He reached the Yukon, partially explored the Koyukuk, then went to St. Michael.[15] In the Kuskokwim the independent trader, R. Sipary, handled goods furnished to him by the company, while on the Nushagak, John W. Clark controlled the trade from his posts at Nushagak, Togiak, and Iliamna.[16]

The fur and ivory trade of the Arctic fell into the hands of the whalers and whiskey traders for many years. It was commented that for a ship with a small stock of trade goods to take one good whale would pay her expense, and she would have a good profit from the proceeds of her barter. The volume must have been considerable when the whale-

bone, the skins of beaver, mink, muskrat, and marten in the
Kobuk and Selawik, and the fox and polar bear of the whole
coast is considered. In 1897, from Kotzebue, it is estimated
that fourteen thousand marten were collected.[17]

In 1883 there was a large unexplored area in the northwest part of Alaska, north and northeast from Kotzebue.
Dr. John Simpson, surgeon of H.M.S. *Plover*, which was on
the search for Franklin's expedition in the Arctic, explored
and mapped Selawik Lake and the south mouth of the Kobuk River for a few miles. Otherwise the vast area from
Kotzebue Sound to the Arctic Ocean was unknown to the
white man.[18]

Lieutenant George M. Stoney was sent by the Government to distribute rewards to the Chukchees for assistance
rendered the officers and crew of the U.S.S. *Rodgers,* which
burned on the Arctic coast below East Cape, on St. Lawrence Bay, while on a relief expedition in search for the
survivors of the *Jeannette*, crushed by ice off the Siberian
coast in 1881. Upon his return he proposed an expedition
to explore the unknown regions.

From 1884 to 1886 Stoney was occupied in explorations
on the Kobuk and adjacent regions, while Ensign W. L. Howard of his party went north to Point Barrow, discovering
and naming the Howard Pass, and going down the Chipp
River to the Arctic Ocean.[19]

The U. S. Revenue Marine at the same time sent a party
under Lieutenant J. C. Cantwell to explore to the head of
the Kobuk River, and Assistant Engineer S. B. McLenegan
followed the Noatak River to its source.[20]

In 1884 the pioneer of the North, Charles D. Brower,
went to Barrow and established his station, the most northerly trading post on the continent of North America. The
broad, level tundra reaches south to the Endicott Mountains, 150 miles, and it stretches 400 miles from west to east,
underlain with veins of coal hundreds of feet in thickness,
alternated with vast beds of the finest of fire clays. There
are seepages of oil, but the present value of that land is the
fur, whalebone, and ivory, that Brower gathers to his warehouses, and the reindeer that pasture on the mosses and
grasses of the tundra lands. He found the Eskimo people of
this northern country fine, clean, upright people, independ-

ent and self-supporting. Chance travelers pick out their strange traits, those which they dislike and do not understand; they choose the worst individuals and then judge the whole people by these poorer specimens. The native people love their country and are glad to live there, even though it is the real Arctic—the only part of Alaska that is actually in the true Arctic Zone. If they have a chance to earn their livelihood from the fish, walrus, and whale of the waters, from the fur and reindeer of the land, they will be a sturdy citizenry that will make a productive area of a seeming waste.[21]

Through all these years the North was governed only by the popular tribunal known as the miners' meeting. There was no other law, but this they obeyed. There was little crime; murder was almost unknown; locks were seldom used.

Of trouble with the Indians, only two cases occurred. In one, Mrs. Bean, the first white woman in the valley of the Tanana River, was killed by a shaman who feared her influence.[22] The other was the murder of John Bremmer, who went to the Yukon with Allen's Expedition in 1886, by an Indian on the Koyukuk. The murder of Mrs. Bean was not avenged. That of Bremmer was summarily and immediately punished by the hanging of the perpetrator, by miners who were on their way up the river on the steamer *Arctic*. Hearing of the outrage while at the mouth of the Koyukuk, they turned the boat up that stream, captured the Indian, brought him down to the Yukon, held a miners' meeting, condemned, and hanged him.[23]

24

Missions and Schools

A STEP HAD BEEN TAKEN TOWARD THE DESTINY OF ALASKA
—a delayed, obstructed, hobbled step. It was still urged that
her resources were negligible—that it had been a mistake to
buy her.

The only resources recognized were those of fur, fish,
trading with the natives in whiskey and goods, and opium
smuggling.[1] Any vested or accrued rights that interfered
with these were struck down, and any mention of other
industries was taboo. Mining law was denied until California
interests secured the Treadwell Mine that afterward yielded
over sixty-five millions in treasure. California and New
England combined to handle the destinies of the land. They
wished to control all legislation in Washington, D. C. It
had a certain resemblance to the regime of the Russian
American Company.[2]

The opposing elements were schools and missions, the
educational forces that spread a knowledge of the conditions. It has been seen that the schools had an intermittent,
precarious existence. The Russian schools withdrew with
the Russian American Company. The efforts of the few
residents at Sitka ended in failure. There were too few
friends to the movement, and too many enemies. The mission schools were the first that were able to maintain a foothold.[3] After the Wrangell school established by the Presby-
terians came the Sitka school, the forerunner of the present
Sheldon Jackson School.[4] The mission school at Haines followed in 1880, when Mrs. Sarah Dickinson, an educated
native woman, went among the Chilkats.[5] Others were
placed among the Hoonahs, and among the Hydahs on
Prince of Wales Island.[6] The Methodists founded the Jesse
Lee Home for Orphan Children at Unalaska in 1890.

Archdeacon Robert McDonald, of the Church of England, had come from the Mackenzie River by way of the
Rat River Portage in the early sixties and was for some time

United States Public School at Wales, Alaska

stationed at Fort Yukon. The Rev. Bompas, of the same church, was in the Yukon in 1869. The Rev. Sims was on the Yukon in 1883 and taught a school at Nukluklayet soon after.[7] Their work at Anvik began in 1887, other stations following later.

The Moravians visited the Kuskokwim in 1884 for the purpose of establishing a mission, which was accomplished in the next year with the Rev. John H. Killbuck as missionary.[8]

In accordance with their lease, the Alaska Commercial Company maintained two schools on the Seal Islands.

The Russian Church re-established two schools in 1884, and others followed until there were seventeen in 1887.

The Roman Catholic Church had missions at Juneau and Wrangell, and in 1886 Bishop Sehgers extended the work to the valley of the Yukon, where he unfortunately met his death at the hands of his traveling companion. Their principal station in the interior is at Holy Cross.[9]

Provisions were made in 1885 for the carrying on of educational work in the new territory by an appropriation of $25,000 for children of school age without reference to race, and $15,000 for support and education of Indian children at industrial schools in Alaska.[10] This was scant provision for a land with an estimated population of 33,426 inhabitants, scattered over 586,000 square miles of territory of almost insurmountable difficulties of travel. Sheldon Jackson was made General Agent of Education for the Territory. There were schoolhouses to build, books to procure, furniture to buy, and transport for thousands of miles. There were teachers to secure for the far, lonely places where there were none other than wild natives.

There were other obstacles than shortage of finances and distance of travel. As the General Agent was embarking on a steamer with equipment for a distant school, the U. S. Attorney had him arrested for obstructing a highway, and confined him in jail until he missed the ship. When parents wished to take their children out under any pretext, the judge ordered the children released, no matter how trivial the reason.[11]

The life of the teachers was trying. Isolated from associates of their color and race, with perhaps none in the village who spoke English, with shamanism and witchcraft to combat, they had to be teacher, doctor, and nurse. A whole winter often passed without the sight of a white man's face. If a schooner beat into the harbor it was likely to be a whiskey smuggler who spread pandemonium among the native dwellers.

As the years passed by there were tragedies among the workers. Professor S. A. Saxman and two of his native workers, Louis Paul and ———— Edgar, were drowned near Cape Fox, in autumn of 1886, while seeking a site for a school.[12] C. H. Edwards was shot to death, along with two of his young native men, by a whiskey smuggler named Malcolm Campbell. Harrison R. Thornton was killed by an Eskimo at Cape Prince of Wales.[13] Mr. and Mrs. V. C. Gambell were lost in a shipwreck of the *Jane Grey* in 1897, on the way to work at St. Lawrence Island, in the Bering Sea.[14]

The work of the teacher is not all irksome, for there are compensations in everything. The joy of teaching the kindly, artless, eager young natives, so free from many of the quarrelsome, grasping ways of civilization, repays for many deprivations and hardships.

The mission of Dr. William Duncan deserves notice as one of the most successful of the northern establishments. He had gone to Old Metlakatla, in British Columbia, in 1857, when it was an abode of primitive savagery, and he had been most successful in his work. In 1887 he obtained permission from the U. S. Government to transfer his settlement to Annette Island, and established it at what is called New Metlakatla. There they built a modern village and today are prosperous and enterprising, owning good homes, a store, salmon cannery, church, waterworks for the town, and modern conveniences equal to many like communities of the United States. White people have at many times endeavored to get a foothold on the island, in order to take advantage of the prosperity of the people, as has been done all the way across the North American continent, but they have not been successful, and the condition of the community is an example of what native people are capable if not unfairly treated. Dr. Duncan, old and feeble, at last turned over the school management to the U. S. Bureau of Education.[15]

The information concerning the country spread by the campaign for a Government brought it into a new light with the people of the United States. People visited the land and went home filled with its wonders to write about it.

The movement marked the dawning of a new era.[16] The first tourists to visit the country were a party with Captain George S. Wright, who visited the Stikine in 1878. The next seems to have been a party with General Nelson A. Miles in 1882. Among the early ones were Eliza Ruhama Scidmore, Charles Hallock, of *Forest and Stream,* and Professor Richardson, an artist from Minneapolis, Minnesota. They visited Glacier Bay in 1883.

The task of organizing the schools and missions in the broad, new, northern country was an enormous one. It was to attempt not only to bring the native out of his primitive, barbarous condition, but there was the degradation of years of misrule and demoralization to repair, in order to bridge the gap between their mode of life and our own. The condition in one place, at Wrangell, was epitomized by Customs Collector Dennis in 1877:

"Did they seek the enlightenment of the Indian, and endeavor to elevate him to a higher moral standard? On this point let the Indians themselves testify. Shakes, Toyatt, and Shustaks, chiefs of the Stikine Indians say this:

" 'For many years we have been desirous of having schools and churches established among us. With the coming of the military among us came a big church "Tyee" who told us that the soldiers were come to protect us, and that he would have schools established and churches built for us. Time passed; no schools were established and no churches built, and, instead of the soldiers being any protection to us they sought to debase and demoralize us. Liquor they sold us that crazed the brain, and trouble came that ended in Captain Smith being killed and one of our men hung.' "[17]

A beginning was being made; the next step was for a Government.

25

The Fight for a Government

ON THE SOUTHEAST COAST OF ALASKA, ON THE SHORES OF the mainland and islands that make the vast fringe of the Alexander Archipelago, real settlers began to wish to make homes. Men came who have lived long lives in that mild, moist, beautiful land. Both natives and whites built homes and hoped to live in them. Unfortunately there was neither title to be had for holding the lands nor a law for transferring them to others, not even for devising them at death. Orders for the military to expel men from lands at the point of the bayonet were the only evidence of interest in the situation by the Government. Not even a town lot could be legally held.[1]

The court jurisdiction was fixed in the State of Oregon, under the Federal judge resident in Portland, more than a thousand miles distant from the nearest point in Alaska. Neither a civil, criminal, nor probate code was provided. One could not procure evidence of birth, a marriage license, nor a death certificate.

The Government had been paying for an expensive military establishment at four or five places for years, whose chief result was to quarrel with the native men and debauch both native men and women.[2] It spent hundreds of thousands in supporting these, finally to withdraw them.[3]

One or two small, swift, effective, well-manned, well-armed boats under competent, upright officers, to capture offenders, and to protect the natives from reprobates, would have evaded the causes of friction and saved hundreds of thousands of dollars. In connection with this a just and equitable court was something one can hardly understand why the Government did not provide. But it did not. It was not for lack of funds, for the revenues from the Seal Islands, after 1870, provided ample returns to meet it.[4]

The United States, with all the history and experience of other nations, from Rome and her provinces to Louis and

MEMBERS OF THE FIRST U. S. COURT IN ALASKA

John H. Kinkead, Governor of Alaska, from Nevada, seated; standing, from left to right: Edwin W. Haskett, attorney, of Iowa; Munson C. Hillyer, marshal, of Nevada; Ward McAllister, Jr., judge, of California; and Andrew T. Lewis, clerk, of Illinois. Snapshot taken in front of Customs House, Sitka, May, 1885.

New France in the time of La Salle; from Spain and Cuba to her own frontier, reverted to type and forgot to provide for her citizens, both native and white, in protection of life and property.

The prayer of the world from time immemorial has been for an upright judge.

Men and women went to Alaska with the fear of the Frigid Zone in their hearts, to find a milder climate along the coasts than prevailed in their Eastern homes. A land like the coast of Norway, with deep, beautiful fjords, narrow valleys between grand mountains, sublime forests down to the water's edge along the network of channels between the islands, was what they saw. They came to distrust; they stayed to learn to love it. They—except a very few—being of the American frontier, did not yet understand how to clear away the little farms from the towering timber. Those who did so found the grass grew lush and rich in the glades, that berries and vegetables were delicious in the gardens, that the dahlias and peonies bloomed in exquisite beauty at their doors. They were possessed of only squatters' rights and had no protection even in those.

The fisheries began to attract capital. The most wonderful run of salmon known in all the world came into the rivers and lakes of the coast along the Pacific. Sometimes, when a storm was on the coast, at the time of the run, the shore was bordered with windrows of these beautiful fish lying dead on the beach. The streams were in places so filled that the bottom could not be seen for the fish. As before stated, the first cannery began in 1878. Rapidly the establishments increased. They spread from southeastern Alaska to Bristol Bay. The cannery from Old Sitka was transferred from there to Kussilof, on Cook Inlet, in 1882, by the Alaska Packing Company of California. This year the first cannery was built at Karluk, where the old Russian fishery of Shelekof was placed in 1785, to make *yukalee,* or sun-dried salmon, for his trading posts. It is one of the most wonderful fishing places in the world. The stream flowed down from clear lakes at the head, where only will the red salmon spawn, filled at times from bank to bank with the struggling fish, so thick in the water that a rowboat could not cross. Seven canneries occupied its banks a few years later. It has been

called the River of Life by some, on account of the marvelous
run of the "Silver Horde." Over 1,200,000 blue-backed or
red salmon were taken in the little river in 1888.[5] The
Alaska Commercial Company was the pioneer in this industry at this place.

The industry was generally richly remunerative. It was
a venture; there were some losses; but plants have been put
in that paid for the first investment, for all expenses, and
returned a large profit in the first year.

The rich companies, financed by men in the States who
had the ear of the politicians, were opposed to the establishment of a government of any kind, except the military,
which was placed there at the request of the company, as
stated before. They feared it would incur taxation and in-
terference with their methods; would encourage settlers
whom they did not want. The fur companies had the use
of the natives to gather their profits. The fishing corporations brought Chinese to their canneries to do their work,
while in Wyoming and California the Chinese were murdered because they were in the country.[6]

The fur and fish barons had senators in Congress at their
call. Senator Stewart is reputed to have been the spokesman
of Hutchinson, Kohl & Co., while the president of the Alaska
Commercial Company was later sent to the Senate.[7]

On the side of the men who asked for a government and
law and order in the communities was arrayed the influence
of the missions. When Dr. Sheldon Jackson returned to the
States after he established the Presbyterian Mission at Wrangell, he devoted his efforts to securing some form of government for the Territory.

The House of Representatives had been favorable to
Alaska's requests from the very first, for bill after bill had
been introduced; the first one being by Representative Ash-
ley on November 26, 1867, "To Organize the Territory of
Alaska." Every bill was killed in the committee rooms.[8]

At Wrangell, in 1877, a memorial was signed by 140
men, asking that a tribunal of justice be constituted, and
that justices of the peace be appointed.[9]

On July 4, 1881, a convention was held at Juneau (then
Harrisburg) to ask for representation and recognition for
the Territory. Mottram D. Ball was elected as a delegate,

and a memorial was drawn up setting forth conditions and asking that the delegate be seated. A bill was introduced, and went to the committee. The majority report was unfavorable, but the minority made a very strong report in favor of the passage. Both agreed that there was imperative need for some form of government. The bill was rejected, and the delegate was refused a seat.[10]

Oregon, under similar conditions, sent Joseph L. Meek to Washington with similar credentials, in 1848. Meek was accredited, and Oregon was constituted a Territory with full power of self-control such as has not been accorded to Alaska after a delay of seventy years.

Undiscouraged by the failures of the efforts, Dr. Jackson continued his fight. He published a series of articles in leading religious papers and made public addresses at missionary and educational conventions, assemblies, synods, and presbyteries, in the principal cities of the East from 1877 to 1884. The schools all over the country took up the fight for a government and for schools for Alaska. Resolution after resolution was passed by teachers' associations and conventions; petitions were circulated by hundreds of teachers, saying: "The promptings of interest, therefore, as well as the considerations of good faith, demand the immediate establishment of civil government in that territory."[11]

The pressure was too great for the demand to be denied. It resulted in the legislation called the Harrison Bill under the title, "An Act Providing a Civil Government for Alaska," which was signed by the President on May 17, 1884. It made provision for a district court, a governor, and for the Deady Code of the Laws of Oregon, to be extended over the new Territory like a cast-off garment. A land district was created, comprising the whole area. The mining laws of the United States were extended to the district, but it was expressly provided that the general land laws were *not* extended to the Territory.

It was the most inadequate and poverty-stricken system of government that has ever been imposed upon any community under the United States flag. In Massachusetts, in 1634, fourteen years after the landing of the Pilgrims at Plymouth Rock, they "chose deputies to consider in advance the duties of the general court," and were electing their own magistrates.[12] That was under Charles the First. In Alaska to this day the magistrates are not chosen by the people. It was 1913 before a legislature met in the Territory, and the legislature has not yet full and usual territorial control over the revenues.

The first governor of the Territory was John H. Kinkead, of Nevada. Ward McAllister, of California, was made judge, and on November 4, 1884, the court was formally organized in a room of the old Russian barracks building at Sitka.[13]

After seventeen years the Territory of Alaska had a governor and a court, but it was still termed a District.

The colonial policy of the United States, if it may be said to have had such, may be considered to have been a colossal failure up to this time. The Act offering this excuse for a government at least had a promise in it—an opportunity for a betterment.

The local situation resolved itself into an effort to amend the law and to do away with the prohibition of intoxicating liquors, which in its enforcement was a farce. If a smuggler was apprehended in the time-honored practice of handling contraband, he was fined an amount equivalent to a small license fee. This was converted into the Government treasury, and the offender was released to repeat the procedure.

To this object was added efforts to secure means to acquire land titles, also to provide town government and public schools.

In the mining sections the old frontier custom of settling difficulties by miners' meetings had prevailed, particularly in the Yukon section and in the Juneau district. In the more remote regions of the west and north there was an entire absence of law, punctuated by an occasional visit of a revenue cutter. The first miners' meeting was probably held at Juneau, about 1880 or 1881.[14]

For years the rails across the continent had been kept bright by nonofficial delegates to Congress, presenting the needs of Alaska to Washington. No less than seven were sent between 1878 and 1902. They rather increased than decreased after the Organic Law was passed.[15]

The definition of one writer describing the form of government provided was that "it became a political preserve for the payment of small debts owed by big politicians to little ones." It might have been added that it was convenient for paying political debts to men of such a character that they dared not appoint to office in the home communities.[16]

The court in the beginning had no jail. Commander Nichols, of the local warship, declined taking charge of criminals at the expense of the Navy. There was no provision for care of the insane, and no funds for deporting them to the States. The marshal was left to struggle with the problem.

The first judge lost the position through shortcomings, and his successor, Judge Dawne, left the Territory under suspicious conditions.

Schools for children of the whites had been and still were supported by subscriptions, no law existing for a tax to be collected for their support.

The importation and sale of intoxicating liquors was forbidden.[17] The Revenue Collector would issue a license to sell. The enforcement of the prohibition of sale was left to the Collector of Customs and a half-dozen deputies, in a country one sixth as large as continental United States and with a coastline as long as that of the seaboard states.

The situation appeared to be almost impossible, but the people were struggling for something better. They had no representative in Congress. The president of the big fur company that controlled all western Alaska was sent to the Senate from California. His interests were not in the advancement of the natives or the upbuilding of other settlements.

The census of 1880 enumerates 33,426 population in Alaska. Of these 430 were white, 1,756 creole, and 31,234 native.[18] The Russians removed their schools with the transfer to the United States. There were no schoolhouses, no schoolbooks, no school furniture or appliances. Very few natives spoke English. The inhabitants were scattered from Portland Canal to Point Barrow, a distance by sea of from 2,000 to 2,500 miles. There were no regular transportation lines over most of the distance. Mail from Sitka to Unalaska and westward points had to be sent to San Francisco, and from there by courtesy of the trading ships of the Alaska Commercial Company.[19]

To begin the establishment of education in this immense

region, and under these difficulties, the appropriation of twenty-five thousand dollars was made, and a General Agent of Education was appointed April 11, 1885. The work was assigned to the Bureau of Education, under the Department of the Interior of the United States.[20]

26

The Progress of Thirty Years

THIRTY YEARS OF UNITED STATES RULE IN ALASKA HAD passed in 1897. The land that had been called Seward's Icebox in 1867 and about which some in Congress inquired "Now that we have it, what shall we do with it?" had produced at the close of 1896 no less than $14,436,130 in gold, or over twice the cost of the whole Territory.[1] It had one stamp mill that had yielded $6,625,045 and had 240 stamps dropping every day in the year—one of the great mines of the world.[2]

In 1867 the fisheries had hardly been touched. The report of the East was that the fish of the Pacific were of an inferior quality because of the lack of salt in the sea. This prophecy shows how little the East knew about the West and its value. The salmon fisheries of Alaska of 1896 produced 909,538 cases of canned salmon, and 15,888 barrels of salted fish. There were 35 canneries, and one company took more than $2,000,000 in fish products out of the country. The pack of 1897 was valued at $2,977,019, or nearly half the purchase price of the country.[3]

There were six newspapers, two in Sitka, three in Juneau, and one in Fort Wrangell. There were twenty-five schools in the Territory, and eight denominations had established missions and churches.[4]

In sea furs the yield of the waters had been over 100,000 sea otter, each of a value of over $100, or a total of over $10,000,000 in 1905.[5] The Seal Islands had produced over 3,345,784 skins between 1867 and 1905, valued at over $47,000,000.[6] The aquatic fur of Alaska had amounted to nearly $60,000,000 during the same time. The whalers took to New England or to San Francisco before the end of 1890 the comfortable sum of $11,057,418. The whole return for the Territory to 1890 had been more than $75,000,000.[7] This was not a bad return upon the purchase price of $7,200,000.

The fisherman, the prospector, the trader, the whaler, and incidentally, the hoochmaker, had far outstripped the Government in progress in the new Territory.

The discovery of the Juneau mines, the Douglas lodes, the placer deposits of Gold Creek and the Silver Bow Basin, the other veins of Sheep Creek and Berners Bay had attracted hundreds of seekers for wealth to southeastern Alaska. The pioneers of the Yukon had uncovered the placers of Fortymile and of Circle City. Hundreds had followed on their trail. Canada had seen fit to send twenty Mounted Police to her side of the Yukon, although nearly all the prospectors were Americans, but our Government had sent none.

The flood of incoming men had made of Juneau a young city of about two thousand people. Among them were miners, newspapermen, merchants, tradesmen, and professional men. The population was stigmatized as temporary, yet there are men there today who came at the beginning of the camp; and many others lived their lives there and found their last resting place there.

The first who came were from Sitka.[8] Then came the Cassiar men, those who had explored the rivers and prospected the gulches of Caribou, Omineeca, and the Cassiar. They came, from Dick Willoughby, with his dance hall, to China Joe, with his laundry and garden.

In 1886 a riot arose in Juneau against the Chinese. Everyone of that nationality, except China Joe, was placed on schooners in the harbor and expelled forcibly from the community. Joe was protected by the old Cassiar miners on account of his friendly acts in the early days of the camp.[9]

The Government bureaus began to awake to an interest in the possibilities of the new land. The Revenue Cutter Service had been on the coast from the beginning. The cutter *Lincoln* initiated the work in 1867, when it carried George Davidson to Unalaska to begin his investigations along the coast. The *Reliance* carried it into the Arctic in 1870, and it continued to the time when the Coast Guard ships took their place.[10]

The Coast and Geodetic Survey began their investigations in 1867 when Davidson went to the coast of Alaska. From it came the valuable series of *Coast Pilots* which have

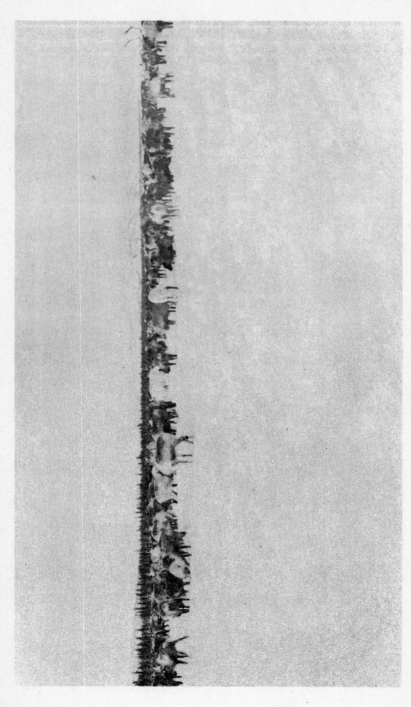

REINDEER IN ALASKA

REINDEER CARCASSES

been issued from 1869 to the present, with surveys of the coast from the southeastern part to Point Barrow.[11]

The Geological Survey made inquiries relating to glacial action in the St. Elias region and in Glacier Bay in 1891, under Russell and Harry Fielding Reid; also in 1895 a small appropriation was made under which W. H. Dall and G. F. Becker opened mineral work on coal and gold deposits. In 1896 Spurr and others went to the Yukon.[12]

Following the discoveries of gold at Juneau in 1880, and the placer deposits at the Fortymile and Circle, in the Yukon, came news of the gold in Cook Inlet, but not in sufficient quantities to stir the fever to a burning heat, although some good ground was found.[13]

Nordenskiold, the Swedish explorer, made the voyage from the Atlantic to the Pacific by way of the northern coast of the Old World, and anchored in Port Clarence in July, 1879.[14]

Water transportation along the coasts had increased with the development of the Juneau mines, and with the increased travel to the Yukon by way of the head of the river. From one little steamer once a month, and a few sailing vessels, the traffic engaged dozens of craft, and no less than five ocean-going steamers were on the run regularly,[15] as far as Juneau, and some plied to the head of Lynn Canal.

On the Yukon River, from the little steamer *Youkon*, taken to St. Michael on the deck of the brig *Commodore*, in 1869, the fleet had increased to eleven steam vessels, and all but two of them were built at St. Michael.[16]

The mail service had improved over 1869, when the Presidential order dated February 20, 1869, was not received at Sitka until April 20, 1869, the delay causing the seizure of a steamer and the sending of it to San Francisco.[17] In 1891 a route had been established from Sitka to Unalaska covering seven monthly trips each year. This replaced the voluntary service of the Alaska Commercial Company by way of San Francisco. To southeastern Alaska the Pacific Coast Steamship Company delivered mail at seven ports two trips a month.[18] Another route served from Wrangell to Klawak and Howkan.

Of lights along the coast there seems to have been none yet provided, the one on Baranof Castle having been discontinued.[19] One beacon had been established on Vitskari Island in Sitka Harbor, which was erected by the U. S. Navy in 1880.[20]

Of surveys along the coasts few seem to have been made. The navigators depended on the old charts of the Russians or the older ones of Vancouver and Cook. Wrangell Narrows were surveyed about 1881 or 1882,[21] and Beardslee did some work around Sitka Sound and in Glacier Bay.[22]

In 1890 the educational system was extended to the Arctic by the establishment of a school at Cape Prince of Wales, under the charge of William T. Lopp and H. R. Thornton; a second at Point Hope with Dr. John B. Driggs as teacher; a third at Barrow, taught by L. M. Stevenson. This was a joint arrangement between the missions and the Bureau, and they were called missionary-teachers, combining the duties of both, and the expense being shared by the two organizations. The first was Congregational, the second Episcopal, the third Presbyterian. This was the first break into the domain of the fur trader and the whaler on the shores of the Arctic Ocean.[23]

At this time the inhabitants of the Arctic were in a deplorable condition, because of the destruction of the whale, walrus, and caribou, or wild reindeer. When Dr. Sheldon Jackson went to inspect for the establishment of the schools he noted the condition and took measures to relieve it by the introduction of domestic reindeer from the herds of the Chukchees, the deermen of Siberia. The first deer were obtained by a subscription of the people of the East, obtained by Dr. Jackson. Later an appropriation was made by Congress for the purpose, the introduction and the distribution to be made through the Bureau of Education. That organization was given charge of them under the Interior Department.[24]

Commencing with 1892, 1280 reindeer were imported during a term of ten years, and were distributed among the native Eskimos on the Arctic coast according to a system of apprenticeship. Herds were also placed in the hands of the missions for distribution under regulations prescribed by the Department of the Interior.[25]

Many obstacles were to be overcome. Buildings for stations were to be constructed, surveys of lands proper for grazing—for the interior was an unknown area—the procuring of suitable apprentices from the surrounding people, the securing of herders to teach the keeping of the herds, the importation of herd dogs, and many other problems were to be solved. The industry was established and carried on in the manner in which reindeer have been cared for and kept domesticated in the Old World as long as reindeer husbandry has been known, for nearly a quarter of a century, when commercialism began to intrude.[26]

Laplanders and dogs were brought from Norway. Buildings were constructed from the driftwood on the beach, for there is no timber over most of the area along the northern sea. Corrals were made of willow, or in the far north, from ice blocks. Herders were trained and went out with their possessions to new grounds, until the industry was spread from Bristol Bay at the south to Point Barrow at the north.[27]

The intention was to give the native a chance for an industry that would keep him from want and make him comfortable in his own country; to give him an education in ownership of property in addition to academic instruction. Knowing the record of the white aggression upon the Indian, rules and regulations were made by the department that the female reindeer should not be sold to other than natives. This was to apply to both the natives and the missions, and all sales were ordered to be subject to the approval of the superintendents of the Bureau of Education.[28] The methods used to circumvent these salutary regulations will be described later.

In 1897 the reindeer herds numbered 4, and the total number of deer was 1466. These were the result of the importation and the increase of five years.[29]

The Territory might in some ways be compared with Oregon after the immigration of the forties, with the difference that Oregon in 1859 was made a State. Alaska in 1897 had only an excuse for a government of a nondescript character. Oregon had land laws, the Donation Act providing a special relief for the settlers, while Alaska in 1880 had none whatever. Large areas of land had been surveyed in Oregon in 1852; it was 1905 before an acre was surveyed for settlement by the Government in Alaska.[30] Instead of considering precedent and trying to improve by the elimination of errors of the past, the Government plunged into new and untried

experiments cruder than those presented in the history of
other territories.

Congress wailed over the cost of maintenance of the
Territory, a great part of which was owing to the unwanted
military that could have been replaced by a more effective
and less expensive means. Another source of trouble arose
from the lack of law to protect the seals and Seal Islands from
pelagic sealing and poachers. The protests of the unprofit-
ableness of the northern dependency were so vehement that
Captain James Carroll, one of the numerous self-appointed
delegates who went to the national capital, appeared before
the House and with a royal gesture offered to take the incubus
off their hands at a valuation of double the purchase price.[31]

No mail route reached the Yukon River, no peace officer
resided on the fifteen hundred miles of waterway from the
boundary line to St. Michael.[32] The transplanted statute book
of Oregon, a municipality more than a thousand miles distant, still served as the code of laws.

For schools, school buildings, salaries of officers, care of
property, freight charges, travel expense, etc., the sum of
$431,500 had been appropriated, to cover a territory of
590,000 square miles in 30 years, and doubtless needing the
benefits of education for those inhabiting it as fully as any
section of the nation. With this there were 21 schools maintained, employing 26 teachers, with an enrollment in 1896-7
of 1,395 pupils. There had been built out of this fund 17
schoolhouses, from Saxman in the southeastern part to Port
Clarence just below the Arctic Circle, while other schools
occupied mission buildings or other structures.[33]

This is in the face of the fact that from the Seal Islands
alone the Secretary of the Treasury reports, on May 3, 1888,
that the sum of $5,059,065.67 had been collected from the
revenue on sealskins at an expense of $299,901.94.[34]

Such were the conditions under which the new Territory
completed its first thirty years under our flag. Of the years
passed, seventeen had been without laws, ten of them under
military rule, seven under the Navy, the remaining thirteen
under a makeshift government.[35]

27

Following the Lure of Gold

DURING THE WINTER OF 1896-7 VAGUE REPORTS CAME OUT from the Yukon that rich deposits of placer gold had been struck on the Klondike, a tributary entering from the east in British territory. A few venturesome men left the States in February or March in time to get down the river before the ice broke.[1]

On July 17, glaring headlines in the Seattle *Post-Intelligencer* declared that the steamer *Portland* was coming in with "A Ton of Gold," a portion of the clean-up of the new gold field.[2] This was wired over the world, and thousands of men from all lands turned their faces toward the new El Dorado. Men and women poured into Seattle, Tacoma, and Vancouver, clamoring for transportation to the new diggings. Some went by St. Michael at the mouth of the Yukon to meet the river steamers that stemmed the stiff current of that stream for sixteen hundred miles. More went by the passes at the head of Lynn Canal and down the river.

At Dyea, at the foot of the Chilkoot Pass, the trading post of Healy and Wilson and two saloons were almost the only buildings. At Skagway stood the little log cabin of Captain William Moore. By an order of July 26, 1897, a port of entry was declared at the head of the canal, without an office or building in which to conduct the business. Ship after ship poured into the port, loaded with everything a mining camp needed and many things that they did not. There was no wharf. The freight was dumped onto lighters, scows, rowboats, rafts—anything that would float to shore. Horses and cattle were dropped from the slings into the water and swam to land. A tide of eighteen feet rose and fell, leaving a half mile of sloping beach at low tide. Up this incline the crowd trampled, carrying freight in the endeavor to get it out of the way of the returning flood. A line of tents rose at the edge of the forest that stood at high-water line. The trampling crowd fought for a place to pitch a tent.[3]

From two landing places, four miles apart, one trail ran up the canyon of the White Pass and another through the gorge of the Chilkoot Pass (Dyea). At the foot of one were pitched the tents of the town of Skagway, and on the beach on the other shore was the town-to-be of Dyea. When the stampeding mob landed they struggled out along the trails, thus making way for another feverish horde. Lumber was dumped on the beach, and foundations of houses, stores, and warehouses were laid. Piles were brought for construction of wharves. It was one of the great movements of the world, comparable only with the "Days of Forty-nine" or the Fraser River excitement of 1858.[4]

The old Indian trail by the Dyea, or Chilkoot, was the best marked and the nearest from tidewater to the head of navigation on the waters of the Yukon. For awhile it had the advantage. The Indians, during the days that they controlled the transportation, charged fifteen cents a pound, and the miners "beefed" at the tariff. Now everyone packed a load and competition raised the price to twenty-five cents, fifty-five cents, and finally a dollar a pound at the height of the panic, from Dyea or Skagway to Bennett. "Skookum Jim"[5] earned his title by carrying two hundred pounds across at one load. The Indians earned fabulous wages bending their brawny backs on the rugged mountain path.[6]

On the Skagway side of the five-thousand-foot mountain that divided the passes, the trail was new. It had to be cut through the forest, graded up the hill at Liarsville, built around Black Lake, Porcupine Hill, and through the river valley to White Pass City. A bridge to cross the river at Skagway was first constructed. Two bridges had to be built to cross the gorges through which the river boiled in a tumbling torrent. From there the summer line climbed the face of the mountain by a zigzag, or as an alternative, went through the Dead Horse Canyon, and up the point where the railway placed the high steel bridge. The winter route ran up the gulch to the summit and then down the lakes on the ice.[7]

In the timber and where there was enough earth to cover the boulders and hold the water it worked into a bottomless pit of muck into which horses sank and died or were shot to end their misery, and the impatient crowd surged over them and trampled the bodies into the quagmire. No one stopped

LAKE BENNETT
SAW MILL
N.W. MOUNTED POLICE POST
CAMP
MUSKEG SWAMPS
TRAIL TO LAKE FLOO-CHI
LOG HOUSE
LAKE LINDERMAN
CAMP
SHALLOW LAKE
CAMP
DEEP LAKE
2FT DEEP FORD
CLEAR BOTTOM
FORD (CROSS ON STEPPING STONES)
CAMP
LONG LAKE
MIDDLE LAKE
CAMP
HAPPY CAMP
1ST SPARSE WOOD
N
DYEA TRAIL
CRATER LAKE
SUMMIT LAKE
CAMP
OLD
SUMMIT OF CHILKOOT PASS
SCALES
STONE HOUSE
MOUNTAINS
TRAIL
SKAGUAY TRAIL
HORSE BRIDGE
SHEEP CAMP
(LAST TIMBER)
SUMMIT
WHITE PASS
CAMP PLEASANT
HORSE BRIDGE
END OF CANYON
BEGINT OF CANYON
CAMP
FORD
CROSSING ON STEPPING STONES
TRAIL
HORSE BRIDGE
CAMP
HORSE BRIDGE
HEAD OF NAVIGATION
FOOT LOG
HORSE BRIDGE
FINIGANS POINT
FORD (2FT DEEP)
CAMP
HORSE BRIDGE
FORD (2FT DEEP)
FERRY
PORCUPINE
CAMP
HORSE BRIDGE
DYEA
DYEA RIVER
CAMP
SKAGUAY RIVER
U.S. COMMISSIONER
HEAD QUARTERS
HORSE BRIDGE
SKAGUAY
INLET

SEATTLE POST-INTELLIGENCER'S
MAP OF THE
DYEA AND SKAGUAY TRAILS

THE LURE OF GOLD
Map showing trails used in the gold rush in Alaska in 1897.

Certificate of Gold Commissioner.

No ......

THIS IS TO CERTIFY THAT *S. Walker*

of *Dawson* in the Yukon Territory, has applied for a certificate, that the royalty has been paid upon *113* ounces of gold which he desires to export from the Yukon Territory in the following *Package* (Name the packages) by the steamer *C. Difton* (Name the Steamer.) , on the *19th* day of *August* A. D. 1901, and by the following route of travel *Whitehorse* (Name the route of travel). *via Skagway*

THIS IS TO CERTIFY That the said *S. Walker* is entitled to export the said quantity of gold in the said packages by the said steamer and by the said route of travel.

Dated at Dawson in the Yukon Territory this *19th* day of *aug* A. D. 1901.

This certificate shall be in force to the *25th* day of *august* A. D. 1901, and after that day, shall be of no avail whatever to prevent confiscation of any gold.

This certificate shall be delivered to the Officer appointed for the purpose at *Whitehorse* in the Yukon Territory before said gold is carried beyond said place; otherwise said gold shall be liable to confiscation.

Gold Commissioner.

A KLONDIKE GOLD CERTIFICATE

for man or beast. The canyon was lined with abandoned implements and portions of outfits discarded as the bearers wearied beyond endurance. Hundreds got "cold feet," turned, and fled for the landing place to sail for "home, sweet home." Keeler's pawnshop was filled with heirlooms pawned by owners to raise funds.[8]

At Skagway and at Dyea typical frontier towns rapidly rose. Every kind of vehicle and every animal was pressed into service to supply transportation. Horses were packed, dogs were loaded, and cattle had loads strapped on their backs.

Stores, blacksmith shops, law offices, and restaurants prospered in tents, then moved into shacks as they were built. A newspaper was published at Skagway on October 15, listing the business houses and professional offices, etc.[9]

The dance halls and the gambling dens of Skagway and Dyea roared and prospered; the "sure-thing men" plied their trade on the trails and rolled the roulette wheel in the dives. The shell game was in evidence at campfires built along the way to tempt the unsophisticated. "Cappers" frequented the trails to "steer" the cheechako to the resorts. The towns were "wide open." So the play went on.[10]

The United States made scant provision to meet the emergency. The Deputy Collector of Customs was sent to open the port without even a tent for shelter, without an entry blank or even a receipt book for duties, or a table to write one upon.

The United States Marshal joined the forces of the bandit gangs until he was arrested and sent to Sitka. The first commissioner was notoriously lax in performance of his duties. Below the boundary on the Yukon there was practically no peace officer in 1897.[11]

The management of the Canadian Government presented a notable contrast. Before the influx of 1897 they sent a force consisting of twenty officers and men to the Fortymile Post.[12] The Minister of the Interior of Canada came out and went over the pass in the fall of 1897 to be able to understand the situation and to make provision to meet it.[13] During the latter part of 1897, fifty-nine members of the Northwest Mounted Police, a registrar and accountant, and two mining inspectors were sent to the Yukon.[14]

The horde of gold seekers fled through the passes and down

the Yukon, wading the rivers, wallowing through the bottomless quagmire, climbing the rock-bound pass, building their Yukon boats and setting out on the lakes and rivers. There was a miniature shipyard in every cove where there was timber for whipsawing the lumber. The white sails flitted down the mountain lakes, through the Fiftymile River, down the Miles Canyon and the Whitehorse Rapids; loaded with men and outfits they streamed on to Dawson.[15]

There was something magnificent in the movement of the host through the defiles of those forbidding mountains. The high spirit that gave the strength to attempt the real trials and terrors of the trail had its elements of greatness. Death by flood or avalanche lurked along the way. Pneumonia and spinal meningitis took their toll. But hope of fortune lured the adventurers on.

Many a man pawned his last vestige of property to procure the price of an outfit, and left wife and children to shift for themselves while he set forth on the search for the pot of gold at the end of the rainbow of the North. It was the strong and steady, the man with patience and courage, that won.

The hardships of the trails brought out the best and the worst of the men who traveled them. The back-packing through swamps and over rock slopes, the plodding through quagmires in the rain, through the snows in the driving northern gales, either made or broke its victim. If he lost his courage on the mountain, or squandered his substance in the gambling dens, it was the end of his cherished hopes.

Many are the tales of the dividing of the outfit with the trailmate, cutting the boat in halves, or splitting the Klondike stove, rather than to have it fall into the hands of the other intact. Bitter were the enmities of the lone trail to the land of gold.

Many a man made the race and got no claim. But if he knew how to fall on his feet and stay there, sometimes other things paid better than mining. Mining is labor, grueling labor for the man without means. To the prospector it means, as the Swede said when he was begged to divulge his luck, "I yust sink holes."

Dawson is in the Yukon Territory, Canada, therefore not a part of this story, but so closely allied and so interesting

The Hudson's Bay Company "Bateau"

THE POLING BOAT

CANOE USED IN THE YUKON

that it is difficult to let it pass. It is a story of its own that has never yet all been told, but has been related in fragments by many persons.

On the trails through the mountains the coming of winter was a blessing, even though the merciless wind blew down the narrow canyons like an icy torrent. Over the summit of the Chilkoot Pass horses could not be used at the steep pitch at the highest point. This was negotiated by backpacking until a tramway was built. The long line of men climbing the steep ascent like a stream of black ants was a familiar picture of the winter of 1897-8.[16]

Interesting as is this great caravan of men and animals wending their way through these rugged passes, we must turn aside to see where other pilgrims, some of them less fortunate, are staking their lives by other trails in the race following the lure of gold.

There were other routes attempted, most of them impracticable. The Teslin Trail was one. It turned aside at Wrangell, followed the Stikine River to Glenora and from there took the line of the old Western Union Telegraph Survey by way of the Teslin Lake and down the Yukon. There was the Edmonton Trail, and the Ashcroft Trail; these being all-Canadian routes they will not be detailed.

Some tried to break through the mountain range from Yakutat Bay, a region filled with glaciers and raging torrents. Some died on the glaciers and others were lost in the rivers.

The Copper River offered a more enticing route, and many went in by the way of Valdez, over the glaciers. Some made their way up the Copper River through the Abercrombie Canyon and the Woods Canyon.[17] This was also a trail of hardship, and only the vanguard penetrated it the fall of 1897. Detachments landed at Valdez and worked out from there, but the great press of travelers did not come until later in the winter.

The other great doorway to the gold country for the summer of 1897 was through St. Michael and up the Yukon River.

28

St. Michael and the Yukon

In June of 1897 the sleepy old Russian town of St. Michael awoke. On the 25th of the month the river steamer *Alice* arrived from Dawson, Y. T., Canada, with twenty-five miners who carried with them half a million dollars in gold dust. It was enough to liven up almost any town, even to see it carried down to an ocean liner and shipped away. Two days later came the *P. B. Weare*, of the North American Transportation and Trading Company, carrying another party of successful men who were staggering under pokes of gold valued at from $55,000 to $175,000, and still others followed.[1]

This was the most convenient and the easiest way to leave or to reach the new gold fields, but the added inconvenience of the early closing of the river was to be considered. The gold went to Seattle, and to San Francisco; then came a stream of boats loaded with passengers and freight, hurrying to get up the river.[2]

The great stream—the Yukon—carrying about two thirds of the volume of water of the Mississippi, in summer is loaded with the soil debris of ground glacial rock and silt of banks cut away by the current. This matter is deposited on the wide, fan-shaped flat reaching out into Bering Sea from its mouth, over which the ocean ships cannot cross to get into the deep current of the stream. All cargoes and passengers must land at St. Michael for transfer to river steamers. At any time after October 1 the northern tributaries may begin to throw out pans of heavy, clear, hard ice that soon batter through the hull of a river boat.

Ship after ship came in, and steamer after steamer went out and up the river, each hurrying to get up before the river closed. The freight piled up on the docks and in the warehouses. The anxious passengers, wild to get to the gold fields where they hoped for a fortune, railed at the masters of the ships that brought them. Some threatened to hang the agents who had solicited their business. An observer ventured to say that the stampeders to the gold fields were not ordinary men—they were gold-crazed lunatics.[3]

Commercial and trading companies built warehouses to facilitate the transfer of goods, and fleets of steamers on which to convey passengers and freight up the Yukon. The Northern Commercial Company, an offshoot of the old Alaska Commercial Company, and the North American Transportation and Trading Company, a rival corporation, had been engaged in the business for years. They enlarged their establishments, and feverishly built new boats. New companies, the Seattle Yukon Transportation Company, the Alaska Exploration Company, and others, sprang up.

Small steamers were shipped on ocean liners to be assembled at St. Michael. An army of men assembled and built steamers, barges, and tugs. River steamers were later built at Seattle and ventured the twenty-three-hundred-mile voyage on the open ocean under their own power or were towed by seagoing ships.

Gangs of gamblers pitched tents along the beach in which they relieved the cheechakos, newly arriving and waiting for transportation, of their spare cash. The War Department established an army post and named it Fort St. Michael. A military reserve of one hundred miles around the fort was set aside by the Government. The Commandant then gave the sports and "sure thing men" notice to vacate the island.

Vessel after vessel hurried away, churning the muddy waters of the Yukon to get to Dawson and the Klondike. One hundred miles a day was all the best steamer could make against the powerful current of the stream, running one half to six miles an hour, and there were sixteen hundred miles to go.

At the northern bend of the river, at Fort Yukon, it is filled with islands till it is fifteen miles from bank to bank. When the frosts of coming winter chill the sources the water falls and the sand bars in the flats lie close to the surface. Then navigation is slow and difficult. Some of the boats had to lighten their cargoes at Fort Yukon, and leave the freight on the bank.

A few of the hurrying carriers reached Dawson; others were caught by the drifting ice and were compelled to find shelter in which to spend the winter. Some did not get away from St. Michael. Between the mouth of the river and the boundary line of Canada fifteen steamers with their passengers and freight were locked in the ice.[4]

In Dawson a panic arose with the fear that supplies would run short and famine ensue. Many boats had carried more firewater than food, as is usual in mining camps. The Northwest Mounted Police began to give "blue tickets" to the undesirables in the town to compel them to drop down the river to Alaskan territory.[5] Disappointed prospectors went down hoping to find gold on the American side.

The Northwest Police put part of the undersirable population on the woodpile, which meant saw wood or freeze. No halfway measures were taken.

At Circle City were old-time miners. Some of them had ordered their winter outfits of food and other supplies the summer before.

Steamers hurried by, striving to reach the Klondike. The men of Birch and Mastodon Creeks became worried. Where were their food supplies to be had? Hunger stared them in the face during the winter unless they got provisions from those boats.

The steamer *P. B. Weare* touched at Circle on her way up-river. A miners' meeting appointed a committee who went on board, took charge of the vessel, opened a warehouse, sent men into the hatches for supplies, took out food and clothing, and sent it up to the storage where there were men who checked and made an account of it. They took thirty tons. The steamer *Bella* came in. The miners went on board her and took possession.

Captain P. H. Ray, U. S. A., was at Circle, having arrived during the season. He opposed the taking of the freight and designated it as unlawful. The miners replied that there was no authority to whom to appeal for relief; that 180 men depended on it for food and that they were going to have it. There were a hundred men and one soldier. Captain Ray asked them to take no more than was actually needed. The men cleared the boat of bystanders, posted guards to prevent theft, and proceeded with their work.[6]

In Dawson excitement ran high. Hundreds were arriving by the upper river with scant provision for the winter, and men began to buy foodstuffs which they cached with intent

The North American Transportation and Trading Company Station at St. Michael, Alaska

THE NORTHERN COMMERCIAL COMPANY STATION AT ST. MICHAEL, ALASKA

to sell when starvation prices arrived. Appeals were sent out to the States for relief. Captain Ray sent a special messenger, Mr. E. Hazard Wells, an old "sourdough" of experience, as a messenger.[7]

Congress passed an appropriation of two hundred thousand dollars for relief purposes. Sheldon Jackson was commissioned to secure five hundred reindeer, sled deer with sledges from Norway, to carry supplies from the head of navigation to Dawson, both the deer and their freight to constitute food, if necessary.[8]

Reindeer to the number of 539 were purchased at $10 each, were shipped to New York, thence to Seattle, and finally landed at Haines Mission, Alaska, on March 27, 1898. The food shortage in Dawson was not so acute as was reported. The reindeer were held at Haines for further instructions as to their disposition.[9]

Meantime the winter closed down on the valley of the Yukon and on the thousands of men seeking gold in the frozen gravels of the Klondike.

At Fort Yukon, where supplies had been left by the boats because of the low water in the river, hundreds of men gathered and attempted to commandeer the food supplies. Captain Ray and his companion, Lieutenant W. P. Richardson, took charge and distributed outfits to the men on condition that they go out to prospect, or that they cut wood for the river boats for the next season, and that they would repay the companies during the coming year at Circle City.[10]

The law of the Yukon for the old miners of the region was to leave the latchstring out, food on the shelf, and wood by the stove with kindling cut for the man who came half-frozen to the shelter. Some of the newcomers, the cheechakos, had no code. They used the cabin, ate the food, and stole the stove on some occasions.[11] Some of them worked the winter, went to Circle and paid their bills; others went out into the woods, ate the supplies, and left the country.[12]

Meanwhile those who had found paying claims were filling five-gallon cans with gold dust from the creeks, and thousands of men were burrowing in the earth like moles, with wood fires to thaw the muck and gravel in the prospect holes. It was the old story of '49, or of the Fraser River of 1858, in a new setting. The miners say, "Gold is where you find it."

29

The Trails of Ninety-eight

WITH THE COMING OF THE SNOWS AND THE COLD OF THE winter of '98, much of the hardship passed, especially on the White Pass. The trail in summer was better on the Dyea Pass;[1] in winter the White Pass excelled. As soon as the streams closed with ice, and the treacherous pits of muck turned to a hard-surfaced track, the long trains of pack animals filed out up the canyons, over the pass, down past Log Cabin, where the Canadian Customs took their tolls, then to Bennett.

Over the Chilkoot Pass the Chilkoot Railroad and Transport Company began their tramway in December. The Dyea and Dawson City Transportation and Trading Company competed for the carrying trade. On the White Pass, George A. Brackett commenced building a wagon road about the same time. Freight rates soon began to drop from those charged in the old days of back-packing. Before the spring came, from Dyea to the Scales, the price went down to four cents a pound, and to Bennett it was as low as thirteen cents.[2]

The snows of winter piled high in the pass and on the mountainsides. When the rising sun of spring and the warmer air of the ocean came with southerly storms, the deep, overhanging drifts above the trails loosened and softened. In March continued storms with heavy snows began and continued into April. On April 3, during a lull in the tempest, men began to travel. Without warning an immense slide came down the mountain with a muffled roar, burying fifty-six men who perished, near the Scales. Some were rescued by relief parties from camps near the scene.[3]

Prospectors searched the country from Teslin Lake to the mouth of the Yukon. On July 29, the news came to Bennett of a gold strike on Atlin Lake, and to this some of the travelers turned aside.[4]

All winter long the throng pressed on. Five thousand people landed at the head of Lynn Canal in February alone, according to the record at the Customs Office.

In the towns the birds of prey, the gamblers, held carnival. The continual influx of men going to the mines, especially the successful ones returning with their pokes of gold, furnished a succession of new victims. Their tactics were not to prey on the people of the town but to reserve their attentions for the passing throng.

With the opening of the ice on the upper Yukon and its tributaries new boats were placed in service, most of them transported over the snow trail in sections and assembled on the lakes.[5] Sawmills buzzed, producing lumber for Yukon boats with which to drift on the river.[6]

To Dyea and Skagway larger vessels were brought, the *Tartar*, the *Athenian*, the *Willamette*, and the *Oregon*. The *Cutch*, formerly the yacht of an Indian rajah, came halfway round the world to enter the trade.

When the ice cleared away from St. Michael, the latter part of June, a squadron met the down-river steamers that carried millions of the winnowings of the clean-up of spring when the water ran in the sluice boxes. The *St. Paul* left St. Michael with over $6,000,000; the *Roanoke* arrived at Seattle on July 20 with $1,500,000, while the *Charles Nelson*, the thirteenth "gold ship," landed on the 26th. The people went wild over gold.[7]

The Spanish-American War drove the Klondike off the front pages of the big dailies, but the stream of gold seekers went on to the North. New steamers for the lower Yukon had been built during the winter. The Moran fleet was the most famous of these—twelve new river boats, just off the ways, in one gay flotilla, with two barges attending them. Storms drove them to shelter, and two were lost on the way, but ten reached their destination safely and for years were well known to the travelers of the North.[8] The *Laurada*, an old blockade runner of the Cuban coast, came around the Horn and towed two steamers up the coast.[9] The *Lotta Talbot*, the *Quickstep*, and others were lying at their moorings, waiting for a tug to take them in tow.[10] The three big "packets" built like the Mississippi steamers, the *Sarah*, the *Susie*, and the *Hannah*, were built at Dutch Harbor and ran to St. Michael under their own steam.

On the river Yukon, before the season of 1898 closed, there were thirty-two companies engaged in transportation, employing sixty steamboats, eight tugs and towboats, and twenty barges.

Prospectors reached out into the wilderness, farther and farther. With the clearing of the ice from the Arctic a little fleet of schooners and other craft went into the Kotzebue Sound, and fifteen hundred men were said to have spread out into the wide region inside the Arctic Circle on the Kobuk, the Selawik, and Noatak Rivers.[11]

The Copper River Valley claimed its share of the adventurers who went into Alaska that year. Hundreds of them passed over the Valdez Glacier before the snow trail broke. On the rivers of the interior many lost everything in small boats and on rafts, then struggled back to the coast. The interior was explored, partly by expeditions sent out by the War Department, largely by the efforts of the ubiquitous prospector. Captain Abercrombie went to Valdez with a detachment of troops and established Fort Liscum at the south of the Inlet. Parties were sent out to the Susitna, to the Copper, and some to Eagle on the Yukon. The captain estimates the people attempting to go through on this route expended $3,700,000 in the effort to establish an all-American route to the interior.[12] The effort was not a loss, for it pioneered the way that led to the discovery of the rich copper deposits that constitute the Kennicott Copper properties; it outlined routes for the telegraph line afterward extended to Eagle; it opened a way to the Richardson Highway, and led to the discovery of the gold placers of the Chisana and other fields.

On the Dalton Trail, up the Chilkat River and north to the Yukon, a pony express was established in the early part of 1898 to carry passengers and mail.[13] This route had been used in 1896 for driving cattle and sheep to the interior.[14] During the winter of 1898 reindeer were brought from Norway as a means of transportation for the relief of miners in Dawson. When it was found that the people were not in a serious condition in that camp, what remained of the animals were taken to the lower Tanana by way of this pass.[15]

The Teslin Trail from the Stikine River north was thronged by men during the spring and summer when the Mackenzie-Mann railway project fell through; from two thousand to three thousand were stranded, and two thousand men held an indignation meeting at Glenora.[16] Then many went back home while others tried the White Pass route.

It is estimated that 28,000 people passed Tagish post of the Northwest Mounted Police during the year 1898. The number of boats was kept as they passed the post, each boat being numbered, and the occupants were required to register at each place they passed on the way down. There were 7,080 boats numbered, and at an average of four persons to a boat the estimate was made. This register enabled the tracing of many persons who were drowned or lost in other ways on their way down the stream.[17]

In Dawson a census was taken which showed 4,236 people in the town, but most of the people were out on the creeks. The whole number in the district, including Fortymile, Selkirk, and the tributaries of the Klondike, was estimated at 18,527. During the fall of 1897 and during 1898 there were estimated to have been 4,000 who went down the river to American territory, or returned to the States.[18]

There were thousands of men who did not get claims in the Klondike, many of whom went to Alaska and sought for other deposits of mineral. Many went back to the American Fortymile, some to Circle City, while still others sought new diggings. One result was the discovery of gold in the sands of Bering Sea that caused an exodus to the barren-looking beach of the Seward Peninsula which was second only to that of the Klondike.

30

"Soapy" Smith and His Gang

ALASKA IS A PEACEFUL LAND, BUT ITS ONE EPIC OF BLOOD-shed came to pass in 1898. Where the carcasses are found the vultures abound. The stream of gold pouring through the roadways to the Klondike caused a flock of the birds of prey to alight at Dyea and Skagway, as well as at St. Michael. Thus they have collected at all great gold stampedes from California to Alaska. They dared not pass to the British soil, for in the autumn of 1897 some fifty-seven stalwart Northwest Mounted Police went into the interior, equipped for business. It was as the Collector of Customs of Alaska wrote in 1874 concerning the gold fields of the Cassiar, "They soon tame our gun and pistol gentry that come over their boundary."

"Soapy" Smith was an affable, adroit, insinuating member of the underworld who had gained his sobriquet by selling soap rolled in five-dollar bills, for a dollar, on the streets of Western cities. He had been known in Seattle and in Creede, Colorado, and did not scorn to grace even smaller cities with his presence. He came up the coast with the hurrying crowd, looked in at various places, but finally "located" at Skagway, collected a force of lieutenants, and opened up for business. The "three-shell game" was one of his principal lures, and the nimble-fingered gentry were to be seen in every favorable place. "Soapy," genial, black-whiskered, alert, was the central figure and dominated the organization. Just how far it extended is not really known, but some of his lieutenants may be recognized in some of the cities of the United States today by one who remembers the old days.

His headquarters were on Sixth Avenue, Skagway. There were little cabins where, when ordinary devices like roulette, blackjack, faro, and the "shell game" did not win, the luckless victim was enticed, and under the guise of "Real Estate" or "Information Office," was received and given audience. A quarrel would ensue over some trivial matter. The lights went out, and roughhouse prevailed for a few moments. When the manhandling was over and the unfortunate subject found himself outside, shorn of money and valuables, there was no one in sight, and the "Office" was vacant.

"Soapy" never descended to the menial occupation of the coarser procedure of his "gang." This he left to his subordinates. He dispensed largess with a liberal hand to those whose favor he desired, and tradesmen whom he patronized were lavishly paid. The boy who delivered the printing from the office to his "Headquarters" was told to "keep the change." He was the "Uncrowned King" of Skagway. His adherents increased till they even are alleged to have included the Deputy U. S. Marshal, and some of the supposedly respectable citizens of the city. He rode in the Fourth of July parade as a marshal. He enlisted a company of volunteers for the war, tendered his services and his command to the President, receiving a letter declining the offer, but which he framed and used as an advertisement on the wall of his resort.[1]

That "Soapy" conducted a correspondence with and enjoyed the friendship of some of the prominent men of the land from East to West, some of the upper and some of the underworld, was shown by the correspondence found in his trunk after his sudden demise.[2]

By March of 1898 the conditions became unbearable to the citizens of the northern town, and a meeting of citizens was called on the case of the murder of a miner named H. Bean, as well as other crimes.[3] This was attended by 101 citizens, and a warning was issued to "all confidence, bunco, and sure-thing men to leave Skagway."

To this the followers of "Soapy" Smith replied with a defiance which purported to be from the "Law and Order Society of 317 Members."[4]

Other meetings were held by the citizens, some of which were "packed" by members of the gang who were informed by traitors to the cause, one being a correspondent of an Eastern newspaper, who was afterward invited to move on.[5]

The climax came in July when a miner from Dawson, J. D. Stewart, came into the town with a poke of gold and was robbed of it, back of "Soapy's" Place. A meeting was held on the Juneau dock, July 8, 1898, and Frank H. Reid[6] was placed as a guard at the entrance to the long viaduct that led to it, so that no unwished-for intruders could attend.

Reid was a quiet, determined man, and was said to be the only man in Skagway for whom "Soapy" entertained a fear. He was stationed about one hundred feet from the end of the long causeway on the piling that led out to the deep water of the bay.

"Soapy" heard of the meeting, took his rifle, a Winchester repeater, drank a big glass of whiskey to reinforce his courage, and swearing that he would "drive the ———— into the bay," started down the street and out on the viaduct. He was followed by some of his gang who kept behind. He was halted by Reid, turned and struck at him with the rifle. Reid caught it with his left hand and forced it aside as he drew his revolver. The first cartridge missed fire.

Gathering his strength, "Soapy" swung the rifle toward Reid and fired. At the same instant the fire flashed from Reid's revolver. An eyewitness states that it looked as though they were spitting fire at each other. Both men crumpled down on the planking and as Reid fell he fired again. "Soapy" was dead, with a ball through his heart and another through his thigh, eight inches above the knee, probably fired by Reid as he fell.

Reid was mortally wounded by the rifle ball that crashed through his groin as he struggled to hold down the weapon that threatened his life and keep it away from his body.

As "Soapy" dropped to the planking, his followers, seeing the fall of their leader, took to their heels up the street. Friends of Reid carried him to the hospital. Others formed in posses, secured arms, and began the search for the members of the gang who had taken to the woods or had hidden in different parts of the town. Guards were stationed on the trails to bar escape by land, and on the wharves to prevent leaving by sea. Captain Yeatman and a squad of soldiers came from Camp Dyea, but upon the assurance of order being kept by the citizens' committee they returned. One by one the outlaws were gathered in and placed under arrest. J. M. Tanner was appointed as Deputy Marshal by United States Commissioner Sehlbrede, and he took the prisoners in charge.

The Citizens' Committee met on the Seattle dock and held an examination. Ten men, finding their presence undesirable in the town, willingly took their departure on the S.S. *Tartar* which was sailing for Southern ports. "Old Tripp," Bowers, Turner Jackson, and others were sent to Sitka to await the action of the Grand Jury.[7]

In this manner ended the most desperate alliance of lawless men that Alaska has known during her history of over sixty years under the flag of the United States.[8]

31

The Building of the White Pass Railway

THE HURRYING, RESTLESS CROWD OF GOLD SEEKERS CAME UP on the steamers and went on over the trail into the Golden Klondike. Soon with them came E. C. Hawkins, a young engineer, with a corps of assistants surveying the path for a railway.[1] Graders and track layers followed; men, wearied on the trail, and wanting funds, turned aside to prepare the roadbed till, by July 2, 1898, the first mile of track was laid, and during that month the first engine pulled up the road on the first railway in Alaska,[2] known as the White Pass & Yukon Route, connecting tidewater of the Pacific at the head of Lynn Canal with the head of navigation on the Yukon River, Canada. It was built under three incorporations—one in Alaska, one in British Columbia, and one in Yukon Territory, and was 110 miles in length. It was financed by British capital, and the president of the road was S. H. Graves.[3] The building was done by the construction company directed by Michael J. Heney, the contractor.[4]

It was a difficult undertaking: rough, craggy mountains scraped clean and smooth by the ice streams that had plowed their way through the gorges, glaciers creeping down the canyons at the sides from vast snowfields along the summits, the unknown dangers of the northern storms. All combined to add to the obstacles presented. Labor was scarce and costly, everyone being desirous to pass on to the promise of the gold fields of the Yukon. Building material must be transported from Seattle on ships already crowded for space to meet the requirements of the passing throng. The excitement of the Spanish-American War, and the demand for men and ships in the military service further complicated the situation.

Another element entered into the construction: the boundary line between the United States and the British possessions was not determined at the summit of the passes. The Canadian authorities claimed as far down as to tidewater

TRAIL SCENE AT THE SUMMIT OF WHITE PASS

COMPLETION OF WHITE PASS RAILWAY AT CARIBOU

SHIPPING AT SKAGWAY

on Lynn Canal and were disposed to defend their claim by the Northwest Mounted Police, some of whom were stationed at Skagway.[5] The United States made good use of its soldiery by establishing Camp Dyea at the head of navigation, thus ending the contest there, but at the summit there was contention. The events, some serious, some comic, ended amicably through an agreement reached between the two countries in 1904.[6]

The roadbed to the summit of the pass, after the first five miles, was almost one continuous piece of rockwork, blasting a ledge in the smooth, solid walls of the canyon. Great snowslides poured down the mountainsides, burying the track, as it was laid, under many feet of snow, and sweeping away every movable thing in its path. Trees were ripped out of the mountain and cast across the path of the trains.

The track was completed to the summit of the pass February 20, 1899; the event was celebrated by appropriate ceremonies in the tents of Contractor Heney, and with true Irish hospitality. Canadian and American guests joined in the pleasure of one of the great industrial accomplishments of the North.[7]

The construction was pushed down the slope of the Yukon Valley, reaching Bennett, on the shores of Lake Bennett on July 6, 1899. The last rail was laid at Carcross, then known as Caribou Crossing, below Lake Bennett, on July 29, 1900, and rail service was completed from ocean to river, putting an end to the old hardships and dangers of the Trail of '97, when thousands of horses and hundreds of men perished on the wild rush to the gold of the Yukon. It is possible to present only the briefest glimpse of those days in these pages, but to those who are interested the tale is told in many volumes of fact and fiction by those who toiled over those passes. The ones who pioneered the way are now old men and women and many of them have already gone over the last lone trail into a far land.[8]

The achievement was a real stride in the progress of the North—a breaking of the bonds of tradition. At first it was looked on as a visionary project—an impossible venture into the forbidden, frost-bound realms of the Arctic world. Once the spell was broken, the mysterious Yukon became so familiar that it had scarcely more terrors than the plains of Montana or the heights of the passes of the Rockies. It began to be realized that the vast valley was in the North Temperate Zone, and was little more rigorous than the climate of Minnesota and Dakota.

32

The Golden Sands of Nome

"THERE'S NEVER A LAW OF GOD OR MAN, RUNS NORTH OF Fifty-three," was one of Kipling's famous epigrams. Nome was well north of fifty-three, and therefore included in its scope. The white whalers swept along the shores, taking the great northern right whale, the bowhead, gathering furs, and peddling ruin and rum. The latter was obtained by the traffic in blackbirds from the Gold Coast of Africa. From start to finish it was mainly a lawless trade, the only limit being the individual conscience of the salty, weatherbeaten captain who walked the quarterdeck, and the discipline enforced by his hard-hitting "bucko" mates. The first semblance of law was presented when the revenue cutter *Reliance* sailed along the shores of the Seward Peninsula and into the Arctic as far as Kotzebue Sound in 1870.[1]

The $2,500,000 of the golden flood of the Klondike in 1897 kindled the fire for gold seeking that swept the land, and the $10,000,000 that poured out in the succeeding year fanned the blaze.[2] The prospectors spread out from the Canadian boundary to the Kotzebue, and in 1898 the news went out that three men, John Brynteson, Erick O. Lindbloom, and Jafet Lindeberg, had discovered rich pay on Anvil Creek on September 20.[3]

Winter was just setting in, and ice was beginning to form in the streams. The discoverers panned and rocked eighteen hundred dollars from the gravels, staked their claims, and returned to their base at Golovin. The news went up the river to Dawson, over the snow trail, fifteen hundred miles, and soon the stampeders were flying down the Yukon to reach the new El Dorado. With the opening of the ice of the next summer a few tents were pitched on the beach at the mouth of the Snake River, where the town of Nome is now situated.

On the water front of Seattle the opening scenes of the drama of 1897 were being re-enacted. Ships, steamers,

schooners, large and small, were being fitted out for the
voyage. The first to reach the Nome coast was the steamer
Garonne, on June 20, 1899. The open, sandy beach, strewn
with driftwood from the Yukon floods, was the only landing
place, utterly no harbor existing, and among the debris the
passengers and freight were landed. The *Roanoke* followed
with other eager treasure seekers. Vessel after vessel hove
in sight and threw their cargoes on the shore. The big
commercial companies of the North, the North American
Trading and Transportation Company, the Alaska Commercial Company, and the Alaska Exploration Company, established trading posts in canvas coverings.

The snows of winter that had covered the frozen tundra
melted away. The rains pelted down, drenching everything
and turning the flat, level-lying stretch of land that lay back
towards the hills into a slippery, muddy quagmire, studded
with niggerhead grass that impeded all travel. Most of the
tents were on the sandspit by the Snake River, from where
they gradually spread to the east side of the stream. Streets
began to be laid out parallel with the water front. As traffic
passed over them the mud became bottomless. Horses mired
and lay helpless until they were pulled out with block and
tackle.

The best of the mankind of the land arrived and, as is
customary in such events, the worst came with them. Pandemonium prevailed. Saloons, dives, and doggeries sprang up.
Claims to town lots were jumped. The cabins that had been
erected were hauled away at night by horses brought by
gangs of men, some of the owners still in the cabins, and before they could get back to their location another structure
would be occupying the ground.

For public safety a form of local government called the
Anvil Townsite Committee was attempted.[4] The town
was first named Anvil City, and a survey was made by George
Harbach. Trouble arose over rich claims being "jumped,"
which means they were claimed by others subsequent to the
original locators. A military post had been established at Fort
St. Michael, and a squad of soldiers was asked from the
fort to preserve order. A miners' meeting was held to declare
the claims vacant, and the contestants were on the ground
to stake on receiving the signal of the action's being taken.

The Only Second Class Saloon in Alaska

The soldiers, under command of Lieutenant Spaulding, dispersed the meeting.[5]

A few days later this excitement was dispelled by the discovery of gold in the very sands of the beach where for nearly a hundred years men had been landing in their voyages along the sea. Thousands of men turned to the strip of riparian, sea-washed gravel. There was no law as to a claim and every man held all that he could control, like a beachmaster on the rookeries of the Seal Islands. More than two million dollars are said to have been taken from these beach diggings.[6]

Thousands of men chased over the tundra, searching for a prospect in the gulches. The whole Seward Peninsula, as large an area as the State of New York, was soon threaded by the hurrying, excited gold hunters. Solomon, Bluff, Council, the Kougarok, Candle, the Immetchuck, Gold Run, were located, and prospect holes were sunk in every corner of the land.[7]

The urgent need of a court was apparent. All Alaska was in one great district, a region as large as all of the states east of the Mississippi and north of Tennessee. The Hon. C. S. Johnson was the judge. He was called to hold court and make a tour of his district, on the circuit covering some seven thousand miles. It was like a judge from New York being called to hold court in San Francisco in 1849. The court sat in a tent. Upon his departure he advised that, in the absence of any legal procedure, a "Consent Government" be organized. This was done, and officers were elected, T. D. Cashel being the first mayor of Nome.[8]

In 1900 there were estimated to have been eighteen thousand people who arrived in Nome and spread over the surrounding country. Nine out of ten of them knew nothing of prospecting or mining, were simply wandering with the hope of striking some source of sudden riches.[9]

Alaska has been visited by several of the miscarriages of justice in the form of appointment of mercenary and unqualified judges to preside over the courts. The distance from authority to furnish relief, and the impossibility of local action by election made the imposition doubly burdensome.

In the spring of 1900, on July 19, Arthur H. Noyes arrived at Nome, Alaska, to fill the position of judge in the newly created Second Judicial District of Alaska. There was ample work for a judge, and before he landed he began by appointing a receiver over a rich mining claim on which a dispute had arisen as to ownership. This course was continued throughout his incumbency. Claim after claim, as rich enough strikes were made to warrant the procedure, were "jumped." The court appointed a receiver who took possession of the ground, the gold already extracted, the machinery, and all appurtenances. The receiver worked the claim, extracted the gold as fast as possible, rendering no more accounts than he saw fit.

A bitter fight ensued between the authority of the court and the defendants who endeavored to protect their property consisting of the richest claims of the creeks back of Nome. The conflict, carried to the Court of Appeals in California, resulted in the imprisonment of the receiver, Alexander Mackenzie, and the removal and fining of Judge Arthur H. Noyes, of the Court of the Second Judicial District of Alaska.[10]

At intervals of several years, strong storms sweep in from the Bering Sea—not so terrific as the typhoons of the Asiatic coast or the hurricanes of the Gulf of Mexico, but devastating to life and property exposed to it. One of these drove on the shore beginning September 11, 1900. Under a continuous southerly wind the waters rose up on the low beach from the shallow sea and flooded the water front, carrying away the buildings on the sandspit, smashing the ends of the structures bordering on the sea, driving ashore vessels lying at anchor in the roadstead and causing a loss of a million dollars. Stocks of goods intended for the winter were utterly destroyed. Stores of coal were strewn along the beach mixed with quarters of beef from the provision warehouses. The great barge *Skookum,* one of the largest on the Pacific Coast, was wrecked and furnished fuel for the winter to those who were destitute.[11]

The community prospered and grew in the following years. The gold of 1899 was $2,400,000, according to the report of the U. S. Assay Office, and this was followed by more than double the yield the next year. A fleet of steamships was employed in the traffic between Nome and Seattle that numbered eighteen vessels in 1907. At one time seventy vessels lay at anchor offshore at Nome.

The traffic by land to the outlying creeks demanded railways, and to meet this the Council City and Solomon River Railroad was built up the Solomon River; and the Seward Peninsula Railway was constructed out from Nome to Dexter Creek and afterward extended to Lanes Landing in the interior of the peninsula.

The gambling instinct, the desire to get sudden riches by means of great ventures, to lay stakes on the roll of the dice, is strong in all races of man. The mining camps, which yield fortunes on a lucky strike in a prospect hole, are hotbeds of every venture that man can suggest. Nome had her stakes on the claims in the tundra and beach sands, in her gambling saloons and dens; but the cleanest and most delirious sport was the great Dog Derby, over the long stretches of white snows four hundred miles to Candle and back. Every year the racing teams of howling huskies or the "Siberian wolfhounds," so called sometimes, were trained for the course. The first sweepstakes was in 1908. The record in 1910, of 74 hours, 14 minutes, 37 seconds, by the "Iron Man," John Johnson, with Ramsay's Siberians, heads the list for the 408 miles.[12]

The story of gold in the sands of Nome goes far back into the misty distance. Like other romances there are only glimpses at intervals of years before the thrilling moment came. Von Bendeleben, of the Western Union Telegraph Company, found a few grains of gold in 1866. Tom Guarick, an Eskimo, gathered half an ounce in 1897, but the real discovery dawned on the world in 1898 when the three men washed eighteen hundred dollars from Anvil Creek with water heated over their campfires. The story developed rapidly. The finding of the beach sand filled with the yellow metal, where for nearly a hundred years the crews of whaling ships had landed, the mining of nearly three million dollars in dust in 1899, fanned the fever in men's blood. The output rose to nearly five million dollars in 1900; discovery of other beach lines buried deep in the tundra back of the growing village, the coming of impatient thousands, marked the progress and gave suspense to the tale.[13]

Six years passed and, in 1906, more than seven millions of gold were taken out of the sands and gravels; but before this another story was unfolding in the heart of Alaska, a thousand miles to the east.

There have been over one hundred and one millions of gold, more than a million in silver, and over a million dollars of tin brought out of this corner of the land that was looked upon as only a playground for polar bears and whales. There is gold of a known value of about one hundred and sixty million dollars awaiting the worker. Every new country is underestimated. Nature does not always leave her gifts exposed to common view; it takes people and years to search out her treasures.[14]

33

Fairbanks, in Alaska's Golden Heart

IN THE TANANA VALLEY, IN THE VERY CENTER OF THE more than a half-million square miles of Alaska, lies a flourishing town, with shops, hostelries, banks, a flour mill for grinding the grains grown on the farms, a college of learning for the building of character in the youth of the land, and charming homes filled with comfort and surrounded by flowers. "Over thousands of square miles the landscape is tinted with wild flowers, from roses to Arctic poppies. Wild birds of 210 different species make their nests and raise their young in the Territory in the short, beautiful summers," Dr. Wm. H. Dall tells us in his *Alaska and its Resources*.

There are farms and dairies adjacent to Fairbanks; ninety-seven homesteads have been filed by men who have come to make a home in the Northland; and a railway connects it with the harbor on the sea at Seward—a harbor open all the year to the largest ships that float.

When, in 1898, Lieutenant Castner and his two half-starved companions landed at the mouth of the Volkmar River and the Indians of the village saved them with food from scanty stores, the region of the Tanana Valley was a wilderness. In the Chena Slough were eighteen white men with two little steamers, nearly at the present site of Fairbanks—the only men from civilization on the length of the five-hundred-mile stretch of the river.[1] Lieutenant Allen and his party of explorers in 1886, and Arthur Harper, the pioneer, were the only ones who preceded them.

Harper is said to have found gold on the river, but it was too costly to work it in that day. A little steamer went into the Chena Slough in 1901, to trade with the Indians. The next year, about twelve miles from this station, Felix Pedro, a prospector, found gold in a creek that has been named Pedro Creek.[2] The next year about forty thousand dollars in dust was washed out, and taken outside during the winter. The inevitable consequence followed—a gold rush.

The spring of 1904 the stampeders threw themselves onto any kind of craft that would float, and pell-mell the rush to the Tanana Valley mines began. The first boat pulled out from Dawson on the 20th of May, following the ice jams down the river. The stream was full of steamers, scows, small boats, and rafts from then forward. Every craft was stored from bulwarks to smokestack with every sort of merchandise that could be used in a new camp. Boats that had burned to the water's edge and sunk in the upper Thirtymile were raised, a hasty house nailed up above the deck, and were stowed with freight and put out downstream. Scows, loaded with fresh fruits and vegetables that had been sledded over the ice from Labarge, came drifting by, steered with long sweeps by the scow captains. They went six hundred miles down the Yukon from the boundary of Canada then three hundred miles up the Tanana River to land at a clearing in the spruce forest splotched with a few log cabins. It was a revival of the days of flatboating on the Ohio and Mississippi.

From Dawson the floating population vacated and moved down. From Nome the restless ones that could not find claims had an exodus, and up the river came the big company boats with barges pushing ahead loaded with freight. The *Will H. Isom* came shoving five great lighters ahead on the towing bitts. The *Louise* drove along with seven, each seemingly as large as the mother boat. The *Isom* is said to have paid for her cost in freight bills, yet did not have a pound on board, all being on the great, roofed-up, square-nosed craft she shoved along in front or that were lashed alongside her guards.[3]

At Eagle, on the boundary line between Canada and Alaska, every boat from Dawson and the Klondike had to stop to enter the ship and to settle for the dues at the United States Customs Office for the foreign goods brought in their holds. Steamer after steamer slid up to the bank and put out their lines to the snubbing posts. At one time five ships, with their square-nosed barges laden with goods, lay alongside the bank. The captains were impatient. "The season is short," they protested as they walked the bank and swore impatient oaths. The owners of goods were petulant, each one seeking the "Pot of Gold at the Foot of the Rainbow," and ranting that he was losing the opportunity of his life.

FLOWER GARDENS IN ALASKA

ALASKAN WILD FLOWERS

Eagle City on the Yukon

Busy Days on the Yukon, 1904

It was a third stampede, only a little less in volume than the Klondike and Nome were in their time. All three were among the great frontier movements of the United States.

At the confluence of the Yukon and the Tanana, all the deeper draft boats of the Yukon transferred passengers and freight to lighter craft to ply the shallower waters and shifting bars of the Tanana River.

Here, in the days before the coming of the white man, was the ancient trading mart of the Indians of the Yukon with those of the Cook Inlet who brought the Russian goods, Kirghiz tobacco, red and blue beads, the red blankets. Here the barter was for the American sable, the otter, and beaver of the Yukon Valley.

The traders of the Hudson's Bay Company, the Russian *promishleniki*, and later the free traders broke up the Indian barter. Al Mayo placed a trading post about eight miles below, on the Yukon, and called it by the old Indian name of *Nukluklayet*. At the confluence a town sprang into existence and there Fort Gibbon of the U. S. Army was placed. Each of the two big trading companies on the river established a station. The Northern Commercial Company post was called Tanana; that of the North American Transportation and Trading Company had the post office and was named Weare. Here again was bustle and excitement.

At Fairbanks all was confusion. Crates of merchandise, kegs of beer, barrels of whiskey, steam thaw-boilers, lumber for buildings, horses and cattle, household goods, all mingled in grand disorder. The local sawmill buzzed night and day cutting lumber for sluice boxes. Out over the tundra and across the marshes men and animals toiled to move the mining machinery out to the claims that had been staked. Great sheet-iron warehouses of the Northern Commercial Company and of the North American Transportation and Trading Company were springing out of the niggerhead grass and spruce stumps that before had occupied the ground. Saloons stood with open doors. The beer barrels cluttered the sidewalks, while inside the white-aproned barkeep swashed his glasses in the bucket under the bar, gave them a swipe to prepare for the next customer and said, "What'll yeh have?" Two or three blocks back from the water front, in the red-light district the dance-halls held their crowds, and after each dance the girls and their partners swaggered up to the bar, with foot on the rail, leaned over and ordered to suit their thirst, each girl getting her commission on the order.

Court was opened; suits were filed to keep pace with the fights over contested claims; lawyers flourished "like a green bay tree." In front of the post office a line of men forty yards long waited in the rain and mud to get to the window to ask for letters from home. Russians, Swedes, Bohunks, Lithuanians, and Germans paced the streets. Even Wada, the Jap, was there as some can testify, truthfully. It was a motley crowd that packed its blankets to some shelter for the night or paid the price for a bunk in some roadhouse or hastily erected building called a hotel. The spirit of the movement infected everyone till he wanted to grab a pick and shovel, borrow a gold pan, and hunt a gravel bar to try for "colors."[4]

Strikes were made on Fairbanks Creek and Fox Gulch, on Ester Creek and on Dome. Chatham had good pay and at Cleary a small metropolis sprang up with establishments of its own. Prospectors pushed out to the Chatanika and the Goodpaster, to the Bonnifield country and to the Kantishna.

Roads were constructed out to the creeks; a telephone system was installed, with branches to outlying centers; little towns sprang up at Dome and Ester. Chena contested for the honor of being the metropolis for a time, but fate and influence were against her; then a railway began construction there and saved her life for awhile.

The Tanana Valley Railway, built by Falcon Joslin, came up to Ester Junction in 1905, branched down to Fairbanks, then wound up the bottoms and over the ridges to the mouth of Cleary Creek.

A telegraph line was extended to Valdez, and a trail was built over the Thompson Pass, through the Copper River Valley, following on some of the trails cut out by the pioneers of 1898. It finally grew into the Richardson Highway, over which auto stages whisk their passengers from Fairbanks to Chitina on the Copper River and Northwestern Railroad, which came years after as the copper of the Chitina Valley became known.

When winter came down and locked the streams tight, the long strings of yellow-eyed dogs trotted along the streets and out on the spruce-bordered trails, eyeing all who passed

THREE QUARTERS OF A MILLION DOLLARS IN GOLD
Photo by Dobbs, Nome, Alaska.

GOLD IN THE GOLD PANS

TANANA VALLEY RAILWAY, 1905

Roadhouse in Copper River Valley

TRANSPORTATION ON THE YUKON

SHIPPING AT TANANA

with a gaze that made one suspicious of their intention. The drivers brought into the metropolis of the mines caribou meat from the divide toward Circle City, moose hams from the Tolovana Flats, the delicious flesh of the mountain sheep from the McKinley Range. At any restaurant the visitor could order a juicy moose steak. All night the roulette wheels spun, and the faro dealer sat at the case while the lookout occupied the high seat at the side with his eye on the dealer and the man who "bucked the game." At the bar the bills were paid with a poke of dust from which the barkeep weighed the yellow grains on the tall, brass scales while the owner looked away in studied indifference. Gold was current at $16.00 an ounce in trade.

The completion of the Alaska Railroad in 1923 to the interior of Alaska was much what the building of the Union Pacific Railway was to the Pacific Coast; it brought it in close touch, summer and winter, with the States.

From the muck and gravels of the Fairbanks, or Tanana, region, in the deep diggings, sometimes 200 feet below the surface, out of the frozen earth where it lay mixed among the bones of mammoth and mastodon of a forgotten age, of skulls of buffalo and extinct wild oxen, the tireless miner extracted $75,000,000 of gold. Out of the Yukon Basin where, at the time congressmen orated in invectives against Seward's Icebox, not a dollar was known to be, there have been taken $171,938,900 of the lifeblood of commerce to the close of 1935. The best authorities of the nation tell us that there are in the unmined gold reserves of the Yukon Basin about $130,000,000.[5]

The prophesies of most politicians regarding the possibilities of the new, unknown lands have generally been false. The prophets have been controlled by the desire for present influence or votes, and it is likely that they will continue so to be. Britain was little esteemed by the Romans when they built the stone wall across Scotland, but it has made good for centuries since.[6]

34

Copper, Coal, and Railways

WHEN LIEUTENANT ALLEN MADE HIS NOTABLE EXPLORA-
tion through the Copper River Valley, Chief Nikolai pointed
out to him the location of a deposit of copper. In 1898, thirteen years later, a party of five men found the vein and named
it the Nikolai Mine.[1] From it and the Bonanza Mine near it,
in one year, there have been taken twenty million dollars of
the finest of copper ore—copper glance, that works almost
as easily as sandstone yet contains 70 per cent of the red metal.
This is the famous Kennicott Copper which is known in all
the market reports of the United States. The deposit was so
rich that the Copper River and Northwestern Railway was
built at a cost of twenty million dollars to bring out the ore,
and the output paid for it in one year.[2]

The copper of that region had been known for more
than one hundred years before the discovery was made.
Baranof knew of it and collected metal from the Indians to
cast a bell. He sent a man to search for it during the last ten
years of the eighteenth century.[3] The Thlingits used it to
make great copper sheets, hand-wrought, which, carved with
heraldic designs, were carried before the chiefs as a mark of
honor, and were valued at many slaves.[4]

The finding of the mountains of red metal was one of
the parts of the story of the Trail of '98, when the gold
seekers passed through the Copper River Valley in the effort
to reach the Klondike, and some of them tarried and found
copper. Not only were the rich deposits of copper glance and
bornite discovered in those stupendous mountains threaded
with glaciers, but pure copper in masses of tons in weight,
silver in nuggets, and placer gold. There are millions yet to
be brought from veins still unworked, some of which are yet
unthought of. Others are just prospects.

The story only began with the finding of the riches, then
the question was, how to bring it out from its fastness? It
was hidden away behind 195 miles of huge mountains; down

THE COPPER RIVER BRIDGE
PHOTO BY C. L. ANDREWS

THE COPPER RIVER BRIDGE

from their gorges ran rivers of ice, miles in width. The green-stone cliffs plunged into canyons through which roared boiling torrents, the Abercrombie Canyon and the Woods Canyon. Hardly an Indian trail threaded the gloomy depths. They portaged the canyons and canoed the swift reaches between.

The first step was the abandonment of the trail over the Valdez Glacier, where so many died on the Trail of '98, and the building of the sled trail over the Thompson Pass, the forerunner of the Richardson Highway of today. By this track, on the snow road of winter, the first ores were brought over the mountains to the coast. The cost of this freighting was hundreds of dollars a ton—a prohibitive rate which precluded the shipping of most ores.

Some of the shareholders in the find died, and some sold out; Stephen Birch bought an interest. Then came the task to secure the capital for the seemingly almost impossible task of building a railway. Two great glaciers, the Miles and the Childs, came out of the mountains to the east and west, almost joined, and the Copper River ran between. Vast lakes of water formed in these ice masses, and when they broke it was like the falling of the Johnstown Dam; a wall of water swept down the glacial valley carrying destruction before it.

The first attempt was from Valdez. Two companies, the Home Railway Company, of Valdez, and the Copper River Company, fought for the right of way in the Keystone Canyon, and men died under rifle fire. There are strange stories about this. This route was then abandoned; Katalla, on the coast, was taken for a base, and a sea-wall harbor was attempted. Another war for the key positions ensued between the company and its opponent in which pile drivers and steam locomotives played a part as war weapons.

A glimpse only of the feat of building the road can be shown. The men who had successfully brought the White Pass Railway through the gorges to the Yukon River shouldered the task, bridged the streams, skirted the immense glaciers, and blasted a way along the cliffs by planting "coyotes" of as much as seventeen tons of powder each, heaving off whole mountain faces.[5]

Finally the harbor at Cordova was chosen as the terminal, and the steel track was finished in 1911 on which millions of pounds of the copper for the World War were shipped to the fighting forces. The great steel bridge that stands between the two glaciers and spans the Copper River was the crucial point, and is a monument to the skill and perseverance of the railway builders.[6]

The years following the gold strikes were the days of railway promotion in Alaska. The finding of gold in so many different parts of the Territory, in the Koyukuk, the Kuskokwim, the Iditarod, the Innoko, at the Manley Hot Springs, and in the headwaters of the Copper River and of the Susitna, all contributed to the call for transportation. The prospecting disclosed many other minerals, platinum, tin, etc., especially immense deposits of coal at or near Katalla and in the Matanuska Valley. Other industries seemed on the eve of development; farmers began to settle in the valleys of the interior although no surveys had been made. The utilization of the coal occupied the attention of prospectors, promoters, and capitalists alike. Many projects were presented for outlets for the product.

Hopes were high for the future of Alaska. Mankind goes by waves, like the sea; when on the top of the billow he is jubilant; it is to be so forever; when he is in the trough of the wave he feels that nothing will ever be good again. Expectations ran high. Capitalists saw fortunes in fish, in gold, and in coal. Plans were set going to gather the harvest. Great financiers visited the new Territory.[7] Promoters painted roseate pictures of riches flowing into the laps of investors. Schemes for a score of railways were in the air; one from Haines Mission to Nome, another from Cook Inlet to Nome, a third from Valdez to Eagle; these, and many others, afterward fell from sight. Not only surveys, but actual construction began on two different routes—the Copper River and Northwestern, already described, and the Alaska Central Railway.

In the United States during the first decade of the twentieth century, a wave of conservation of resources swept the land. It was a worthy cause, for the nation had been for three hundred years burning, wasting, destroying, as well as using and developing the resources of America. It had devoured the inheritance of the Indian with the wealth he had accumulated through ages. The burden fell on Alaska. The other commonwealths had squandered their patrimony, or had placed it in private hands where it was beyond reach. Immediately the Government proceeded to withdraw the coal and oil lands, to reserve the forests of Alaska, and to place vast areas in bird reserves or fish preserves, in which there were privileges rented or given to certain parties.[8]

General development halted; the country began to slide into the trough of depression. Railway construction ceased. The Copper River and Northwestern Railway stopped construction on its branch to the Bering River coal deposits. The Alaska Central was seventy-nine miles on the way to Matanuska mines and the Fairbanks gold fields; track laying was discontinued, and a little gasoline engine became the only vehicle on the right of way, while the grass grew waist-high between the rails.

A clamor was raised that if the wealth was to be reserved by the United States then the nation should develop the resources by building the railways and highways. Citizens of Cordova shoveled foreign coal into the bay as a protest against the withdrawal of their coal from entry. It was carried to Congress. Secretary Fisher, of the Interior Department, made a visit to Alaska to get firsthand information. A commission was appointed to investigate routes.

A law was passed by Congress authorizing the President to locate, construct, and operate railroads in Alaska; approved March 12, 1914. In pursuance of this the Alaskan Engineering Commission was appointed to investigate and report on available routes. The route of the old Alaska Central road from Resurrection Bay was chosen; the rights and construction work of the company were purchased; the amount of thirty-five million dollars[9] was authorized for construction. The Government Railroad, afterward known as the Alaska Railroad, extending from the new town of Seward on the coast, to Fairbanks in the Tanana Valley, came into existence. The main line between the terminals was 467.6 miles. The Tanana Valley Railway was acquired as part of the system.

The building of the road had hardly begun when the war cloud rose in Europe. The cost of construction was increased, and men began to cross the line to Canada to enlist in the British armies. Conditions grew worse, men became scarce, the prices of commodities rose, the difficulties of construction increased, the authorization for the road was exhausted, and the work was not finished. An additional seventeen million dollars was provided; then the commercial artery to the interior of Alaska was completed, and rail communication to the interior of the Territory was established from the navigable waters of the southern coast, free from ice through all the year. In 1923 President Harding made the first journey to Alaska that was ever made by the ruler of the nation, and he passed over the Alaska Railroad to the gold fields of the Tanana.

The Government, however, neglected to put out effort to secure traffic for its road as a private corporation would. It seemed to take for granted that if it built the railway the people would advertise and furnish the tonnage.

When Jim Hill built the Great Northern Railway he commenced reaching out for tonnage as soon as he laid his first mile of rail. He furnished farmers better seed, and he loaned them blooded bulls to get their produce to carry. He laid machinery at the mines to get the tonnage of the ores. What did the Government do till the road was finished? When did it put out its first literature? Did it give low settlers' rates as Hill did on the Great Northern in 1890? A paper, the *Railroad Record,* was published to record progress, but it told nothing of the facilities to farmers, or miners, or dairymen.

The railway has laid the coal of Nenana at Fairbanks at five dollars a ton by the carload, and has increased the output of the placer mines of the interior to $5,474,000 in 1934, the highest since 1921. Ditches have been built, huge dredgers constructed, and the Fairbanks Exploration Company is said to have expended the sum of eight million dollars on their plant. The output will increase. The hard times of the older centers squeezes the swarms out of the seething hives of the cities and sends them out to the unpeopled lands. Gold is sought as it becomes valuable in proportion to other commodities. So the yellow metal in the northern hills and valleys will again be the lodestone to draw men to Alaska, and they will stay to farm, to cut the forests, to raise stock and keep dairies as do men in Denmark and Sweden and Norway. Necessity is the impelling force.

The Alaskan interior has ceased to be a land of mystery.[10]

TRAIN AND TOURISTS ON GOVERNMENT RAILWAY

Government Train and Depot at Seward, Alaska

35

Forty Years' Development

FORTY YEARS HAVE PASSED SINCE THE HEADLINES OF "A Ton of Gold" across the morning daily at Seattle electrified the nation. Out of Seward's Icebox has rolled, since the last summing up in 1897, no less than $1,887,941,309 of wealth of mineral, fishery, and fur products; etc., shipped to the United States. Much of the results of the deep-sea whaling escaped record and went to fill the coffers of New England and San Francisco shipowners without Alaska's having the credit of origin.

This is not a bad showing for a country once decried and derided. The functions of government have progressed but not in the degree that would be expected. With the cry of gold came the obligation to extend the operations of the governmental agencies that promote development of the riches newly discovered.

Mail service for the miners of the Yukon Basin was one of the first crying needs. A contract for a service along the river was given, but the immense distances, the inexperience of the contractor, the difficulty of procuring the supplies, all combined with the severity of weather to delay the accomplishment of the result. Elie Verreau lost his canoe in an ice jam, barely escaped with his life, and his mail was found in the flats of the Yukon, 180 miles below, when the ice melted in the spring. Abandoned mail was scattered along the trail over the Valdez Glacier the winter of 1898. Eskimos carried mail with reindeer in the far Northwest. Gradually routes were established; from Dawson, Y. T., Canada, to St. Michael, Alaska; from Valdez to Eagle; from Unalakleet over the snow trail to Kotzebue and Barrow.[1]

Finally came the day of the air mail, and the service was extended to Alaska. The birdmen of the skies now have their routes from the railhead of the Government Railway to Nome, and flyers make their way to Kotzebue and to Barrow as occasion demands it, while flying routes have been established down the Yukon and Kuskokwim. The service is as efficient as can be expected, but some of the postal rates in Alaska militate against the development of the country. It costs as much to send a package by parcel post for ten miles between post offices, even where rail or steamboat connections are available, as it costs to send it from San Francisco to New York. All zones are the same in Alaska, and the highest rate applies.[2]

At the beginning of the forty years the discarded Deady Code of Oregon was the law of the land. A criminal code for Alaska was enacted in 1899. A tax on business and trades came with it—the first in more than thirty years of United States dominion. The land had been favored in the absence of taxation, and likewise in an absence of revenue and improvements. Over fifteen million dollars in gold had gone out of the Territory without yielding a penny for the upbuilding of the local conveniences of civilization. Scarcely a light glimmered along the headlands; scarcely ten miles of wagon road existed.

The tax was imposed by the United States and was unequal in its rates. A dock paid 10c a ton on all freight passing over. At a wharfage of $1 a ton this was 10 per cent. A quartz mill paid $3 to a stamp. In 1899 the Treadwell milling machinery comprised 880 stamps and yielded $1,611,856 or $1,831 a stamp, on which the tax was about 15/100 of 1 per cent. Salmon was taxed 4c a case, and 10c a barrel for salted fish. The value of the output was $3,843,734 for 1899 on 1,065,-880 cases and 22,382 barrels, or about 1.17 per cent on the product with no property tax on the plant.[3]

The Alaska Civil Code was passed in 1900 superseding the obsolete Oregon Code. The whole was codified in 1906 under the Charlton Code, issued by the general government.

At this time there was no legislative body. The chief executive officer was the governor, appointed by the President of the United States. There were three judicial divisions with headquarters at Juneau, Nome, and Valdez. Every department of the United States except the State Department exercised jurisdiction and was represented in Alaska. There was a lack of co-ordination and much interlocking of authority.[4] Juneau was made the capital by the Act of June 6, 1900.

The land laws lagged behind the march of progress. It was not possible to file a homestead until 1898, and the privilege was extended only to entries on surveyed lands, of which there were none in Alaska, a system of surveys not yet being provided for. The next year the surveys were provided, but the first base line was not established until 1905. The situation was alleviated in 1903 when surveyed or unsurveyed lands were permitted to be taken. Before this the only titles given were under soldier's scrip, by means of which valuable areas, worth hundreds of thousands of dollars for trap sites, etc., were secured at a trifling cost.[5]

In June, 1900, the mining laws were amended; this same year saw the coal land laws put in operation, and the capital was transferred from the old historic town of Sitka to the newer metropolis at Juneau. The following year the incorporation of towns became possible, and several of the communities availed themselves of the opportunity afforded. Other notable events in the life of the Territory were the convention on the national boundary in 1903, the creating of road districts the succeeding year, and the care and custody of the insane receiving attention, with maintenance of same, provided by sending them to Oregon to an asylum.

On a November day of 1905 Captain Roald Amundsen came in on Norwegian skis to Eagle, Alaska, to report his arrival at the farthest outpost of the telegraph, and that he had succeeded in bringing the first ship through the Northwest Passage.

The most notable advance in a series of years was the election of a delegate from Alaska to the National Congress, in 1906. Over twenty-five years of effort and petition at last resulted in the right to send a delegate who would be recognized on the floor of Congress by the Government, and who had a right to speak for Alaska in the councils of the nation. He was elected to represent more than fifty thousand people but had no vote in the assembly.[6]

Vast reservations were made of forests, bird sanctuaries, game preserves, including other withdrawals of public lands, the Bering Sea Reserve, Pribilof Reserve, Forrester Island Reserve. Tongass Forest Reserve and Chugach Forest Reserve were enlarged. The Alaska Fund was created to provide for maintenance of roads, schools, and care of insane.

A law was made to exempt fisheries from tax, provided salmon fry were hatched and released.[7]

The furs, those rich pelts of the North, so much sought for all over the world and over which so much romance had lingered, became scarce in Alaska: first, the pelagic animals, as the seal and sea otter; later, the land animals, the beaver and otter, and others. Fox farming began. Islands were leased, and choice breeds of the white and blue, silver, and cross foxes were planted. Other fur bearers, as mink and marten, began to be considered for cultivation. A new era in the fur trade was opening.

The greatest step forward was when, after forty-five years of petition, Alaska was granted a legislative assembly, thus placing them in that way equal to the Massachusetts Colony in 1636, but not yet electing its magistrates. This law was passed August 24, 1912, and the next year the first legislature of Alaska convened at Juneau, the capital of the Territory.[8]

The upper house, called the senate, consists of eight members, two from each judicial division, while the lower house, called the representatives, numbers sixteen, four from each judicial division of the Territory. The first legislature met on the first Monday in March, 1913, and to convene each two years thereafter for a session of not longer than sixty days. Special sessions may be called by the governor.

The Geological Survey of the United States sent out parties that explored and surveyed the Territory from north to south, making detailed examination in important places, and published a comprehensive series of bulletins, monographs, and professional papers that are a library in themselves and a monument to the memory of the late chief of the Alaska division, Dr. Alfred H. Brooks.[9]

The Coast and Geodetic Survey began a series of surveys, relieving the mariners from the danger of depending on the old charts of Vancouver and the Russians for southeastern Alaska, and of Cook and Beechey for the Arctic Coast. The drag survey was put in force, locating hidden rocks that at other times required the loss of a ship to find. Lighthouses sprang up along the southern coast and on the headlands of the southern ocean beginning with southeast Five Fingers Island in Stephens Passage, and Sentinel Island Light on Lynn

DOG TEAM IN ALASKA
The last mail before the ice broke.

THE AIRPLANE COMES TO ALASKA

THE PIONEER CHURCH, JUNEAU, 1892

THE NEW FEDERAL BUILDING,
JUNEAU, ALASKA

THE ALASKA JUNEAU GOLD MINE

A BIRCHBARK CANOE OF THE YUKON

A YUKON STEAMER
The cut in the sky line is the Alaska-Canada Boundary.

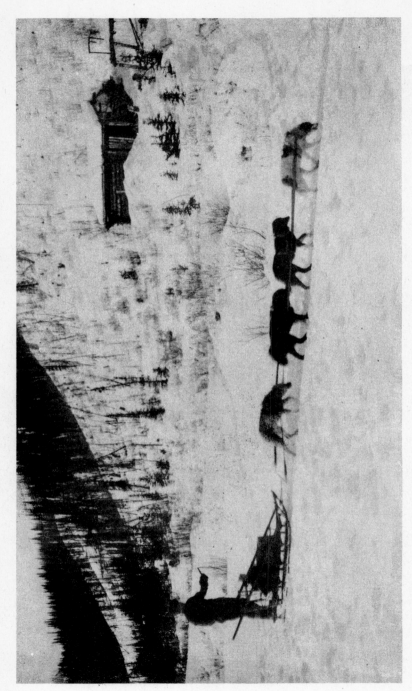

A Dog Team in the Yukon Valley

Canal, in 1902. The lights and fog signals are a marked relief from the old days when ships felt their way up the rock-walled channels by listening for the echoes of the whistle from the cliffs.

The Alaska boundary became an acute question between Great Britain and the United States during the closing years of the nineteenth century. Troubles arose along the Stikine River soon after the transfer of the Territory.

The indefiniteness of the description of the treaty made in 1825 between Great Britain and Russia describing the line along the southeast coast as follows:

"shall ascend to the North along the Channel called *Portland Channel*, as far as the point of the Continent where it strikes the 56th degree of North Latitude; from this last mentioned Point the line of demarcation shall follow the summit of the mountains situated parallel to the coast, as far as the intersection of the 141st Degree of West Longitude (of the same meridian); and, finally, from the said point of intersection, the said Meridian Line of the 141st Degree, in its prolongation as far as the Frozen Ocean."

gave rise to contention. There proved to be no well-defined chain of mountains situated parallel to the coast, within distance of ten marine leagues which the treaty prescribed as the extreme limit of the Russian possessions from the coast. A Canadian surveyor made a survey in 1877.[10] This was followed by a message of the President in 1889.[11] The matter remained in quiet until the gold excitement and the consequent transport of goods and people over the passes called it up. The White Pass, at the head of Lynn Canal, where the town of Skagway is situated, became the crucial point of contention.[12]

The decision was made by the Alaskan Boundary Tribunal, signed at Washington, D. C., January 24, 1903, fixing the boundary between the countries.[13]

The Alaska Road Commission was formed under the Act of Congress approved January 27, 1905, to provide for the construction and maintenance of roads in Alaska, and is composed of three retired officers of the Army of the United States. Under their direction a system of roads and trails has been constructed over the Territory, and the work is carried on each year from funds appropriated by Congress or apportioned from the Alaska Fund.[14]

Trunk lines such as the Richardson Highway, from which branches reach out into tributary districts have been built. From these the trails reach out into the distant, thinly populated, and little-known sections. There are roads among the islands of the southeastern portions, and trails are staked as far north as Point Barrow. Shelter cabins are maintained along the far reaches where the mail carriers and other lone travelers can find protection from the storm and cold. The last and perhaps the greatest of all these projects is the all-land route of the International Highway through Canada to Alaska. When this is complete the auto owner may take his car, and, leaving Seattle, travel to the Yukon and then back to the coast at Valdez or Seward.

The building of the railways, from the White Pass and Yukon route to the completion of the Alaska Railroad, in a few years changed the whole system of transportation in the Yukon Valley. The change was hastened by the World War's drawing the miners from the gold fields.

From a fleet of more than ninety steamers and barges plying between St. Michael and Dawson or Fairbanks, today there are but two steamers from Dawson to Nenana, and two from Nenana down the Yukon. The beautiful flotilla that pushed its way against the strong current of the Yukon lies at St. Michael, drawn up on the ways, or rotting at the water's edge, a million-dollar junk pile.

It was a part of the swift change of modern transportation, from watercraft to rail, auto, and aircraft. Where forty years ago the river system was ice locked from October to May, today the railways, auto highways, and airplanes reach to the farthest limits throughout the year. A dog team trail of yesterday that took a month is now a matter of hours.

The first airplane expedition to Alaska reached Nome in 1920, on August 24.

The World War drew heavily on Alaska, and more men went to the front in proportion to the population than went from any state of the Union. Men volunteered for the Canadian Army before the United States entered the conflict. Men volunteered for our forces, and, following this, the compulsory service brought men from the outlying districts hundreds of miles to reach the settlements to respond to the call.

To the War Funds and the Red Cross the natives respond-ed nobly. From the villages of southeastern Alaska came $12,320.85 for war relief, for Liberty Bonds $9,700.00, and Savings Stamps $283.70; from Point Barrow came hundreds of pounds of eiderdown for comfort pillows for the soldiers; and White Mountain gave a fund of $100.00 that they had saved toward a sawmill for their community.[15]

The Spanish influenza fell perhaps more heavily on Alaska than on any part of the world. Through lack of medical assistance, the conditions under which many lived, in isolated villages, with scant accommodations and no medi-cines, whole communities perished. On the Seward Peninsula 1,500 are estimated to have been lost through this disease. At Unalaska and Bristol Bay 258 orphans were all that were remaining of a population of from 800 to 1,000.[16] It took more than 2,000 people as its toll. The story of the misery of those days will never be known.

The pioneer in the telegraphic industry was the Russian extension of the Western Union Telegraph Company in 1866, already mentioned. The principal communities of the Terri-tory installed systems of telephones before 1900, while the first telegraphic service completed to Alaska was by the Canadian line through the Hazelton route to Whitehorse and back to Skagway. This was over the old line proposed by the Western Union.

May 26, 1900, for the purpose of connecting head-quarters of the Department of Alaska at St. Michael with other points, an appropriation was made for a military tele-graph line to Alaska. In pursuance of this plan, cables, land lines and wireless systems have formed a network over the Territory. Mercantile and private parties have installed wireless plants until Alaska is in touch with all parts of the world.

The Bureau of Education extended its service over the land from north to south; from the humble beginning it has been enlarged until in 1936 the record shows 4,464 pupils in the native schools comprising four different peoples living in diverse regions—the Thlingits and Hydahs of southeastern Alaska; the Aleuts of southwestern Alaska on the Aleutian Islands, the Eskimos of western and northern Alaska; and the Tinneh or Athabaskan Indians of central Alaska. Eleven grades are taught. The total enrollment is 4,464 pupils. The average attendance was 3225.3 for 1936, and the average cost for each pupil was $139.80.[17]

From a total expenditure of $437.77, in 1884-5, the amount allowed for education in the Territory became $690,-000.00 for 1937-8, and an additional appropriation of $37,-000.00 for medical purposes was made. [18]

In 1936 there were 101 stations under the charge of the Bureau, and two industrial schools. The motorship *Boxer* and the *North Star* convey teachers and freight to remote schools, then, returning, bring cargoes of ivory and reindeer meat to Seattle. In 1931 the educational work was transferred to the Bureau of Indian Affairs, and the general office was transferred from Seattle to Juneau, Alaska.[19]

The Reindeer Service of the Bureau of Education, under the Interior Department, shows an increase from the herds in 1897 of 1,466 reindeer clustered around the stations of Port Clarence, Golovin, Eaton and Wales, to half a million deer today in herds extending from the Alaska Peninsula to Point Barrow. Of these reindeer the natives own about 70 per cent, which represents a capital of about $1,000,000, the larger part of the income of which is consumed in the maintenance of from 5,000 to 10,000 Eskimos who are largely dependent on these animals for their food and clothing. From the sinews their thread is made. From the fawnskins warm, durable parkas, or storm shirts—the finest Arctic clothing ever worn in the winter blasts—are sewn by the skillful needlewomen of the North; and from the skins of the legs, boots that protect the feet are fashioned. The reindeer is to the Eskimo what the buffalo was to the Sioux and the Shoshone. If the native is not delivered to a grasping commercialism under special privilege, he will, under a little encouragement and oversight of a wise nature, be as well fitted to meet the future in his Northern home as are the dwellers of the South. If he is permitted to be robbed of this industry, as the Indian has been of all he possessed in most of the United States, it will mean beggary and starvation to him in the future. In 1929 the reindeer herds were transferred from the Bureau of Education to the management of the governor of Alaska.[20] In 1937 the service was placed under the office of Indian Affairs.

A separate system of schools is maintained for the Territory of Alaska. In 1897 there were none. Today there are 17 schools in incorporated towns, and 66 outside, while there are 12 high schools maintained in the principal places. These have an enrollment of 3,480 pupils and they are taught by 253 teachers who are required to maintain a high grade in order to remain in the service. The graduates of Ketchikan, Juneau, and Fairbanks are recognized and have the same rank as those from the schools of the States.

The financing system is largely provided by the appropriations of the Territorial Legislature. To this is added 25 per cent of the Alaska Fund, composed of the Federal taxes collected in Alaska. This system was inaugurated under the law of March 3, 1917, passed by Congress, amending the Organic Act of Alaska. The Territorial Department of Education presides over these schools, with the Commissioner of Education, chief executive, resident at Juneau.[21]

The Alaska Agricultural College and School of Mines, situated at Fairbanks, Alaska, was dedicated September 13, 1922, and was opened on the 18th of that month. The Territory made the first appropriation of sixty thousand dollars in 1917, which was later followed by others and in 1922-3 a Federal Endowment was added. It has since become the University of Alaska.

A Reindeer and Agricultural Experiment Station is also maintained, in connection with the College. A museum, in co-operation with the Museum of Natural History, has an interesting display of Pleistocene animal remains. A library of over eleven thousand books belongs to the institution. It possesses a fine collection of Eskimo implements and artifacts, and co-operation between the Bureau of Mines and the College gives special opportunities to students in the rich mining region surrounding. An Aeronautical Engineering Building in memory of Col. Ben Eielson will be one of the distinctive features of the institution.

The college newspaper, the *Farthest North Collegian*, issued its first number in February of 1923. Thirteen other newspapers pass the happenings of the world to the readers, two of them daily.[22]

The Historical Library and Museum at Juneau is rich in files of periodicals of the Territory and in articles of native manufacture. Other libraries supply the needs of the communities from Ketchikan to Nome.

The library brought to Kodiak by Rezanof was transferred to Sitka by Baranof at a later date. It is estimated by Khlebnikof as being of about 1,200 volumes, 600 Russian, 300 French, 130 German and the remainder English, Latin, Swedish, and so forth.[23]

It was later enlarged by additions, some valuable historical and other books being added by Mr. Khlebnikof after he left Sitka. This was the only library of the Russians in their colonies.

After the transfer to the United States the library was lost sight of. Mention is made in the Sitka *Times*, May 14, 1869, of a library of several hundred volumes at the fort at Sitka, but it is quite evident that it does not refer to the Russian collection. In the report of the Bureau of Education for 1894, it is mentioned that the books of the public library were lost, strayed, or stolen, but which library is referred to is not clearly designated.

That H. M. Hutchinson took the books to San Francisco as being purchased with the other property of the Russian American Company is the most plausible solution of the matter. This is borne out by the recent discovery of a portion of the books, clearly identified by a memo in one of the volumes, "To the Kodiak Library, from the Court Chamberlain Rezanof."[24]

In some of the books is the stamp of the Mercantile Library, of San Francisco, a long defunct institution. This indicates that it was presented to that organization, and passed into private hands on its dissolution.

The Western Union Telegraph Company's Russian Extension Party brought a small collection of books to Libbysville, R. A., in 1866, this being the first library placed in what is now Alaska by people from the United States.[25]

Collector of Customs William Gouverneur Morris attempted to establish a library at Sitka in 1882, but his death probably prevented his accomplishing this object. In the town of Circle City, in 1895, George Baldwin was instrumental in forming a considerable collection of books for the miners. Others followed, until at the present there is a library in almost every village or town in the Territory.

The literary treasures of the Territory have been greatly enriched in recent years. The Territorial University secured a donation of seventeen thousand dollars from the Rockefeller Foundation for the purpose of translating the Russian material on Alaskan history into English for the library of the institution.

The Territorial Library of Alaska acquired the library of the late Judge James Wickersham, which is the greatest known collection of material on Alaska. The Legislature of Alaska appropriated twenty thousand dollars for the purchase, for cataloging, and for other expenses in connection with the acquisition.

The productions of the country, not including the consumption of the population, rose from about seven million dollars in 1897, to over sixty-eight million dollars in 1936.

The sixty thousand people of Alaska poured into the lap of trade over thirteen hundred dollars per capita of the best materials of commerce, created wealth, torn from the mountains, waters, and valleys of Alaska.

Of gold alone, the most desired of metals, it sent eighteen million dollars, three hundred dollars each for every man, woman, and child in the Territory, to be stored in the coffers at Knoxville.

This is the development of Alaska for forty years.

36

The Alaska of Today

ALASKA, THE NEWEST AND LEAST-KNOWN OF THE COMMON-
wealths under our flag, is the largest single area of our holdings.
Twice the size of Texas, it embraces in its confines not only
an immense area of soils in the North Temperate Zone, adaptable to agriculture, but it has many other and varied resources.

ARMY OCCUPATION

Alaska has changed: the only frontier is beyond the Arctic
Ranges; a new people have come in, soldiers and roadmakers;
it is practically under military occupation since Japan made
her attack on the Aleutian Islands.

The army has retained Fort Wm. H. Seward, acquired in
1898. It has added to this an air base at Anchorage, called
Fort Richardson, Ladd Field at Fairbanks, Fort Raymond at
Seward, Fort Ray at Sitka, Fort Greely at Kodiak, and
others. Airfields are scattered all over the Territory. It is
stated that twenty-two million dollars have been expended
on air bases in the past two years. Thousands of young men
are getting their first knowledge of Alaska, and after the war
is over many of them will return to the Territory to build up
the country and become enterprising citizens. This is the
compensation hoped for from the intrusion Alaska has
suffered from Japan.

WAR WITH JAPAN

For thirty years and more the Japanese have been spying
on our coast, sounding our harbors, running over the hills
with plane tables, making surveys, photographs, and maps.
An attaché of the Japanese Legation in Washington, D. C.,
a commander in the Japanese Navy, traveled along the
southern coast of the Territory in 1911. At every port he was
out under the pilot house scanning the harbor, noting, with
his field glass, the buoys and landmarks. He scrutinized the
native villages and photographed the inhabitants.

Brailing a Salmon Trap in Alaska

PALMER, THE COLONY CENTER OF MATANUSKA COLONY, 1936

Mt. Lituya, 11,832 Feet, and Mt. Crillon. 15,900 Feet

Eskimo School Children at White Mountain

Japanese government boats entered the western harbors of Attu and Atka, and the agents spent days noting the harbor, studying it in every way, and questioning the government schoolteachers. Nothing escaped their notice. In their boats they haunted the Pribilof Islands and scoured the coast of St. Lawrence Island.

General William Mitchell called the attention of the United States government to the strategic importance of the Aleutian Islands. General Homer Lea, in his book issued after the Boxer Rebellion, sounded a warning years ago of the intentions of Japan. The "Tanaka Memorial" was a declaration of the Japanese government, just as Hitler's *Mein Kampf* was a declaration of German intentions. Both were unheeded until actual blows were struck, and we were unprepared. Attu and Kiska were taken and occupied. After about a year we recaptured Attu, and lately Kiska has been recovered. We awoke to the necessity of having other lines of communication between Alaska and the States, when we saw Japanese submarines off the coast of California, and shells were sent ashore at Astoria, Oregon, and along the California coast.

ROADS AND HIGHWAYS

Road making had progressed, slowly but steadily, for several years. But the necessity of a land route through Canada, as a protection from foreign attack, was difficult to bring to the favorable attention of the United States government. A petition was presented for an Internation Highway, to extend Highway 99, which is connected with the Pan-American Highway in Mexico, through Canada to the Alaskan line. Meetings were held, speeches made, Chambers of commerce of cities of the coast were enlisted, the project was taken to Congress. An Act was passed on May 15, 1930, providing for commissioners to be appointed by the United States and Canada, to study the matter of construction of a highway to connect the northwestern part of the United States with British Columbia, Yukon Territory, and Alaska. It provided ten thousand dollars for the purpose.

The history of the movement is vague in the beginning, but in 1929 International Highway associations for promotion of the project were formed in Fairbanks, Alaska, and in

Dawson, Canada. Their object was to bring the project to notice in Canada and the United States, and to secure necessary legislation. On April 17, 1929, the Legislature of Alaska adopted a memorial to Congress, endorsing the project. It appropriated funds to provide for advertising the work. The Department of the Interior took great interest, especially Assistant Secretary Ernest Walker Sawyer. The Alaska Road Commission conducted a survey in 1931, to determine the best route from the Yukon frontier of Canada to Fairbanks. Report was made on this survey by Mr. Donald MacDonald, leading engineer.

The premier of British Columbia, the Honorable Simon Fraser Tolmie, conducted an international automobile caravan from Vancouver, B. C., to Hazelton, B. C., to explore the road and advocate the system. "The Pacific Yukon Highway," was the name selected by this group for the project.

Ed Borders, a young Alaska University student, made a snowshoe journey over the route in winter to demonstrate its practicability.

Airplane and ground reconnaissance was made in 1930 by the British Columbia government, in the northern part of the province, for locating the most favorable route. A meeting of the Canadian Committee with the American Commissioners was held in Victoria, B. C., October 9, 1931, for joint consideration of the matter.

In 1933 the report of the commission was made, and was printed by the government in Washington, D.C.—*Department of State, Conference Series,* No. 14. It advised the route from Hazelton to Whitehorse, Yukon Territory—635 miles.

At this point it would connect with the river transportation 2,160 miles by the Yukon to St. Michael on Bering Sea. Between Whitehorse and Fairbanks, Alaska, three routes were considered. One was by way of Dawson; the second from Fairbanks, following the Tanana River to the source, thence to Whitehorse; the other to start from the Richardson Highway at Gulkana, extend east to Kluanne Lake, B. C., thence to Whitehorse. This would be 390 miles in Alaska, and 300 miles in Yukon Territory, Canada.

Action on the matter was dilatory, although urged by Alaska and British Columbia and Pacific states' interests.

With the attack of the Japanese on Attu and Kiska, and the raid on Dutch Harbor, June 3, 1942, the United States was suddenly awakened to the importance of Alaska, and the need of adequate protection of and transportation to that outlying dependency of the nation. The fate of Manila and the Philippines was an appalling warning. The exigencies of war demanded immediate action. For some reason not known exactly, another route, a line from Edmonton in the Mackenzie River Valley, was selected without notice, and work was begun at once by army engineers of the United States. A large part of the construction is understood to have been done under contracts of cost plus 10 per cent or more. The work was prosecuted under pressure, regardless of cost, beginning in March, 1942, and was reported finished in December of that year. The surfacing is yet to be done and the permanent bridgework is just beginning. The road runs through difficult terrain, and with frequent muskegs which are especially troublesome. During this season it is impassable.

The work was completed in record time and was a great achievement. But to the people of the Pacific Coast it is a disappointment. People who have for many years done business in Alaska have to go fifteen hundred miles east to take the new route. This is irksome, to escape a thousand mile voyage by sea. But it avoids the submarine dangers.

The tourist trade of Alaska has been entirely destroyed by the war. Military regulations on transportation are delaying and difficult even where business transactions are involved, and a strict censorship of letter mail is maintained between Alaska and other United States' territory.

Delegate Anthony J. Dimond, representing Alaska in Congress, is endeavoring to have a highway constructed from Prince George, B. C., to connect with the Alaska military highway. He has the support of the Pacific coast states.

The cost of the International Highway is not officially known, but unofficial estimates are around one hundred million dollars. The United States is furnishing the funds, but when the war is over the highway is to belong to Canada, and will constitute a feeder to the Canadian Pacific Railway.

RAILWAYS

Only one addition has been made to the railway system of Alaska in recent years: the building of a branch line from the Alaska Railway, at the head of Turnagain Arm to Portage Bay on Prince William Sound, as authorized by Congress in 1941. The work was completed on November 19, 1942. The town of Whittier, on Portage Bay of Prince William Sound, is the eastern terminus.[1]

With the exhaustion of the Kennicott Mine, the Copper River and Northwestern Railway that served the Copper River region ceased operation and closed down in 1938.

ALASKAN OIL RESERVE EXTENDED

The Alaskan oil reserve, previously set aside in the Point Barrow region, was extended during 1943 to include the area from Point Hope at the west to the Canadian boundary at the east. Otherwise the coal and oil situation remains unchanged.

Alaska has the greatest fisheries of our nation.

Its mineral region, in variety and quantity of deposits combined, exceeds that of any state of the Union.

Its stands of merchantable timber are fourth in rank in our country.

Its potential water power approximates that of any of the states.

Its scenery is unsurpassed.

Alaska's salmon pack leads the world. Its halibut and cod banks are broad in extent. The halibut products totaled to 48,730,886 pounds in 1936.

Of the halibut taken in Alaskan waters, but a small part is landed at Alaskan ports and goes into the statistics of the Alaskan fisheries. There are over ten million pounds that find their way to Prince Rupert, B. C.; the larger part goes to Seattle, which holds its position of the greatest market, and only eight or nine million pounds are landed in Alaskan ports.

Schools of herring are marvelous, and as fine in quality as the Yarmouth bloaters. It has 135 species of fish, of which 62 are valuable for food.[2] Of fresh-water fishes there are 27 species, among them trout, lake, Dolly Varden, Clark's, Gardner's, Beardslee's; they kill trout to get rid of them in

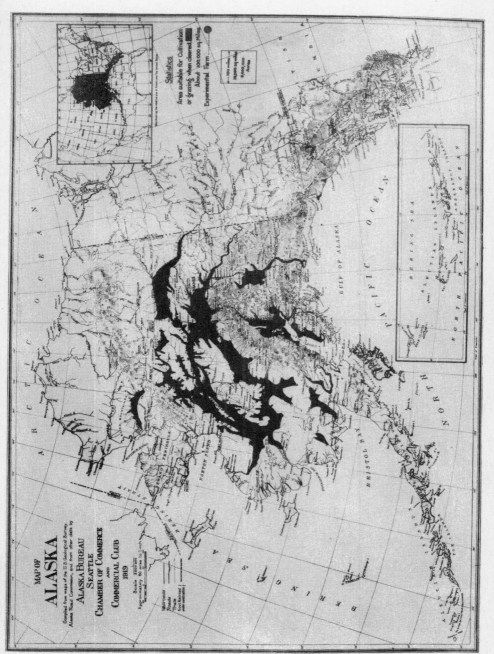

AGRICULTURAL LANDS

Photostat by Asahel Curtis.

Oat Field in Matanuska Valley, 1911

Potato Field at Knik, 1911

POTATO FIELD AT EAGLE, ALASKA

A GARDEN AT EAGLE, ALASKA, JUNE 23, 1908

A GARDEN AT EAGLE, ALASKA, JULY 24, 1908

Alaska. The salmon are of five kinds; several different white-fish. Burbot in the Yukon attain a length of 5 feet and a weight of 60 pounds. The greyling frequents the streams of the interior valleys. In the sea the flounder is nearly every-where present. Halibut of 300 pounds have been taken.

The fisheries of Alaska yield more than those of any state in the Union. They are greater than Norway, France, or Greece. They totaled $52,783,457 in value in 1936.

The salmon pack of the Territory is more than all the rest of the world. In 1936 the canned pack was nearly two thirds of the whole of all the countries bordering on the Pacific, being 8,454,948 cases out of 13,127,643.

Each spring millions on millions of salmon swim into the clear, fresh waters of the streams that pour into the sea, seeking the gravel beds of the crystal lakes and rippling rapids that flow over the bars, where they deposit the eggs for the new life of another year.

Into the North goes a fleet of ships each year to carry provisions and supplies for gathering the harvest. An army of men run the ships, gather the "silver horde," fill the cans, then drop the sails of their fishing craft and return to the States to receive their pay for their summer work. Ship after ship brings the products to the markets.

Fishing boats numbering 2,923 and 447 traps take the fish. Seven hundred and sixty-one power boats tow the catch to the canneries in 416 lighters and scows.

The harvest consists of more than 100,000,000 of salmon that in 1936 filled 8,454,948 cases of 48 one-pound cans.

California began canning salmon in 1864 on the Sacramento River; the first were packed in 1866 on the Columbia River; British Columbia began in 1876; and Puget Sound in the next year. Siberia entered the field in 1910, and Japan in 1913. The whole of the canned product from the inception of the industry to 1931, is 236,962,750 cases of 48 one-pound cans. Of these Alaska furnished 122,779,525 cases, although her first fish were put up as late as 1878, which is more than half of the whole production.

The whale fishery has sadly diminished from the days when hundreds of ships came from New England to take the bone and oil. The present output is nearly all from the shore fisheries. A few are taken by the Eskimos on the Arctic shores. The whales are killed by harpoon guns fired from the decks of ships, and the glory of putting the lance "into the life" of the greatest game of the world is gone forever with the white-winged barks that sailed round the world from New Bedford for the Arctic Ocean in the past century.

The fisheries continued normally until war conditions interfered. In 1941 the product was valued at $63,477,295, an increase over the previous year of $27,636,635. The war has made information difficult to procure, but indications are that there will be a large pack of salmon, most of which will be applied to army needs.

The Japanese have for years been poaching on the fisheries in Bering Sea. Their fleet in 1941 comprised the floating plant for preparing the fish as taken, the *Kosei Maru* of Tokyo, with eight trawlers of about one hundred tons each, the *Tenyu Maru* and the *Seguru Maru,* with several small tenders. They worked off the Aleutian Islands and also around the Pribilof Islands and Nunivak Island. They have taken salmon, crabs, halibut, and cod. Then they came with the crab pack and sold it to our dealers in competition with our product. Some of the American fishermen sent for rifles and threatened to clean the sea of poachers. Then the Japanese shifted their fleet to other banks. They withdrew from the Alaskan coast in July.

FUR SEAL FISHERIES

The fur seal fisheries of the Pribilof Islands yielded 95,013 skins in 1911, the largest take since 1889. The by-products' plant produced 35,000 gallons of first class oil and 16,910 gallons of second class. Fertilizer to the amount of 747,546 pounds was manufactured. The count of the seals in 1940 was 2,338,312. The sales of fur sealskins brought $1,382,987.50.

The seal herds have nearly reached the number estimated on the islands in 1870, judging by the take of seals. At that time it was considered that 100,000 skins a year could be taken, and it was so provided in the lease of that year to the Alaska Commercial Company. The take of 1940 almost reached that amount. In 1942 all the seal killers and their families were evacuated from the islands as a war measure, and no killing was done. It is understood that the Aleuts

THE ALASKA OF TODAY

were returned this year. The loss of the oil was unfortunate, considering the demand for grease during the year.

Around Kodiak Island from 1835 to 1845 was the greatest right-whaling ground of the world. This right whale produced both bone and oil, and consequently was most sought of all the species. The grounds were so devastated that today, at the shore whaling stations, out of a take of about four hundred whales a year, there is seldom more than one right whale.

WHALING

Whaling statistics have not been published since 1939. The take in that year was by the Akutan Station of the American Pacific Whaling Company, that being the only plant in operation. It took 171 whales, with products valued at $136,941. In 1929 the catch of whale was 385 animals. Among them was only one right whale. In 1939 there was no right whale taken. That indicates that the right whale grounds around Kodiak Island, which from 1835 to 1840 were the greatest in the world, are almost completely exhausted. The industry in Alaska seems to be no longer profitable.

The United States must protect its interests in the fishing on the offshore banks, or fish products will go to foreign fishermen. Four- to five-thousand-ton ships are lying at anchor with full equipment of cannery machinery just off our coast, while a fleet of fishing craft with trawls and nets are taking the fish, and the indications are that the intention is to pack the salmon before they return to their usual spawning waters in the annual run.[3]

When Vitus Bering made his voyages the Arctic and North Pacific Oceans and Bering Sea were filled with a sea life in whale, sea otter, fur seal, and walrus.

Commercialized civilization has pursued all these forms of sea life almost to the verge of extermination in the past and almost to the destruction of the industries. It still continues. There is urgent need of conservation to prevent this vast area's becoming a barren waste of waters. It will probably require international action to secure this. A foundation was laid in the convention of 1910 on the fur seal and sea otter. Whether this course will be followed or the devastation will continue should be determined at an early date.

Alaska employed 29,283 persons in her fisheries in 1929, nearly half as many as her census credits on her population, but most of them come from the States each spring and return in the fall to spend their earnings in the Western cities. Some 20,000 men go North in each year and are paid on their return to the States, leaving nothing in the country where they spend their summer fishing.[4]

MINERAL PRODUCTION

The minerals of Alaska comprise almost all that are valuable that are known to the commercial world. In gold production she is exceeded by but two states—California and South Dakota—in annual output. In 1897 the first shipment of the washings of the Klondike was heralded by the headlines in the morning paper as "A TON OF GOLD," and the world went wild. Now $18,000,000 a year come down, and no one is in the least excited, although it is of a weight of several tons. In 1936 Alaska produced $18,433,000. Had this been predicted in 1867 it would have been hailed with riotous unbelief.[5]

The mountains are filled with copper, from Kasaan to Copper River and beyond—bornite, chalcopyrite, copper glance, or chalcocite, as well as free copper in the ore or in placer deposits. The mining of this metal is but in its infancy. Some of the deposits are wonderfully rich. At present there are about one hundred localities where the lodes promise to be commercially valuable. Over two hundred millions have been taken out since the first ore was mined by old Baranovich on Karta Bay.

Of silver over $12,000,000 has been recovered, entirely as a by-product of the gold and copper mining, the ores not having been worked for the silver alone.

Lead, platinum, chromite, molybdenum, tungsten, and antimony are found in many different localities. Marble is found in large quantities among the islands of the southeast coast, as well as in other places. Deposits of iron have not yet attracted the prospector although its existence has been known for a century past. Only 35 per cent of the Territory has been geologically surveyed, yet the estimate of thirty billion tons of coal has been made. Of oil there are five prospective fields; there are seepages on the Arctic Coast east of

Barrow, and there are producing wells yielding high-grade gasoline near Katalla.[6]

Mining has suffered from the effects of war, gold mining having been diminished by the turning of miners from that metal to the development of metals needed for war purposes, such as tin, copper, chrome, nickel, molybdenum, and others.

AGRICULTURE

The agricultural possibilities of Alaska are as great as those of Norway, Sweden, and Finland combined, while the area is greater. Wheat has been ripened each year for many years; barley, rye, and oats produce well. Hay may be cut from native grasses. Berries of fifteen kinds, not including several varieties of the same berry—as of six kinds of huckleberries, five kinds of currants, and so forth—grow in vast quantities, wild, while cultivated berries produce abundantly.

More than three fourths of the area of Alaska lies within the North Temperate Zone, and may be utilized for the grazing of dairy herds or for sheep or hogs.[7] Of farming lands the reports of the Government show that in the Yukon and Tanana Valleys there are 4,500,000 acres, in the Cook Inlet-Susitna Valley region 1,296,000.

More than one hundred years ago the Indians of the southeast coast grew potatoes and sometimes sold as much as one hundred barrels at a time to the Yankee trading ships or to the Russians at Sitka. Jack McQuesten raised turnips in the Yukon Valley in 1893. As early as 1847 Murray planted potatoes that were carried from the Mackenzie River across the divide and down the Porcupine River to Fort Yukon.

Clarke at Skagway, Anway at Haines, Knudson at Juneau, began farms about forty years ago.

The Matanuska Colony is an experiment in agriculture. In 1911 there were excellent gardens and small fields of excellent oats at Knik Landing. In 1916 men were taking homesteads over different parts of the valley. Many of these men still live there.

In 1935 two hundred families were colonized at and near Palmer, on the Government Railway. Some of them were of poor character for opening new lands. The plan was not well co-ordinated. Within a month ninety persons left to return to the States. In a year one fourth of the colonists had deserted. They were of different mettle from those who crossed the Great Plains with ox teams in the forties and fifties of the last century.

Some are staying and making good. In July and August of 1936 there were excellent gardens and some good stands of grain.

The Matanuska is a beautiful valley. It has miles of birch, spruce, poplar, and other timber. Sparkling mountain streams course through it. It is dotted with lakes. Grand mountains are to south, east, and north. Beds of anthracite and bituminous coal lie a few miles up the valley.

The soil is an ashy loam, underlain with glacial deposits, and all is covered with a leaf mold from the forest.

There is no good reason why the colony should not be successful, and it will be a beginning of a population that must arrive before Alaska comes to its own.

Agriculture has progressed slowly but healthily in Alaska in recent years, new settlers coming and taking homes. The most rapidly increasing farming community is on the east side of the Book Inlet. The settlers there have their farms upon which to live, and in the season they work in the salmon fisheries on that inlet. This is the kind of a community to be encouraged.

The Matanuska Colony begun in 1935, is prospering, notwithstanding the fact that 104 of the 200 families returned to the States at the expense of Uncle Sam, who expended the sum of $3,641,082 on the project. Their places have been partly filled by men who came to Alaska "on their own." The products of the colony are reported to be worth over a million dollars this year. Many of the colonists who returned to the States went to get on relief there. The wrong kind of material had been selected in too many cases. They were no more fitted to encounter the hardships of a new country than they were those of the older settlement. There would have been thousands who would have gone "on their own" had they been given transportation for themselves and families, with implements and livestock which at present rates cost a small fortune to the settler, as the government found by its colonial experiment. In too many cases the colonists were not workers, and such are not fitted for new settlements and conditions.

When they went to the valley, there were there men who had been in the valley for twenty years, with no aid from the government. They came in 1916, and were as many in number as the new colonists.

The policy of withdrawing the lands along the new highway is a mistake patterned after some former acts of the kind.

THE CLIMATE

The climate of Alaska varies from the mild, damp seacoast where the cold seldom drops below zero, and where the rain and snowfall are heavy, to the cold of the Arctic. Passing from the southern coastal region through the mountain chains to the interior, the air is drier, colder in winter, with bright, clear summer days. North of the Endicott Mountain Chain lies the true Arctic. About three fourths of the Territory lies in the North Temperate Zone.

The temperature, precipitation, and so forth, of different localities is shown in the following table:

	Ketch-ikan	Ju-neau	Cor-dova	Mata-nuska	Fair-banks	Bar-row	New York
Highest Temperature Recorded	96	89	87	82	99	75	102
Lowest Temperature Recorded	-8	-15	-7	-34	-65	-55	-13
Mean Annual Precipitation—rain	157	80	132	14	12	5	43
Mean Annual Precipitation—snow	40	114	150	39	47	55	35

Data furnished by Weather Bureau, Seattle, Washington.

FURS

Alaska is the home of some of the finest of the fur bearers, and from its forests and waters have been gathered over $138,000,000 in value of these delightful luxuries of civilized and savage peoples. The richest and most valuable of these, the sea otter, has been so nearly exterminated that for twenty years it has been forbidden to kill them. It will be many more years before the waters will be restocked. Other of the peltry producers, as the beaver, are dangerously near the state of depletion. Under careful selection and management the seals of the Fur Seal Islands are increasing and again

number more than a million animals. The farming of furs
is becoming an important industry, but the fur trade suffered
perhaps more keenly than any other in Alaska because of
the depression of financial conditions. The present production of fur may be kept at the present rate in the future by
careful and reasonable oversight. The total production of
fur in Alaska since 1867 has been over $138,000,000.[8]

REINDEER

In the western, northern, and central portions of Alaska
there grows a white moss that constitutes the winter food of
the reindeer. These animals had increased under the management of the Bureau of Education of the Interior Department
until in 1930 there were five hundred thousand animals.

Aggressions against the native industry by non-native interests, beginning in 1914, increased until by 1928 or 1929 one
corporation had in its herds about twenty thousand reindeer
of native ownership, which the corporation was using almost
as its own. It was increasing its holdings by all the invidious
methods of the Western cattle days. It was making an attack
by driving wedges like military spearheads into the native
herds, with the view of consolidating the pincers and mopping
up. Protests were made against this procedure in 1929. It
was placed in the hands of the Secretary of the Interior and
was under consideration until Congress decided to purchase
the non-native interests in 1940.

The management of the reindeer was placed in the hands
of the Governor of Alaska in 1930. He had had no experience
with the industry. The idea of open herding had been urged
on the natives and was practiced by the non-native white
owners. This was opening an opportunity for the wolf packs
to prey on the unguarded herds which were handled but once
or twice a year to count or to butcher for market. White
men without scrupples preyed on the herds. Mavericking
became a regular trade. In one herd a corporation in one year
profited by 713 mavericks. But under these methods even
they were threatened by imminent bankruptcy, for the industry is one only for an owner who can follow the herd and
endure the rigor of the climate, like an Eskimo or a Lap. The
herds soon became wild, like the caribou, the wild reindeer.

During the controversy over the matter, insult was added

Comparative Map of Alaska and Scandinavia

to injury to the Eskimo owners, by a law removing the CON-
TROL of the reindeer from the natives, although they had
spent a lifetime of forty years in building up and caring for
the industry. The natives became discouraged. Their herds
were mixed; they lost interest in their property, for they got
no protection when they complained. As a result the industry
went to pieces rapidly.

In 1940 the government made a roundup at a cost of
about seventy-five thousand dollars, and reported that there
were 252,550 reindeer. The government bought the non-
native held reindeer, numbered at 82,442, for the sum of
$328,326. Range appliances were purchased for $112,925.72.

The industry had been established and carried on by a
superintendent under the Bureau of Education, with the
assistance of the schoolteachers at places where herds of reindeer were kept. In 1914, when the white owners intruded,
the appropriation was only $5,000 annually.

The policy adopted in Washington was to eliminate the
men who had built up the industry. This is shown by the
testimony before the Committee on Appropriations of the
Interior Department, proceedings for the fiscal year 1935,
page 970, as follows:

"Mr. Burlew: 'They have had the assistance of schoolteachers but we want to get away from that. The schoolteachers do not have the necessary experience in range management.'

"Mr. Murphy: 'Are they not going to lose the supervision
of the schoolteachers?'

"Mr. Burlew: 'We hope so.' "

A law was passed providing for a change in the law that
had been in force for many years and had facilitated the education of the natives in the care and management of the
reindeer. The elimination of the words, "of Alaskan natives,"
and an amendment providing that "no part of this appropriation shall be available for the payment of employees who are
not experienced in animal industry," effectively cut off the
Eskimo from the reindeer industry.

The superintendent and the schoolteachers used as local
superintendents were the only ones outside of the intruding
white owners who had any experience with reindeer management. The universities do not teach reindeer management.

Neither do agricultural colleges. The intention clearly appears to have been to get a new set of men who had no interest in the native, and to eliminate those who had built up the native industry.

This shot the industry to pieces, the number of reindeer dropped from 500,000 in 1930, to 252,550 in 1940. It fell further by 1942 to a count of 119,336, and an estimate of a total counted and uncounted of 169,723.

The appropriation has been over $90,000 each year in the past two years, instead of the $5,000 of 1914 to 1918. It is hoped that the management may soon be such that the native industry will be restored to its former healthy condition.

However, the capacity of the Alaskan ranges for reindeer has been greatly overestimated. Some have believed it to be five million.

The Old World has kept reindeer since before history began. It has twice the amount of reindeer grazing land that America has, including Canada and Alaska. The Old World has about 2,500,000. This would indicate a capacity of about 1,250,000 for America, and perhaps 500,000 to 700,000 for Alaska.[9]

FORESTS

The forests of Alaska are the fourth in rank in the stand of merchantable timber standing in the states today,[10] with 84,760,000,000 board feet measure.[11]

There are two great National Forests in the Territory, the Tongass Forest and the Chugach Forest. The first contains approximately 16,547,000 acres, the second, 4,800,000 acres.[12] The estimate of the Forestry Bureau is that a billion feet may be cut annually from this without decreasing the supply. This is all standing ready for the cutter's ax.

The forests are of hemlock, spruce, red and yellow cedar, birch, and smaller trees. Hemlock and spruce predominate, and a large part of the growth is adaptable to the manufacture of paper pulp. An aerial survey of the coast region has been made and applications for two units, for construction of paper mills, covering five billion board feet have been filed with the Forest Service.

The forests of the interior, while of wide extent, are not

so valuable, and consist of spruce, larch, birch, cottonwood, and so forth. But little timber has been cut in Alaska. For many years the export was forbidden. The total cut of saw timber for 1929 was 47,500,000 feet, and the value of the export was $178,114.[13] Nearly all of Alaska's wealth in her forests is yet untouched. The virgin growth of spruce and hemlock that clothes the mountainsides is as yet hardly scarred by saw or ax, and fire has not yet consumed any considerable amount. In this region alone of our vast domain can the primeval forest be seen so easily and so completely. Beautiful mountain lakes, forested to the water's edge, are nestled between beetling mountains whose summits hold glittering masses of blue ice between their peaks, the remainder of the ice rivers that wound down the gorges in the remote past.

Alaska has 59,278 people enumerated in its census. Of these there is the white population; the Eskimos, who live from Kodiak north to Barrow and east to the Canadian boundary; the Aleuts, who inhabit the long chain of the Aleutian Islands; the Tinneh, or Athabaskan, Indians of the Interior; and the Thlingit, Hydah, and Tsimpsien Indian peoples of the southeastern coast.[14]

New countries increase in population slowly. Alaska had 33,426 in 1880, of whom 430 were white, 17,617 were mixed white and native, and the others native. In 1930 there were 59,278; in 1939, 72,524. In the last ten years Alaska has gained nearly as many people as there were in Oregon according to the census of 1850; Oregon then had 13,294.

The state of New York was first settled by the Dutch in 1624, and in 1790 had but 340,120 inhabitants. Oregon was admitted as a state in 1859. In 1860 her census shows but 52,465. Delaware had but 59,096 people when admitted as a state. Rhode Island had 68,825; Tennessee had 35,691, and Nevada had 42,491, when they were admitted to statehood. All these had smaller populations than Alaska has today. Why, then, has Alaska no voice in the election of her governor, of the President, and no vote in Congress? It is like "a bound boy at a shuckin'."

Alaska should have a place in the sisterhood of states.

The area of the Territory is 590,000 square miles, which gives about 10 square miles to an inhabitant. It is the land of the broad open spaces. The total exports of the land in

1936 were $78,561,667,[15] and included a wide range of commodities valuable to the United States. This was over $1,300 for every man, woman, and child of Alaska; an unparalleled record. The gold production of 1936 was $18,433,000, or over $300 per capita.[16]

The total exports of the Territory since 1867 have been over $2,000,000,000 in value. No country of so few inhabitants can show such an export of products.

The climate is as varied as the people. The southeast coast is mild and rainy; the heavy precipitation of moisture gives a luxuriant growth of forest and vegetable. The Aleutian Islands are moist and foggy, owing to the cold waters of the Bering Sea condensing the moisture that is borne by the warm Japan Current that washes the shores at the south. The slopes of the mountains are wonderful grasslands, estimated by the Government to be ten thousand square miles in extent.[17] The interior valleys are cold in winter and warm in summer, much like Montana and Dakota, but not subject to the terrible blizzards of that region. The lands lying on the Arctic slope north of the Endicott Range are the only truly frigid portions of the land.

Alaska is the last storehouse of undeveloped and largely unexploited resources of our nation. There is room for homes for millions of people.

In 1940 Alaska sent to the United States raw materials valued at $61,560,540, for use in our factories and mills. Her total shipments since 1867 have been $2,041,641,790.

From our mills and factories she has purchased $44,189,-431 worth of manufactured products.

In 1938 Alaska shipped raw materials to the value of $77,658,397. With a population of 72,524 people—men, women, and children—this is over $1,000 a year for each and every one. It would appear to be greater than any other country's exports. In fact, it establishes a record.

37

The Alaska of the Future

THE VALUE OF A NEW COUNTRY IS ALWAYS UNDERESTIMATED. The difficulties of an unknown region are feared and dreaded. The man who has never laid the foundations of a building where no other existed before cannot understand the work of years that it requires to improve a land, to build the material things that make it inhabitable and desirable. The child born in a home built and furnished never knows the toil that raised the pillars of the house. The man who looks over the uncultivated valleys and the forested mountains does not envision the future of the land when the work of years will have changed its face.

The man who sees the cities that have been built, the paved streets and highways, the lands that have been drained and cultivated, the plowed fields, looks over them and says, "If I had been here when the country was new, I'd have been rich."

The productions of Alaska give the lie to the predictions of its lack of value made sixty years ago. But there are pessimists who cannot yet see its future, even from the standpoint of seeing what has been accomplished. When the White Pass Railway was built there were many who said that it was impossible. Today we know that roads of all kinds may be constructed in Alaska, just as well as in the United States or in Norway.

Alaska is the great, unexploited, almost untouched storehouse of raw material for the United States. It will take the toil of millions to make it available. The most that has been done to the present time is to despoil the land of the richest and easiest wealth that can be removed. Four hundred and sixty-nine million, one hundred and fourteen thousand dollars in gold has been taken out and exported—little has remained in Alaska. One mine has produced over $65,000,000 and all that marks the spot is a shaft filled with water. The fisheries produce $50,000,000 annually, and the most that

Alaska retains is the license tax on the product and the wages of one third of the laborers. The rest goes south to build noble edifices in the cities, to enrich the coffers of the investors of the East and West. Thus Britain drew from the colonies; in this way Rome fattened on Gaul. It is one of the griefs of the new countries that is inflicted on those who go out to the far places. It will pass, and Alaska will come to its own.

Had the Government protected her people in the new lands it would have been better; Alaska would have prospered more, and the nation would have been enriched. In the beginning of her occupation, just as it was with Russia, the native fur gatherer was the one who produced the wealth. The traders swept along the coasts and with rum and disease depleted the fur gatherer, and both the peltry and the native faded away. Smallpox, venereal diseases, measles, influenza, all unknown before the coming of the white man, swept them off like sheep with the rot, while the sea otter disappeared from the ocean. The whalers combed the seas and boiled the whale and walrus to take the oil to New England.

Then the United States began to build highways and railways. There are those who would remove the railway. They forget that Norway has 1960 miles of Government-owned railway, yet does not pull up the rails.[1] And Norway is not a new land to develop. The Union Pacific with a land grant and a subsidy did not pay in the beginning. The Northern Pacific, with a magnificent gift of lands, broke Jay Cooke and strained the finances of Henry Villard before it built up Oregon and Washington.

SCENERY

Another vast and permanent source of profit of future years is the wonderful scenery. Glaciers greater than those of Norway or Switzerland, mountains overtopping the Alps of Europe, lakes that rival Lucerne, are there in rich profusion. It is a land of deep fjords, beautiful lakes, and noble rivers. It has the highest mountain of the continent, the fourth river in length, and the greatest glaciers of the mainland.

The tourist travel began with the party of General Miles in 1882; Captain Carroll took the *Ancon* into Glacier Bay to view the wonderful Muir Glacier in 1883; by 1892 there were over two thousand pleasure seekers who traveled in Alaska. They come in increasing numbers every year. Switzerland claims two hundred millions of dollars of profit from her tourist trade annually. Alaska has more and greater natural riches to please the eye than all Europe.

ALASKA IS THE GREATER SCANDINAVIA

Alaska is a greater area than that of Norway, Sweden, Finland, and Denmark combined. They have nearly sixteen million people,[2] while Alaska has about sixty thousand. They have been drawing on their natural resources for hundreds of years. Alaska is almost a virgin country. Alaska has almost every resource that those lands have and yet others that they have not.

Those countries are under the same parallels as Alaska; the same isothermic lines cross them.

Finland has 1,871,865 cattle, 1,368,113 sheep, and 395,-968 horses; the capital invested in agriculture is $491,000,000.

Norway takes from her forests $250,000,000; she has 250,000 farms, with 182,401 horses, 1,220,875 cattle, 1,654,-448 sheep, and 282,709 pigs. About 800,000 of her people live in whole or in part on the agriculture.

Sweden has 10,377 miles of railway, of which 4,014 are state-owned. She has 430,000 farms. Half of her population lives from the lands.[3]

Those lands have little or no copper; Alaska is rich in this metal. Those countries produce no gold; Alaska sent out over eighteen millions of dollars in gold last year. They have small stores of coal; Alaska has billions of tons.

Across the channel from the old Treadwell Mine, where the water broke into the galleries in 1917, the Alaska-Juneau Mine and Mill mines and mills 10,000 tons of ore a day, which has already produced more than $46,000,000 in gold. The Yukon Basin poured out $7,115,000 in 1935 of placer. Nome diggings yielded on the Seward Peninsula an estimated $2,-327,000, $1,000,000 more than in 1934. This is an index to what may be done by enterprise and interest in Alaska.

Alaska has room for millions—when they come she will be greater than all those nations. *Alaska needs citizens to develop her resources.* The decline in her population from 1910 to 1920 was not because of any fault in herself. Her people were drained away by the World War. Her men went to the armies. Their families went to the States while their breadwinners were away, for the necessities of life were high in that far land. Wages in the shipyards drew other men away. Mines closed where millions of dollars were invested, because the cost of extracting a dollar in gold became greater than the value of the dollar. The prospector became almost extinct, and his occupation no longer paid for the hardship and expense.

Mining will again prosper. The prospector will again go to the mountains to search for the hidden treasure. Conditions will permit present prospects to be developed into mines. New ore bodies will be discovered. Cripple Creek and Tonopah were not discovered until Virginia City was almost forgotten. The Chicagof Mine was not found until twenty years after Nicholas Haley began his quest for the golden lure at Sitka.

THE ALASKA OF THE FUTURE

The Government has built a road and a railroad to the interior. It has imported a colony of two hundred families. Those who came in this manner were imported and their way paid. Those who made it possible to get this done, the natives who for a hundred years combed the waters and threaded the forests to get the furs that made the profit, and the prospector, the miners, the pioneer farmers, those who showed that it was a land in which men could live and be prosperous, did not have their way paid with Uncle Sam's gold and have a silver spoon put in their mouths. They paid their own passage, and built their own cabins. Places were not made for them; no salaries awaited them on their arrival, nor food at the commissary.

Now, strikers try to starve those who made the country livable, for the miner, the prospector, and the old-timer pay the bill.

The railway of the Government, in place of making low freight rates so that new farms and mines may be developed and rates be made reasonable by more volume of trade, proposes to raise rates.

The men who made the country what it is got no vacations except on their own expense.

This policy will only delay the coming to its own of Alaska.

Next to the lack of people who will transform the raw material of the latent resources of Alaska into the finished product for the market, and the high-grading of the rich spots, leaving none of the values in sight, the obstacle that stands in the way of development is the promotion of worthless projects. In these, millions of dollars have been squandered, perhaps with some benefit to the promoters, but with deadly effect upon all else. The Bear's Nest at Juneau, the Pande Basin farce at Sitka, the Reynolds-Alaska fiasco at Valdez, are examples in point, and others might be mentioned in the past and in the present. These have damaged the country under the pretext of development and have discouraged honest progress.

The fisheries are not yet at their height. There are miles of banks along the Aleutian Islands and in Bering Sea that have not been touched. The fished-out halibut banks near shore can be rehabilitated. Conserve the known assets. Develop the latent resources. Care for the native people. They are citizens who will live in the land and produce wealth. Give them an education by which they may live. They are worth it. They make good citizens. Do not send them judges who wink at the debauchery of the native by truculent traders and licentious soldiery and who say, "I do not like laws that make my friends criminals," instead of enforcing the laws as they stand on the statute books.

Rome did not destroy her conquered peoples. She was lenient toward their customs and their religions. The Hudson's Bay Company and the Russian American Company had a kind of a consideration toward the wild tribes, so they did not wither away before the breath of the white men as our tribes have from the Atlantic to the Pacific. The United States has been slow to learn how to treat her native subjects, yet she was glad to have the same Indians who were only counted as good when they were dead, to fight in the battle line in Europe in the World War.

Had one hundred thousand Russians lived in the Russian possessions in America, the United States could not have become the purchaser of Alaska. And America did not appreciate the value of her purchase. Like Louis of France, when he let the colony of La Salle starve on the shore in Texas, in one of the richest spots of the South, she did not know its worth. The trade of the empire of the Valley of the Mississippi was meagre when Roosevelt, in *The Winning of the West,* tells that the only exports across the mountains were strings of pack horses loaded with furs and deerskins. Washington lost money trying to provide a canal up the Potomac to reach the interior. Chicago was one little cabin of a trading post in 1821, at the mouth of a marshy river. Seattle in 1880 could hardly scrape 3,500 inhabitants, and the forest stared at it from the top of the first hill.

After sixty-four years Alaska has not the territorial rights that were granted to Oregon upon her first request, only six years after it was a joint possession with Great Britain. Oregon was made a Territory in 1848; in 1850 she had only 13,-294 population. In 1859 she was made a state; in 1860 she had 52,465 according to the census. Alaska has had more than that for over 20 years, yet it is not even a full territory. Nevada was made a state October 31, 1864. In 1870 her enumeration shows but 42,491 people.[4] Play fair with Alaska. Make her responsible. Give her equal rights with sister communities. Let her people have a pride in their homeland. Do not make them feel that their chosen country is a stepsister in the national family, or a Cinderella.

Robert W. Service was a man of the North with a vision of a seer when he wrote "The Spell of the Yukon" and said:

> "Dreaming of men who will bless me,
>   Of women esteeming me good,
> Of children born in my borders,
>   Of radiant womanhood,
> Of cities leaping to stature,
>   Of fame like a flag unfurled,
> As I pour the wealth of my riches
>   In the eager lap of the world."

Alaska's growth will be gradual. It will not come in a flood like the Klondike invasion. It is well that it will not. Settlers cannot take a wagon, load family, goods, chattels and household goods, and drive overland as the emigrants crossed to Oregon. A sea voyage intervenes like that which lay between England and America when the Pilgrims came. They will settle along the coast. The development of the pulp timber will be the first step. Already permits have been applied for on two units that will employ a thousand men each. By the time that the nineteen units are occupied by producing mills it will add more than a hundred thousand to the population—nearly twice as many as the past half century shows.

As to the future I shall quote Dr. Alfred H. Brooks, already referred to and a true friend of Alaska, where he says, "We may confidently expect the time will come when Alaska will support a population of 10,000,000 people."[5]

The army of men who stampeded over the passes to the Klondike in 1897 is fast disappearing over the Last Divide. Many of them saw a vision in that northern land. For some it came true in the golden gravels, and they rioted in its riches. Others saw farther—their hope is not yet fulfilled; they must yet look to the *Future of Alaska.*

APPENDIX

Value of Shipments From Alaska to U. S.
1867 to 1940 Inclusive

Minerals
1867-1940 Inclusive

Commodity	
Gold	$562,114,000
Copper	227,422,200
Silver	13,765,000
Platinum group: platinum, iridium, osmium, et al.	3,716,900
Coal	12,904,400
Lead	2,672,600
Tin	1,635,800
Other minerals, antimony, quicksilver, petroleum, limestone, gypsum, nickel, chrome, and sulphur	7,353,100
Total	**$831,584,000**

The statistics on minerals are from the work of the Geological Survey. Platinum has increased rapidly in production in recent years.

Chromite is known to exist on the Kenai Peninsula. The deposits near Seldovia were examined by A. C. Gill of the Geological Survey, U. S., in 1940. J. B. Mertie also made investigations for Survey in 1917. From the examination so far made it is estimated that the total exportable ore in the Kenai Peninsula is 150,000 tons.

Large quantities of iron ore are known to exist on the Kasaan Peninsula, Prince of Wales Island, Alaska.

Fishery Products
1867-1940 Inclusive

Commodity	
Salmon	$1,105,023,832
Halibut	40,945,421
Cod	12,347,836
Herring	27,279,931
Trout	115,990
Shellfish	111,342,479
Whalebone	11,402,479
Whale oil	12,397,900
Whale fertilizer	1,857,165
Fish oil	18,538,669
Fish fertilizer	9,420,004
Miscellaneous fish products	6,817,582
Total	**$1,259,489,219**

Miscellaneous—All Other

Fur	$154,501,959
Wood and lumber	2,624,393
Wool, unm'fd	7,685,197
Reindeer meat	1,319,658
Ivory	182,364
All other products	5,948,092
Total	$176,261,219
GRAND TOTAL	$2,246,080,036

The 1930 census for Alaska showed 59,278 population. This is an annual shipment of more than $1100 per capita, for every person, man, woman, or child, and of the very best raw materials, of which our country has need.

Post Offices Established in Alaska

On page 133 it was stated that Sitka Post Office was established in October, 1885. Recent information from the office of the postmaster general states that Sitka Post Office was established at Sitka, Russian America, July 23, 1867, John H. Kinkead, Postmaster.

Wrangell P. O., established October 6, 1869, first as Fort Wrangell, R. R. Lear, Postmaster.

Unalaska P. O., established as Ounalaska, July 22, 1892, and changed to Unalaska, August 26, 1898.

St. Michael, Alaska, established as St. Michaels, June 12, 1897, changed to St. Michael, January 17, 1898.

Circle, Alaska, established March 19, 1896, Leroy N. McQuesten, Postmaster.

Kodiak, Alaska, January 29, 1869, H. N. Cope, Postmaster.

Fort Tongass, established October 6, 1869, Chas. C. Walden, Postmaster.

Information About Early Alaskan Mail Routes

Mr. Ralph A. Miller, News and Notes, paper, on postal information, of Chilton, Wisconsin, informs me that on July 31, 1867, the postmaster at San Francisco, Cal., was authorized to arrange a special service from San Francisco to Sitka, Alaska, and that one trip was made under this authority by the steamer *John L. Stephens,* prior to December 28, 1867.

October 5, 1869, a contract was entered into by H. M. Hutchison, of Washington, D. C., on mail route No. 17,601, from Port Townsend, Washington Territory, by Fort Tongass, and Fort Wrangell, to Sitka and return, once a month from October 1, 1869, to June 30, 1870.

Ships of U. S. Navy Stationed at Sitka, Alaska, During Occupation of the Territory by the Navy

U. S. S. *Alaska,* Captain George Brown commanding, arrived April 3, 1879 at Sitka. Departed June 16, 1879.

U. S. S. *Jamestown,* Commander Captain L. A. Beardslee, arrived at Sitka, June 14, 1879. Commander Henry Glass relieved Commander Beardslee, September 13, 1880. The *Jamestown* left Sitka August 9, 1881.

The U. S. S. *Wachusetts,* Commander Edward P. Lull commanding, arrived at Sitka July 30, 1881. Commander Henry Glass relieved Commander Lull October 19, 1881. The *Wachusetts* left Sitka, January 11, 1882, but returned on March 4, and Commander Frederick Pearson took command March 13. She finally left Sitka October 3, 1882.

The U. S. S. *Adams,* Commander Edgar C. Merriman, sailed from Mare Island September 11, 1882, for Sitka. Commander Joseph B. Coghlan took command September 14, 1884, when the *Adams* left for California.

The U. S. S. *Pinta,* Lt. Commander Albert G. Caldwell, arrived at Sitka August 17, 1884, to relieve the *Adams.* Lt. Commander Henry E. Nichols took command on September 14, 1884, and on September 15 fired a salute of 17 guns in honor of John H. Kinkead, the first Civil Governor of Alaska. The *Pinta* remained in Alaskan waters until June 30, 1897. Officers commanding during the period were:

Lt. Commander John S. Newell, Nov. 27, 1887
Lt. Comdr. Oscar W. Farenholt, Sept. 16, 1889
Lt. Comdr. Washburn Maynard, Sept. 24, 1891
Lt. Comdr. Wm. T. Burwell, Feb. 25, 1894
Lt. Comdr. Albert L. Cowden, Sept. 26, 1894.
Lt. Comdr. Frederick M. Symonds, Oct. 9, 1896.

NOTES
Part One—1728-1867

1

Russian Voyages of Discovery

[1] In 1639-1642 Ivan Moskovitin came to the Sea of Okhotsk and explored along its shore. Between 1643 and 1646 Vasili Poyarkof went to the Sea of Okhotsk in three small vessels and surveyed southward toward the Amoor. In 1647 Michael Stadukin traveled from the Kolima River to the Anadyr in winter.

Simon Deshnef, a Cossack, appears to have been the first to pass through Bering Strait in 1648. He mentioned the Diomede Islands and "men who have their lips cut and wear a tooth of ivory."

Vladimir Atlassof discovered the Kamchatka Peninsula in 1697-1699. Peter Popof describes what he called *Bolshaya Zemla,* or the Great Land, in 1711.

Ivan Fedorof and Michael Gvozdef in 1732 visited the *Bolshaya Zemla.* See F. A. Golder, *Russian Expansion of the Pacific,* 1914.

The Academy of Sciences of the U. S. S. R. published *The Pacific Russian Scientific Investigations* in Leningrad in 1926, which contains data relating to these early voyages.

[2] Vitus Bering was born at Horsens, Denmark, in 1681, and entered the Russian Navy under the name of Ivanovich Bering in 1703 as a Second Lieutenant. He was promoted to the rank of Captain of the first class in 1724, and in 1725 was given command of this expedition. *Obshii Morskoi Spisok* (General Marine Register) Part 1, p. 40, St. Petersburg, 1885.

[3] All the dates given during the Russian occupation are Old Style. To correspond to New Style, twelve days should be added. The nautical day began in Bering's time at 12 M.

[4] The distance from St. Petersburg to Okhotsk was as follows:

St. Petersburg to Moscow	734 versts
Moscow to Tobolsk	2385 versts
Tobolsk to Irkutsk	2918 versts
Irkutsk to Yakutsk	2433 versts
Yakutsk to Okhotsk	927 versts
Total	9,397 versts

or 6229 miles.

The Russian verst is 3,500 feet.

Coxe, *Account of the Russian Discoveries between Asia and America,* p. 248, London, 1780.

[5] The pole of extreme cold in the northern hemisphere lies near Krasnoyarsk, Siberia, and the lowest known average temperature (monthly) in degrees Fahrenheit, is that of Verkhoyansk, Siberia.

[6] The Diomedes are a group of three islands, Big Diomede, Little Diomede, and Fairway Rock, lying in Bering Strait. The International

Boundary passes between Big and Little Diomede Islands. Big Diomede belongs to Russia and the Little Diomede to the United States. Big Diomede has at times been called Ratmanof, or Noonarbook, while Little Diomede has at times been called Krusenstern, and at other times Ingalook.

[7] P. Tikhmenef, *Historical Sketch of the Russian American Company*, Part 1, p. 1, St. Petersburg, 1861.

[8] Alexei Ilich Chirikof entered the Russian naval service as a midshipman in 1716, and was made an underlieutenant in 1721. In 1725 he was promoted to the rank of Lieutenant and was assigned to Bering's command. In 1747 he was promoted to Captain-Commander. His death was in December, 1748. *Obshii Morskoi Spisok*, Part 1, p. 414.

[9] Martin Petrovich Spanberg was born in Denmark and died in 1761 with the rank of Captain of the first class.

[10] The Hudson's Bay Company lined their boats, called *bateaux*, up the Columbia River at the time they traded in Oregon and Washington.

[11] George Wilhelm Steller, a native of Winsheim, Franconia, was born March 10, 1709. He accompanied Bering and after his return to Kamchatka attempted to cross Siberia but died of a fever at Tumen, in December, 1746. Part of his journal is included in Coxe, *Account of the Russian Discoveries between Asia and America*, 1803 Ed.

[12] George Davidson, *Landfalls of Chirikof and Bering*.

[13] G. F. Muller, *Voyages from Asia to America*, London, 1761; Coxe, *op. cit.*, 1803 Ed., p. 40; Martin Sauer, *An Account of a Geographical and Astronomical Expedition, etc., by Joseph Billings in 1785-94*, London, 1802; F. A. Golder and Leonard Stejneger, *Bering's Voyages*, 2 vols., American Geographical Society, New York, 1922-1925.

[14] They experienced a series of storms, such as appall the most courageous spirit, which induced the pilot, Hasselberg, to declare that during an experience of fifty years he had never witnessed such violent tempests. "Steller's Journal," Coxe, *op. cit.*, 1803 Ed., p. 65.

[15] *Ibid.*, p. 137.

[16] The foxes were so abundant and bold that they were pests. They stole Steller's notebooks and pencils when he was working and were so tame that they were killed with hatchets and daggers. *Ibid.*, pp. 73 *et seq.*; F. A. Golder, and L. Stejneger, *op. cit.*; "Steller's Journal," Coxe, *op. cit.*, 1803 Ed.

[17] The sea cow, *manati*, or rhytina, was an immense animal found on Bering Island and in adjacent waters, which weighed as much as eight thousand pounds, and the flesh resembled beef. It was hunted by the Russians for food for their expeditions in search of furs and soon became extinct, the last one being killed in 1768, according to Sauer, *op. cit.*, p. 181. "Steller's Beasts of the Sea," *Fur Seals and Fur-Seal Islands of the North Pacific Ocean*, Part 3, p. 182, Gov't Ptg. Off., 1899.

2

Russian Fur Trade and Voyages of Fur Hunters

[1] Muller, *Voyages,* p. 59; Coxe, *Early Russian Discoveries,* p. 13, London, 1789.

[2] The trade on the frontier was estimated on the silver ruble. Coxe says the ruble varied from three shillings eight pence, to four shillings two pence, or about an average of four shillings. Coxe, *Account of the Russian Discoveries between Asia and America,* p. 13, London, 1780.

[3] *Ibid.,* p. 211.

[4] Captain-Lieutenant Golovin, "Obzor Russkikh Kolonii iv Amerike," ("Review of the Russian Colonies in America"), *Morskoi Sbornik,* January, 1862.

[5] Pallas's cormorant, the largest of its family, possessing rich plumage, was a bird from twelve to fourteen pounds weight. It was found only on Bering Island, where it was discovered by Steller, and it became extinct in about a hundred years from that time. *Report, National Museum,* p. 641, 1889.

[6] The "*Sheetika* or *shitika;* a large boat sheathed with plank, which is fastened to the timbers with twisted oziers; the interstices are stuffed with moss, instead of with calking; and the seams are covered with lath about two inches wide, to prevent the washing out of the moss; these are enclosed in the oziers. The name implies sewn, as they are made without nails or pegs." Martin Sauer, *Account of a Geographical and Astronomical Expedition, etc.,* p. 16.

[7] Vasili M. Berkh, *Chronological History of the Discovery of the Aleutian Islands (Kronologicheskaya Istoria, etc.)* p. 4, St. Petersburg, 1820.

[8] The group of islands now known as the Near Islands were at first designated as the Aleutian Islands, but this term was later applied to the whole Aleutian Chain from the Peninsula of Alaska westward, including the Near Islands. *See* the Russian chart of 1802 (facsimile in *Fur Seal Arbitration,* vol. 5, 1895).

[9] A party from the ship killed fifteen Aleuts in order to get their women. The Cossack, Shekhurdin, protested to the commander of the ship against the act. The commander answered him with a pretense of regret at the occurrence and sent more powder and lead to the murderers. Coxe, *op. cit.,* 1803 Ed., p. 117.

[10] *Op. cit.,* 1780 Ed., p. 49.

[11] *Ibid.,* p. 67.

[12] *Op. cit.,* 1803 Ed., pp. 146-8.

[13] Tolstykh was very successful in his voyages. In 1759 he secured a cargo containing 5,360 sea otter, which was valued at 317,541 rubles. Berkh, *op. cit.*

[14] The date of the removal of the tribute is given by Shelekof, August

30, 1789, in a letter to Delaref. Tikhmenef, *Historical Sketch of the Russian American Company*, vol. 2, p. 25, Appendix. Berkh, *op. cit.*, p. 80, says it was prohibited in 1779.

3

Rebellion of the Aleuts

[1] Coxe, *Account of the Russian Discoveries between Asia and America,* 1803 Ed., p. 187.

[2] Bancroft, *History of Alaska*, pp. 144-147.

[3] Coxe, *op. cit.*, pp. 162 *et seq.*

[4] The *bidar* of the Russians is the same boat known as the *oomiak* of the Eskimo. It is built of sea-lion or walrus skins stretched over a wooden frame. The frame is made without iron and is lashed together at all points with rawhide thongs. It is the native whaleboat and will carry a dozen people and a ton of meat on a voyage.

[5] Ivan Veniaminof, *Works of Innokentius*, vol. 3, p. 397, and pp. 90-91, Moscow, 1888.

[6] Coxe, *op. cit.*, 1803 Ed.

[7] Veniaminof, *op. cit.*, vol. 3, p. 399. For further information about Solovief, *see* Berkh, *Chronological History of the Discovery of the Aleutian Islands,* p. 76, St. Petersburg, 1820; Davidof, *Dvukratnoe Puteschestvie iv Ameriky Morskikh Ofitzerof Khvostova i Davidova (Two Voyages to America by Marine Officers Khvostof and Davidof)* Part 2, p. 108, St. Petersburg, 1810 and 1812.

4

Later Russian Voyages

[1] Coxe, *Account of the Russian Discoveries between Asia and America,* 1780 Ed., p. 300; William H. Dall, "Review of Bering's First Expedition," *National Geographic Magazine,* May, 1890, pp. 18-19.

[2] Coxe, *op. cit.*, p. 251.

[3] Maurice A. Benyowski, *Memoirs and Travels*, London, 1780.

[4] Berkh, *Chronological History and Review of the Fur Trade*, St. Petersburg, 1820.

[5] Twenty-nine ships hunted on the islands between 1765 and 1786. The most valuable cargo was of the amount of 300,416 rubles. *Ibid.*

[6] *Ibid.*, p. 90.

[7] Tikhmenef, *Historical Sketch of the Russian American Company*, Part 2, p. 1.

[8] "Twenty-four hours after his departure from Unalaska he dis-

covered land." Martin Sauer, *Account of a Geographical and Astronomical Expedition, etc.*, p. 211, London, 1802.

The cargo secured by Pribilof consisted of 2,720 sea-otter tails, 31,150 sealskins, 6,794 white fox, 11¼ poods of walrus tusks, and 15 poods of whalebone. Berkh, *op. cit.* Shelekof says there were 2,000 sea otter, 40,000 sealskins, 6,000 blue fox, and 1,000 poods of walrus ivory. Tikhmenef, *op. cit.*, Part 2, p. 23, Appendix.

[9] The *bidarka* is the same as the *kyak* of the Eskimo—a boat with a frame of wood, covered with skin and decked over, with two or three manholes in which the occupants sit. The waterproof shirt, called a *kamlika*, made of intestines of the whale or walrus, and worn by the paddler, is lashed tightly about the rim of the manhole, or hatch, and thus the boat is made entirely watertight and will withstand almost any sea if properly handled. It is one of the most wonderful of sea boats of small size, and some of the natives are so skilled in its use that they turn the boat upside down and then right it again. The Russians made them with two and three hatches, while the natives usually made only the one-hatched boat.

5

First Russian Colony in America

[1] G. Shelekof, *Puteschestvie* (Voyages), St. Petersburg, 1812.

[2] Tikhmenef, *Historical Sketch of the Russian American Company*, vol. 1, p. 12. A post seems to have been placed on Montague Island, for Shelekof says: "I sent five Russians to build a fortress at Cape St. Elias . . . those who had sailed to Cape St. Elias began their work, and left a party to finish the fort which I had ordered to be constructed at that place." Coxe, *Account of the Russian Discoveries between Asia and America*, 1803 Ed., pp. 288-290.

This was not Cape St. Elias of the present maps and was probably the southern end of Montague Island, for he says: "Suklia, one of the most southerly of the islands of the Bay of Chugach, and the one which in the expedition of Bering was called St. Elias." *Ibid.*, p. 304. The Russians called Montague Island by the name Suklia in many places in their records, and Shelekof was evidently not very clear in his understanding of the St. Elias Island of Bering.

[3] Tikhmenef, *op. cit.*, vol. 2, p. 8, Appendix.

[4] *Ibid.*, pp. 19-21.

[5] Gavrila Andreevich Sarychef, *Account of a Voyage of Discovery, etc.*, vol. 2, London, 1806-7.

[6] Martin Sauer, *Account of a Geographical and Astronomical Expedition*, pp. 172-3, London, 1802.

[7] *Ibid.*, p. 193.

[8] The Russian Hydrographic Office published an *Atlas of Northwestern America, Northeastern Asia, and the Waters Between*, in 1826, under the

direction of Vice-Admiral Gavrila Andreevich Sarychef. It comprised thirty-three double-page sheets, of which twenty-six were charts and seven were views. A description is given by Marcus Baker, *National Geographic Magazine*, March, 1902, p. 86.

[9] Delaref came to the islands in command of a ship in the fur trade. On the arrival of Baranof he returned to St. Petersburg and was made a director of the company.

[10] Shelekof, *op. cit.*, Part 2; Coxe, *op. cit.*, 1803 Ed.

[11] Tikhmenef, *op. cit.*, vol. 1, p. 30.

6

Other Nations on Northwest Coast of America

[1] "Our early explorers failed to make known their discoveries to the world, but their journals and reports were delivered to the government, which at that time, following the example of the Spaniards, kept them all secret and thus deprived the navigators of their fame." Golofnin, *Materialui dlya Istorii Russkikh Zaselenii po beregam Vostochnoi Okeana (Materials for the History of the Russian Settlements on the Shores of the Eastern Ocean)* Part 4, pp. 107-8, St. Petersburg, 1861.

[2] Juan Perez, *Diario*, Santiago, 1774, MS., Bancroft Library.

[3] The voyage of Bodega y Quadra is described in Daines Barrington, *Miscellanies*, pp. 469-524, London, 1781. Bancroft, *History of Alaska*, San Francisco, 1886, gives an account of the voyage and quotes *Viajes al Norte*, MS. 25, in the Bancroft Library, University of California, Berkeley, Cal. See pp. 197-202.

[4] Bancroft, *op. cit.*, states that the anchorage was in Port Mary, Shelekof Bay, but the soundings of "not less than sixty-six fathoms," and "protected from the north by Cape Engano," (Barrington, *op. cit.*) of this narrative will not admit of this construction, as Shelekof Bay has no soundings of over sixteen fathoms.

[5] Captain James Cook and Captain James King, *Voyage to the Pacific Ocean*, in three volumes; 1 and 2, by Captain Cook; 3, by Captain King; vol. 2, pp. 344-527, and vol. 3, pp. 244-278. London, 1785, 3rd Ed.

[6] *Ibid.*, vol. 2, p. 344.

[7] *Ibid.*, p. 345.

[8] *Ibid.*, p. 353.

[9] Of Cook Inlet, a footnote says: "Captain Cook having left a blank which he had not filled up with any particular name, Lord Sandwich directed with the greatest propriety that it should be called Cook's River." *Ibid.*, p. 396.

[10] *Ibid.*, vol. 3, p. 46.

[11] While making the survey on Buçareli Bay, at a point near Cape Bartholomew, a village was discovered, "which had belonged to the Indians, situated at the top of a steep hill, whose sides were so precipitous that in

order to climb it, that it was necessary to use long ladders. . . . When viewed from below, the structure, as regards its situation, resembled an inaccessible fortress." Maurelle, Journal, MS., Bancroft Library.

[12] Robert Greenhow, librarian of the State Department, in *History of Oregon and California and other Territories on the Northwest Coast of America*, p. 125, London, 1844, sketches this voyage. In a footnote he says, "The papers relative to this voyage, have been obtained from Madrid, from the Hydrographical Department . . . are the official account of the whole expedition—and the journals of Bodega and Maurelle—accompanied by several tables, etc. . . . A translation of a part of Maurelle's journal may be found in the first part of the narrative of the expedition of La Perouse. . . . "

Copies of the MSS. are in the Bancroft Library, and Bancroft, *op. cit.*, gives an account at pp. 217-221.

This area from Oregon to Cook Inlet was generally known among the shipmasters of the trade, as the Old Northwest Coast.

[13] LaPerouse, *Voyage Round the World*, 2 vols., London, 1798.

[14] Etienne Marchand, *Voyage Round the World*, 2 vols., London, 1801.

[15] Captain George Dixon, *Voyage Round the World*, p. 316, London, 1789.

[16] *Ibid.*, p. 198.

[17] Captain Nathaniel Portlock, *Voyage Round the World*, 1785-8, London, 1789.

[18] James Meares, *Voyages, Made in 1788-9*, 2 vols., London, 1791.

[19] Haswell, Journal, MS., Library of University of Washington; Robert Greenhow, *op. cit.*, London, 1844.

[20] *Diario de la Navigacion*, MS., Bancroft Library.

[21] Fidalgo is mentioned by Bancroft, *op. cit.*, pp. 273-4; Greenhow, *op. cit.*, mentions Fidalgo's voyage at p. 220, and a footnote states: "Manuscript journal of the voyage of Fidalgo, among the documents obtained from the hydrographical department of Madrid."

[22] Alessandro Malaspina, *Viaje politico-cientifico alrededor del mundo por las corbetas Descubierta y Artevida (A Political-Scientific Voyage around the World in the Ships "Descubierta" and "Atrevida")* Madrid, 1885, describes his expedition; Bancroft, *op. cit.*, p. 249; Greenhow, *op. cit.*, p. 222; and *The Early Literature of the Northwest Coast*, Publication of the Transactions of the Royal Society of Canada, 3rd Series, Ottawa, 1924, all have much interesting information about the ships that sailed in those waters in those years.

[23] "The unfortunate commander, having given some offense to Godey, who then ruled Spain without restriction, was, on his return to Europe in 1794, confined in a dungeon at Corunna and kept there as a prisoner until 1802, when he was liberated, after the peace of Amiens, at the express desire of Napoleon." Greenhow, *op. cit.*, p. 222.

[24] Salva y Baranda, *Coleccion de Documentos Ineditos*, vol. 15, pp. 323-363, Madrid, 1849.

[25] George Vancouver was born about 1758 and entered the British Navy as a midshipman at the age of thirteen years. As a midshipman he accompanied Captain Cook on his second voyage and as an able seaman was also with Cook on his third voyage and was made a Lieutenant in 1780. In 1790 he was promoted to the rank of Commander and appointed to the command of this expedition. He died in 1798, at the early age of forty years. Edmond S. Meany, *Vancouver's Discovery of Puget Sound*, New York, 1907; George Vancouver, *Voyage of Discovery to the North Pacific Ocean*, 3 vols., 4to, Atlas of Maps, London, 1798.

[26] Captain Brown was killed by the natives at Woahoo, H. I., in January, 1795. William Robert Broughton, *Voyage of Discovery to the North Pacific Ocean*, London, 1804.

[27] Peter Puget entered the British Navy in August, 1778; in 1790 he went as Lieutenant under Vancouver, and January 14, 1793, was placed in command of the *Chatham*. He was made a Captain in 1797, and in 1821 was promoted to Vice-Admiral. He died October 31, 1822. Meany, *op. cit.*

[28] Vancouver, *op. cit.* A second edition was issued in 6 vols., 8vo., London, 1801.

7

The Colony Under Baranof

[1] Kyril Khlebnikof, *Zhzineopisanie Aleksandra Andreevicha Baranova (Life of Alexander Andreevich Baranof)*, St. Petersburg, 1835. The name of the author is not on the title page, but from the preface it is plainly the work of Kyril Khlebnikof, the *Glavnia Kontora*, or chief of the counting-house, under the successor to Baranof.

Baranof was born about 1746, according to A. A. Polovinof, *Russkii Biographicheskii Slovar (Russian Biographical Cyclopedia)*.

[2] Khlebnikof, *op. cit.*, p. 6.

[3] "Send a clergyman of learning, mild, not superstitious, and not a bigot," wrote Baranof. When Shelekof complied with the request he sent ten clergymen. *Ibid.*, p. 9.

[4] "At Chiniak I made arrangements for the building of a harbor . . . it should be named *Paulovski* in honor of the Prince Imperial," according to a letter to Shelekof. Tikhmenef, *Historical Sketch of the Russian American Company*, vol. 2, p. 35, Appendix.

[5] The tribes of natives from Yakutat southward, even as far as the Columbia River, were called Kolosh by the Russians.

[6] The name of the English shipwright was Iakof Shiltz, according to F. A. Golder, *Guide to Materials for American History in Russian Archives*, p. 118.

[7] The exact location of the shipyard is not known. The Rev. L. H. Pederson, formerly of Seward, Alaska, devoted much time to searching for it and believes that it was on the west side of Resurrection Bay, a little way

below Seward, and says that some traces still exist on the ground. The map in Tikhmenef, *op. cit.*, places it near the present town of Seward. It was occupied for some years as a trading station but there were no other boats built there.

[8] Letter, Baranof to Shelekof. Tikhmenef, *op. cit.*, vol. 2, pp. 85 *et seq.*

[9] *Ibid.*, vol. 1, p. 40.

[10] Khlebnikof, *op. cit.*, p. 25.

[11] Tikhmenef, *op. cit.*, vol. 1, p. 30.

[12] Vancouver, *Voyage of Discovery to the North Pacific Ocean*, vol. 5, pp. 238-9, London, 1801.

[13] Tikhmenef, *op. cit.*, vol. 1, p. 57.

[14] The word *toyon* is a Yakut term, meaning leader, or chief. The Russians appointed a *toyon* in each village, and depended on him to recruit the hunting parties, etc. The system was not used farther north than about St. Michael.

[15] A description of the hunt for sea otter as given by Baranof himself is contained in Tikhmenef, *op. cit.*, Part 1, pp. 126-7.

[16] Report of Igor Purtof. *Ibid.*, vol. 2, p. 60, Appendix.

[17] The fate of all the settlers is not known. Probably twenty families were sent to Yakutat, of which number some died of scurvy and the others were killed by the Kolosh in 1805. Two families were sent to the Kenai Gulf, and one was sent to the neighborhood of Cape St. Elias, according to Tikhmenef, *op. cit.*, vol. 2, p. 95, Appendix. Four men returned to Russia in 1821, according to the *Russian American Archives*.

Of the missionaries, Archimandrite Joassaf was lost on the *Phoenix* in 1799; Hieromonk Juvenal was killed at Iliamna in 1796; Hieromonk Afanasia returned to Russia in 1825; Hierodiakon Nektar returned to Irkutsk in 1806; Monk Joassaf died in Kodiak in 1823; Monk Herman died on Yelovie Island (Spruce Island) near Kodiak in 1837; Hieromonk Makar was lost on the *Phoenix*, as was Hieromonk Stephen.

[18] Tikhmenef, *op. cit.*, vol. 2, p. 101, Appendix.

[19] *Ibid.*, p. 77. Baranof made a speech to his rebellious traders in May, 1794, according to *ibid.*, Part 2, pp. 47-8, Appendix.

[20] Khlebnikof, *op. cit.*, p. 33.

[21] In the Bancroft Library, Berkeley, Calif., is a MS. purporting to be the Journal of Father Juvenal, which was preserved by his boy Nikita and given to the Russians. It says that upon the father's preaching against polygamy the chief offered one of his wives, which was at once refused. After this, the Journal continues, "In the middle of the night I awoke to find myself in the arms of a woman, and a grievous sin was committed before I could extricate myself." The next day the women laughed at him, and when he insisted to the chief that he put away his wives, the natives killed him. Journal of Father Juvenal, MS., Bancroft Library, University of California; Bancroft, *History of Alaska*, p. 371.

[22] Khlebnikof, *op. cit.*, p. 30.

[23] On this voyage he passed through a strait on the north side of Mt.

Edgecumbe, gave it the name of Olga Strait, and lay on anchor in a small harbor where, on shore, he placed a cross and called the harbor Krestof Bay. Golofnin, *Materialui dlya Istorii Russkikh Zaselenii, etc.*, Part 4, p. 41, St. Petersburg, 1862.

8

The Founding of New Archangel

[1] Ivan Alexandrovich Kuskof was Baranof's most trusted assistant. He was a merchant of Totemsk and came to the colony as a clerk with Baranof; he was promoted, made a Commercial Counsellor in the company, and was awarded a gold medal. In 1812 he built the post at Russian River, California, and in 1821 he resigned, returned to Russia by way of Okhotsk, and died at Totemsk in 1823. Khlebnikof, *Zhizneopisanie Aleksandra Andreevicha Baranova*, p. 35.

[2] Under date of May 20, 1795, Baranof wrote to Shelekof: "Old age is approaching. . . . At night I must use a glass to read and write and my cheerful spirit is on the wane. I feel it is beyond my power to fulfill and attend in person to all the important duties imposed upon me. Besides this I hear that you take heed of every breath of calumny and slander that reaches you against me. . . . If long and faithful services have not gained me your confidence it is better that they should at once be severed." Tikhmenef, *Historical Sketch of the Russian American Company*, vol. 2, p. 100, Appendix.

[3] Khlebnikof, *op. cit.*, p. 46; Golofnin, *Materialui dlya Istorii Russkikh Zaselenii, etc.*, Part 4, p. 42; Tikhmenef, *op. cit.*, vol. 2, pp. 136-9, Appendix.

[4] Khlebnikof, *op. cit.*, p. 49.

[5] Richard Cleveland, *Narrative of Voyages*, Cambridge, 1842.

[6] "Even cannon of 4 pound calibre," says Khlebnikof, *op. cit.*, p. 52.

[7] *Ibid.*, p. 52.

[8] Tikhmenef, *op. cit.*, vol. 2, p. 131, Appendix; Khlebnikof, *op. cit.*, p. 51.

[9] Golofnin, *op. cit.*, Part 4, p. 44; Khlebnikof, *op. cit.*, p. 54; Tikhmenef, *op. cit.*, vol. 2, p. 147, Appendix.

[10] Tikhmenef, *op. cit.*, vol. 1, p. 83. The port was called Redoubt St. Archangel Michael.

[11] The *Elizabeth*, which arrived from Okhotsk, seems to have been the first vessel for four years. She arrived in November, 1802.

[12] Khlebnikof, *op. cit.*, p. 63.

[13] Ivan Ivanovich Banner (called Bander by Langsdorff) was a titular counsellor in the service of the Russian American Co. He had been in the Crown Service at Irkutsk, and was also land inspector at Zasheversk. After leaving that service he went with the company and was sent with a ship to found a settlement on Bering Strait for trade with the Chukchees

and Eskimos. His ship was damaged in the passage, and he ran in at Unalaska, where Larionof, who was in charge, detained him, and advised him to discontinue the effort to place the post in the North. He was later sent to Kodiak, where he remained in charge for several years. He died at Kodiak in 1816. Mrs. Banner was appointed as teacher of girls at Kodiak in 1806, and was probably the first woman teacher in Russian America. *Ibid.*, p. 66.

9

The Organization of the Russian American Company

[1] Golofnin, *Materialui dlya Istorii Russkikh Zaselenii, etc.*, Part 1, p. 55.
[2] The terms of the Charter are in *ibid.*, Part 1, pp. 77-80.

10

Destruction of Old Sitka

[1] "The conduct of the Russians at Sitka was not likely to inspire the Kolosh with a very high opinion of them." Davidof, *Dvukratnoe Puteschestvie iv Ameriky Morskikh Ofitzerof Khvostovi i Davidova (Two Voyages to America)*. (By Marine Officers Khvostof and Davidof).

[2] Tikhmenef, *Historical Sketch of the Russian American Company*, Part 1, p. 88, gives a brief account of the massacre. In *ibid.*, pp. 174 *et seq.*, Appendix, are statements of the survivors. This text is chiefly from Khlebnikof's letters to the journal *Raduga*, Revel, 1833, and reprinted in *Materialui dlya Istorii Russkikh Zaselenii, etc.*, Part 4, pp. 45 *et seq.*

[3] *Ibid.*, p. 50.

[4] *Ibid.*, p. 50. Barber went to the Sandwich Islands and there, hearing that war existed between Russia and England, planned to go back and attack Kodiak with the design of capturing the furs at that station. The later news of peace prevented his doing so. Tikhmenef, *op. cit.*, Part 1, p. 89.

[5] "Khlebnikof's Letters," *Raduga*.

[6] *Ibid.*, p. 53.

[7] *Ibid.*, p. 54: "Toyon Kanagit, in the assembly in Khutznof, took on himself the obligation to get powder, muskets, and guns, assuring the other Kolosh that the foreigners would give them as much as they would need if they would only destroy the Russians and Aleuts."

[8] Baranof was so pleased that he donated a thousand rubles to the school at Kodiak. Khlebnikof, *Zhizneopisanie Aleksandra Andreevicha Baranova* p. 66.

[9] *Ibid.*, p. 74. Davidof, *Dvukratnoe Puteschetsvie, etc.*, tells of his arrival and stay in the colonies.

[10] Statements of the survivors describing the massacre and their escape can be found in Tikhmenef, *op. cit.*, Part 2, pp. 174, Appendix.

11

Battle at Sitka and Re-establishment of the Post

[1] Tikhmenef, *Historical Sketch of the Russian American Company*, Part 1, p. 106.

[2] *Ibid.*, vol. 2, p. 183, Appendix.

[3] *Ibid.*, vol. 2, p. 183, Appendix; Khlebnikof, *Zhizneopisanie Aleksandra Andreevicha Baranova*, p. 82; Urey Lisianski, *Voyage Round the World, 1803-1806*, p. 149, London, 1814.

[4] A. J. Krusenstern, *Voyage Round the World*, 2 vols., London, 1813.

[5] Lisianski, *op. cit.*, p. 147.

[6] *Ibid.*, p. 151.

[7] The fort contained at least eight hundred inhabitants. *Ibid.*, p. 163.

[8] The Kolosh settlement was around the Baranof Hill, or Katlean's Rock, as it is called in some accounts. *Ibid.*, pp. 240-1.

[9] A few Kolosh lurked in the forest and killed eight Aleuts on Jamestown Bay on Oct. 25. Khlebnikof, *op. cit.*, p. 88.

[10] "The Song of Baranof" was published in the *Muscovitian*, Moscow, Russia, and a copy is in the Library of Congress. It was composed in 1799, and was probably first sung at the founding of Sitka. Photostat copy, Andrews Collection.

A translation was made by Henry W. Elliott, which was published in the *Overland Magazine*, of San Francisco, Cal. Another translation is found in C. L. Andrews, *Nuggets of Verse Panned from the Gravels of the Past*, p. 3, 1936.

12

Rezanof and His Policies

[1] Lisianski, *Voyage Round the World, 1803-1806*, p. 217.

[2] Tikhmenef, *Historical Sketch of the Russian American Company*, vol. 2, p. 192.

[3] Letter of Rezanof from Sitka, November 6, 1805. *Ibid.*, p. 197: "The immense number of wooded islands in the vast bay furnish excellent anchorage for ships as well as a charming view. On one of them a tower and beacon light has been erected." This was probably the first attempt at establishing a lighthouse service in southeastern Alaska.

[4] Khlebnikof, *Zhizneopisanie Aleksandra Andreevicha Baranova*, p. 99.

[5] Letter of the agent at Fort Constantine to Baranof, September 24, 1805. Tikhmenef, *op. cit.*, vol. 2, p. 195, Appendix.

[6] Khlebnikof, *op. cit.*, p. 101; Khlebnikof, *Materialui dlya Istorii Russkikh Zaselenii, etc.*, Part 3, p. 6.

[7] Khlebnikof, *op. cit.*, p. 103.

[8] G. H. von Langsdorff, *Voyages and Travels*, London, 1813; Wilfred Harold Munro, *Tales of an Old Seaport*, pp. 129 *et seq.*, Princeton Press, 1917.

[9] "When there is a possibility of making a settlement on the Columbia River, it (Sitka) will be still a central point from where it would be easy to seize Kaigan Island (Prince of Wales) ... found a settlement on the Columbia from which we could gradually advance toward the south to the port of San Francisco, which forms the boundary line of California." "Report of Rezanof"; Tikhmenef, *op. cit.*, Part 2, Appendix, pp. 232-3; *ibid.*, vol. 2, p. 253.

[10] *Op. cit.*, vol. 1, p. 162.

[11] Rezanof's Japanese expedition led to the capture of Captain V. M. Golofnin by the Japanese, and to the Captain's being treated with great severity by them.

Relating to Japonski Island at Sitka, Golofnin states: "I am ashamed to say, but must: Rezanof wished to capture Japanese, to settle in America and to use them on company work; he designated for their settlement an island and named it Japonski Island, which to this time among the Russian *promishleniki* carries that name." *Works of V. M. Golofnin,* vol. 5, p. 170, St. Petersburg, 1864.

13

Trade Extension and Shipbuilding

[1] Khlebnikof, *Zhizneopisanie Aleksandra Andreevicha Baranova*, pp. 75-77.

[2] *Ibid.*, pp. 96-148, gives the ships and their catch.

[3] On his return from Kodiak, Baranof moved his records and thereafter made Sitka his head factory. *Ibid.*, p. 123.

[4] *Ibid.*, p. 118.

[5] The Kolosh killed some Aleut fishermen before they dispersed. *Ibid.*, p. 115.

[6] Khlebnikof, *Materialui dlya Istorii Russkikh Zaselenii, etc.*, Part 3, pp. 12-13.

[7] Khlebnikof, *op. cit.*, p. 127.

[8] *Ibid.*, pp. 127 *et seq.* The sentence is in the *Russian American Archives*, Correspondence, vol. 1, March 22, 1817.

[9] Khlebnikof, *op cit.*, p. 135.

[10] *Ibid.*, p. 138.

[11] Washington Irving, *Astoria.*

[12] Khlebnikof, *op. cit.*, p. 145.

14

Ross Colony

[1] The wreck of the *St. Nicholas* is told by Golofnin in *Remarkable Shipwrecks of Russian Navigators.* Some of the Russians, including the wife of Captain Bulagin, were captured by the Indians. The rest wandered in the forest until hunger compelled their surrender to the Indians, after which Bulagin, his wife, two other Russians, and two Kodiak men died. The rest were ransomed by Captain Brown and taken to Sitka.
Tikhmenef, *Historical Sketch of the Russian American Company*, vol. 1, p. 207; *Washington Historical Quarterly*, January, 1922.

[2] Khlebnikof, *Zhizneopisanie Aleksandra Andreevicha Baranova*, p. 126.

[3] *Ibid.*, p. 146; R. A. Thompson, *Russian Settlement in California*, Santa Rosa, California, 1906.

[4] The American sea captains visiting the islands in the earlier years are reputed to have taken as many as ten thousand sealskins in a year. Khlebnikof, *Materialui dlya Istorii Russkikh Zaselenii, etc.*, Part 3, p. 157.

[5] Captain Golofnin on his voyage around the world in the sloop *Kamchatka* visited Ross and described it. He tells of explorations made by the Russians on the interior rivers, "for example, two rivers entering into the bay, on the north side of the bay of San Francisco, to the Spanish entirely unknown." Golofnin, *op. cit.*, Part 4, p. 122.

[6] Khlebnikof, *Materialui, etc.*, Part 3, pp. 151-6.

[7] Khlebnikof, *Zhizneopisanie, etc., op. cit.*, p. 170.

[8] Khlebnikof, *op. cit.*, Part 3, p. 149.

[9] Bancroft, *History of California*, vol. 4, p. 159.

[10] Sir George Simpson, *Journey Round the World*, p. 283, London, 1847 (Simpson was governor of the Hudson's Bay Company); Tikhmenef, *op. cit.*, Part 1, p. 366; *Dielo o Kolonii Ross (Affairs of Ross Colony)*, St. Petersburg, 1866.
Russians in California, California Historical Society, San Francisco, treats it from the Spanish side.

15

The Closing Years of Baranof's Management

[1] Khlebnikof, *Zhizneopisanie Aleksandra Andreevicha Baranova*, p. 149; Golofnin, *Remarkable Shipwrecks of Russian Navigators*, vol. 4, p. 444, St. Petersburg, 1864.

[2] Khlebnikof, *op. cit.*, p. 151.

[3] *Archives of the Russian American Company*, vol. 1, p. 188.

[4] A Russian fort appears to have been partly constructed on the present site of the city of Honolulu, for Dr. Gowen, in his work on Kamehameha, says: "It seems to have included the fort which the Russians had left unfinished." Herbert H. Gowen, *The Napoleon on the Pacific, Kamehameha the Great*, p. 302, New York, 1919.

[5] Khlebnikof, *op. cit.*, pp. 161-9.

[6] In a letter to Hagemeister dated April, 1819. *Archives of the Russian American Company*, p. 242.

[7] Otto von Kotzebue, *Voyage of Discovery*, London, 1821. Kotzebue returned to the colonies in 1823-6. Kotzebue, *New Voyage Round the World*, 2 vols. London, 1830.

[8] *Archives of the Russian American Company*, vol. 1, p. 73; Khlebnikof, *op. cit.*, p. 172.

[9] Tikhmenef, *Historical Sketch of the Russian American Company*, vol. 1, p. 248.

[10] M. de Roquefeuil, *Voyage Round the World*, London, 1823.

[11] Tikhmenef, *op. cit.*, vol. 1, p. 244.

[12] Golofnin pretended to be Baranof's friend, yet in some of his reports he said some very unkind things of him personally. *See* Golofnin, *Materialui dlya Istorii Russkikh Zaselenii, etc.*, Part 1, p. 53; Khlebnikof, *op. cit.*, p. 175.

[13] *Ibid.*, p. 176. Baranof gave a shirt of mail, made of small links of steel, to one of the Auk chiefs at the time of his departure. This was kept as a valued treasure and passed down with the chieftainship until a few years ago, when Father Sergius, George Kostromitinof, secured it from the Auks at the time of the death of their last chief, and deposited it in the National Museum at Washington, D. C. Scrap Book of Father Sergius, Sitka, Alaska.

[14] *Archives of the Russian American Company*, Journal, vol. 1, p. 112.

[15] Khlebnikof, *op. cit.*, p. 177.

16

The Second Charter, 1821-1842

[1] Tikhmenef, *Historical Sketch of the Russian American Company*, vol. 1, p. 41 *et seq.*, Appendix, gives a copy of the Charter. It is also quoted in the *Alaska Boundary Tribunal* (U. S. Gov't Ptg. Off.) "Case of U. S.," Appendix.

[2] P. H. Golovin, "Review of the Russian Colonies," p. 112, St. Petersburg, 1861.

[3] "To facilitate the settlement of accounts in the colony the general administration has established checks of 10, 5, and 1 ruble, 50 and 25

kopeks, amounting in 1817 to 12,000 rubles, but as they were worn out in traffic they issued anew 30,000 rubles in 1822 (of which 6,000 was placed at Kadiak and 3,000 each at Unalaska and Ross). The first issue was retired and sent back, and the new checks were distributed over the colonies and used among the Russians and Aleuts." "The Colonial Government always kept on hand in the treasury a certain amount of Spanish piastres for the purchase of breadstuffs or goods in California." Khlebnikof, *Materialui dlya Istorii Russkikh Zaselenii, etc.*, Part 3, p. 107.

[4] *Russian American Archives*, vol. 1, p. 41, Correspondence.

[5] "Case of U. S.," *Alaska Boundary Tribunal*, p. 8, Appendix.

[6] *Ibid.*, p. 12.

[7] "They claim we have seized the place to which they possessed the right of priority, that we have made it impossible for them to realize any profits on their furs and that we have taken away the best localities for catching fish. Khlebnikof, *op. cit.*, Part 3, p. 130.

[8] Golovin, *op. cit.*, p. 49.

[9] Tikhmenef, *op. cit.*, pp. 330-333.

[10] *Ibid.*, Part 1, p. 274.

[11] *Ibid.*, p. 281.

[12] Frederick William Beechey, *Narrative of a Voyage to the Pacific and Bering Strait*, London, 1831.

[13] Ivan Veniaminof, *Works of Innokentius; Zapiska ob Ostrovakh Oonalashkinskago Otdyela*, Part 2, pp. 368 *et seq.*, Moscow, 1886.

[14] Tikhmenef, *op. cit.*, Part 1, p. 283.

[15] *Ibid.*, Part 1, p. 285.

[16] *Ibid.*, pp. 286-7.

[17] "Case of U. S.," *Alaska Boundary Tribunal*, p. 266, Appendix.

[18] Robert Campbell, MS., Journal, Andrews Collection. In 1837 Sir George Simpson, governor of the Hudson's Bay Company, wrote to Campbell: "Robert Campbell is not the man I take him to be unless in due time he plants the Hudson's Bay standard on the shores of the Pacific."

[19] "Case of U. S.," *Alaska Boundary Tribunal*, p. 279, Appendix.

[20] Sir James Douglas, Journal, M.S., Bancroft Library; Copy, Andrews Collection.

[21] Sir George Simpson, *Narrative of a Journey Round the World*, London, 1847.

[22] "Case of U. S.," *Alaska Boundary Tribunal*, p. 276; *Archives of the Russian American Company*, vol. 12, No. 1.

[23] Tikhmenef, *Historical Sketch of the Russian American Company*, vol. 1, p. 287. Some accounts indicate that the attacking party was from Ahyak, or Sledge Island.

[24] Sir Edward Belcher, *Narrative of a Voyage Round the World*, London, 1847.

[25] Simpson, *Narrative of the Discoveries on the North Side of America*, London, 1843.

[26] Tikhmenef, *op. cit.*, vol. 1, p. 280.

[27] Golovin, "Review of the Russian Colonies," *Morskoi Sbornik*, St. Petersburg; Tikhmenef, *op. cit.*, vol. 1, p. 314.

[28] *Ibid.*, p. 330.

[29] A. Zagoskin, *Pyeshekhodnia Opis Chasti Russkikh Vladenie iv Amerika (Pedestrian Exploration of Parts of the Russian Possessions in America)*, 2 vols., 1847.

[30] Tikhmenef, *op. cit.*, vol. 2, pp. 203-4; *Archives of the Russian American Company*, vol. 22, p. 550; *Journal No. 23*, No. 311, p. 282.

[31] Simpson, *Journey Round the World*, vol. 2, pp. 182-9.

[32] Tikhmenef, *op. cit.*, Part 1, p. 366. Ross sold to Sutter.

17

Third Charter

[1] Tikhmenef, *Historical Sketch of the Russian American Company*, vol. 2, p. 12, Appendix; Khlebnikof, *Zhizneopisanie Aleksandra Andreevich Baranof*, p. 190.

[2] The term "Creole" as used here is given as legally defined by the Russian authorities and as used in the colonies. In the southern United States and in the West Indies it is held to include only children of Spanish or French descent born in America of European parents. The term is technically defined in the Appendix to Tikhmenef, *op. cit.*, p. 55.

[3] P. N. Golovin, "Review of the Russian Colonies," *Morskoi Sbornik*, St. Petersburg, p. 121.

[4] Tikhmenef, *op. cit.*, Part 1, pp. 310, 312; Part 2, p. 243.

[5] *Ibid.*, Part 2, p. 243.

[6] *Ibid.*, p. 86, Appendix.

[7] Starbuck, *History of American Whale Fishery*, pp. 155-7.

[8] Tikhmenef, *op. cit.*, Part 2, p. 129.

[9] Alexander H. Murray, *Journal of the Yukon*, Ottawa, 1910.

[10] At the time of the establishing of Fort Yukon and for many years afterward the returns from the station reached the market only after seven years. *See* George M. Dawson, *The Yukon Territory*, p. 352, London, 1898.

[11] Dall, *Alaska and Its Resources*, p. 276.

[12] Tikhmenef, *op. cit.*, Part 2, p. 204.

[13] Barthold Seeman, *Voyage of "H.M.S. Herald,"* London, 1853; Lieut. W. H. Hooper, *Ten Months Among the Tents of the Tuski*, London, 1853; Richardson, *Polar Regions*, p. 172; Captain McClintock, *Narrative of the Fate of Sir John Franklin*, Boston, 1859; Captain Richard Collinson, *Journal of "H.M.S. Enterprise," 1850-1855*; Captain Sherard Osborne, *The Discovery of a Northwest Passage*, London, 1855.

In the *Parliamentary Papers* and the *Blue Books* of the British Government; in what are called "Franklin's Papers"; "*Further Correspondence and*

Proceedings Connected with the Arctic Expedition"; "Further papers . . . in search of Sir John Franklin . . . " are records of the time that are valuable original sources little known to the general public. They constitute the most interesting and romantic story of the North.

[14] Tikhmenef, *op. cit.*, Part 2, p. 207.

[15] "Report of Chief Manager Voevodski," *Archives of the Russian American Company*, June 6, 1855, p. 74.

[16] Cession Papers, Russian America *Ex. Doc. 177, Fortieth Congress, Second Session*, H. R., p. 263; Lewis & Dryden, *Marine History of the Pacific Northwest*, Portland, Oregon, 1895.

[17] Bancroft, *History of British Columbia*, p. 599. Captain Moore came to the U. S. about 1842, served in the U. S. Navy during the Mexican War, and later came to the Pacific Coast, June 24, 1862, he arrived at the Stikine River with the Str. *Flying Dutchman*, and a barge on board which there were 140 passengers. In 1887 he went over the White Pass for William Ogilvie, Canadian Dominion Surveyor, who was on his way to the Yukon, and in 1888 he established a trading post at the site of the present town of Skagway. He carried the first mail out from Dawson by way of the upper Yukon during the winter of 1896-7, although he was over 70 years old at the time. "Biography of Captain William Moore," *Washington Historical Quarterly*, 1930.

[18] W. H. Dall, *Alaska and Its Resources*, Boston, 1870. The project of the telegraph line by this route was the predecessor of another scheme. In 1897-8 Count Loicq de Lobel, a Frenchman residing in Dawson, Y. T., conceived the idea of a railway from America to Asia by way of Bering Strait. What was looked upon as a most visionary proposition at that time may not be considered so impossible fifty years hence.

[19] Captain-Lieutenant Paul Nikolevich Golovin was sent in 1861 to make a survey of the colonies, going to Sitka by way of New York and San Francisco. His report was published in the *Morski Sbornik* (Marine Journal) at St. Petersburg, under the title *Obzor Russkikh Kolonii iv Amerike*, or, "Review of the Russian Colonies in America."

[20] Sea otter taken from the Colonies by Russian fur-traders from 1741 to 1862:

1741, Bering's crew on Bering Island	900
1745 to 1803, the free traders	96,047
1786 to 1797, The Shelekof Company	15,647
1798 to 1821, The Russian American Company	86,644
1822 to 1841, The Russian American Company	25,416
1842 to 1862, The Russian American Company	25,899
Total	250,553

Other Fur Taken:

	Seal	Blue and White Fox	Red Fox Black Fox	Beaver	Marten
1798 to 1821	1,767,340	51,034	75,103	56,001	17,921
1821 to 1842	458,502	79,352	89,352	162,034	15,666
1842 to 1862	372,894	54,434	77,847	157,484	12,782
Total	2,598,736	184,820	242,302	375,519	46,369

Berkh, *Chronological History of the Discovery of the Aleutian Islands,* Appendix; Tikhmenef, *op. cit.,* Part 1, p. 327; Part 2, p. 327; Part 2, p. 221.

[21] Letter No. 937, September 19, 1863, of the Russian American Company, to Manager Furuhelm, tells of a holding company to buy the stock of the Hudson's Bay Company, etc. *Archives of the Russian American Company,* vol. 24, p. 378.

A letter from Thomas Fraser, secretary, Hudson's Bay House, London, refers to a letter of July 4, 1861, saying, "It is stated that the trade of this company has been so seriously affected by the encroachments of petty traders and the introduction of ardent spirits as greatly to diminish the value of the territory as a fur trading district. . . ." *Archives of the Russian American Company,* vol. 24, p. 137.

[22] Victor J. Farrar, "The Background of the Purchase of Alaska," *Washington Historical Quarterly,* April, 1922.

[23] The text of the treaty is given in full in the Cession Papers, Russian America, *op. cit.*

NOTES
Part Two—1867-1930

18

The Transfer to the United States

[1] "Official Report of General Jefferson C. Davis," in Cession Papers, Russian America, *Ex. Doc. 177, Fortieth Congress, Second Session, H. R.,* p. 108; also p. 72; *Ex. Doc. 125, Fortieth Congress, Second Session, H. R.* cited in the *Washington Historical Quarterly,* Oct., 1908. In the harbor were the Russian ships *Czarevich, Constantine, Menshikoff, Politofski,* and *Olga,* which were transferred to the U. S. flag. Customs Records, Alaska.

[2] "Of American ladies, six were present: the wives of General Davis, Colonel Weeks, Major Wood, and Rev. Mr. Rainier of the *John L. Stephens,* the wife of Mr. Dodge, Collector of Customs, and the wife of Captain MacDougall of the *Jamestown.* Six Russian ladies were also present: the Princess Maksoutoff, the wife and daughter of Vice-Governor Gardsishoff, and three whose names I do not know." *Ibid.,* p. 72.

[3] The records in the State Department at present are: Correspondence files, vols. 1 to 25, 1802 to 1866; Journals of outgoing papers, vols. 1 to 34; Journals of outgoing papers, unnumbered, 5 vols.; Journals of exploration, 2 vols.; Logbooks of vessels, 16 vols.; total, 82 vols.

Bancroft, *History of Alaska,* bibliography, gives 182. It is probably an error in the number. The original list made out by Pestchouroff is on the front of vol. 1 of the correspondence, and lists from 1818 to 1867, signed, "Rec'd Sitka, A. T., April 7, 1867, Edward G. Fast, 2nd Lieut." The papers for the last half of 1831 are missing and very few papers are dated before 1818. The record begins with the management of Yanovski. Hagemeister perhaps took all the Baranof records to St. Petersburg.

[4] Alaska Customs, Record of Manifests.

[5] *Ibid.; Alaska Herald,* San Francisco, Cal., Sept. 15, 1868.

[6] The Treaty of Cession, concluded March 30, 1867; ratified by the United States May 28, 1867; exchanged June 20, 1867, and proclaimed by the U. S., June 20, 1867, states: "The inhabitants of the ceded territory, according to their choice, reserving their natural allegiance, may return to Russia within three years; but if they prefer to remain in the ceded territory, they, with the exception of the uncivilized native tribes, shall be admitted to the enjoyment of all the rights, advantages and immunities of citizens of the U. S., and shall be maintained and protected in the free enjoyment of their liberty, property, and religion." *Ex. Doc. 177,* Part 1, p. 8.

[7] In 1860 the number of people in the dependency of the colonies who were counted as Christians was: Russians, 784; Creoles, 1676; natives, 9,568; total, 12,028. Tikhmenef, *Historical Sketch of the Russian American Company,* Part 2, p. 264.

[8] The first troops ordered to Alaska were two companies, one of infantry, one of artillery. *Ex. Doc. 177*, Part 1, p. 97.

[9] "It is clearly of my opinion that troops in Alaska are to a great extent needless. . . . With two efficient gunboats carrying out the policy of British Columbia, punishing summarily and justly any outrage committed by the Indians, the territory would be better off, and the country as a whole advanced in prosperity." "Colyer's Report to the Secretary of the Interior," *Ex. Doc. 177, Forty-first Congress, Second Session*, pp. 1030-31.

[10] Instructions, Treasury Department, U. S., August 15, 1867, Customs Records, Alaska.

[11] Letter, Collector of Customs, W. S. Dodge, to Secy. of Treas., Jan. 16, 1868, Customs Records, Alaska.

[12] *Ex. Doc. 177*, p. 122.

[13] "Mr. Loan of Mo.," *Congressional Globe*, 1868, p. 3807.

19

The Military Occupation

[1] For the transfer to the United States the best authority is *Ex. Doc. 177, Fortieth Congress, Second Session, H. R.* It contains the important state papers of the Cession, Sumner's speech before the Senate, and the reports by Davidson and others of the survey of the cost.

In addition to this I have quoted from the Customs Records of the District of Alaska, on file at Sitka. Notes of sailing of ships are from the port clearances at Sitka, Seattle *Post-Intelligencer* files and Victoria, B. C., *British Colonist*.

[2] Customs Files, District of Alaska, correspondence files, etc., Alaska.

[3] Marcus Baker, *Geographic Dictionary of Alaska*, Gov't Ptg. Off., states, post office, Sitka, and Wrangell, established October, 1885.

[4] Letters, Collector of Customs, District of Alaska, Nov. 10, 1867; Letter, Chairman of Lighthouse Board, Nov. 11, 1868, Customs Records, Alaska.

[5] *Ex. Doc. 177*, pp. 195, *et seq.*

[6] *Coast Pilot of Alaska*, Part 1, First Edition, Gov't Ptg. Off., 1869.

[7] *Compiled Laws of Alaska*, title 1, chap. 1, sections 1 and 2, Gov't Ptg. Off., 1913.

[8] How unhappy the situation must have been is shown by the statement of W. S. Dodge, Collector of Customs, to the Hon. Vincent Colyer: "The great mass of the soldiers were either desperate or very immoral men. . . . Not only contaminating the Indians, but in fact demoralizing and making the inhabitants of Sitka what Dante characterized Italy: 'a grand house of ill-fame.'" "Colyer's Report," *Report of the Secretary of the Interior for 1869-70*, p. 1030.

[9] Letter, Collector of Customs, District of Alaska, March 2, 1870; Special Military Orders No. 18, Sitka, Alaska, March 8, 1870.

[10] "Colyer's Report," *loc. cit.*, p. 999.

[11] *Report on Education in Alaska*, Appendix J, p. 75. The last entry was made Feb. 4, 1873. *See* also Wm. Sumner Dodge, *Address*, Sitka, July 4, 1868. The officers were: Mayor, W. S. Dodge; Recorder, G. R. McKnight; Surveyor, J. A. Fuller; Constable, P. B. Ryan; Councilmen, J. A. Fuller, C. A. Kinkaid, Frank Mahoney, Isaac Bergman, and J. Halstead. Bancroft, *History of Alaska*, p. 601. One difficulty encountered was that the majority of the population was from foreign countries and unused to self-government.

[12] Report of Collector of Customs, Alaska, May 21, 1870, Customs Records, Alaska. *Ibid.*, July 12, 1870.

[13] The art of distilling is said to have been taught to the Indians by a discharged soldier named Doyle at Hootznahoo, from which the liquor derived its name of hooch. For the effects and for the method of production, see William Gouverneur Morris, "Report on Customs District, etc., 1879," *Ex. Doc. 59, Forty-fifth Congress, Third Session, H. R.*, pp. 61-2.

[14] "Colyer's Report," *op. cit.*, p. 996; *Ibid.*, p. 1031; "Case of U. S.," *Alaska Boundary Tribunal*, p. 358.

Nearly twenty years afterward, Quan-ni-ne-qua, a Kake Indian, was arrested for the crime. He told of how he asked for pay for his brother's death, and how he was told: "Indians are no good anyhow," and that he was so angry that he killed the men. Only one family was interested in the killing but thirty-six houses were burned. Sitka *Alaskan*, January 16, 1886.

[15] "Colyer's Report," *op. cit.*, p. 996. Appendix R, p. 1015.

[16] *Ibid.*, p. 1047.

[17] "Lieut. Borrowe's Report," *Ex. Doc. 67, Forty-first Congress*.

[18] *Life of William H. Seward*, vol. 3, pp. 424 *et seq.*

[19] Moore MS.; Delaney MS., Andrews Collection.

[20] *Ibid.*; Choquette had a trading post on the river.

[21] "Yukon Gold District," *U. S. Geological Survey*, p. 133. Bancroft, *History of British Columbia*, p. 561.

[22] Customs Records, District of Alaska; Moore MSS., Andrews Collection.

[23] "Schuck's Basin Mines." Juneau Gold Belt, *Geological Survey, Bulletin 287*, p. 2.

[24] "Report of Captain L. A. Beardslee," June 15, 1879, to Jan. 22, 1880, p. 24.

[25] *Boundary Tribunal*, Appendix, p. 346, Gov't Ptg. Off.; *General Orders No. 1*, Secretary of War.

20

The White Whalers

[1] The *Shenandoah* entered the Arctic in 1865. June 20 she burned five ships and barks in Bering Strait. On June 27 she found nine ships

where they had found the *Brunswick* fast in the ice and were helping her. She destroyed nine of them. For description of the Stone Fleets and for the raid of the *Shenandoah, see* Starbuck, *History of American Whaling,* vol. 2, No. 107, pp. 102 *et seq.*

[2] The disaster of 1871 is detailed in *ibid.,* pp. 103 *et seq.*

[3] For the wrecks of 1876, *see ibid.,* p. 109; *The Fishery Industries of the U. S.,* Sec. 5, vol. 2, p. 158. Spears, *Story of the New England Whalers,* pp. 402 *et seq.,* tells of the wrecks.

[4] Some of the ships went as far as Return Reef. *Fisheries Industries,* 1887, pp. 74-77. Gov't Ptg. Office.

[5] *Fishery Industries,* vol. 2, sec. 5, p. 318. The value of the products of the walrus from 1870 to 1880 was $1,260,000.00. In 1880 the value of the ivory was from $1 to $1.25 a pound. At the present it sells at about $ .75 a pound. A walrus will weigh 2,000 pounds and some of them are estimated to reach from 3,000 to 4,000 pounds. The largest tusks weigh as much as 20 pounds for the pair. The average is about 4 or 5 pounds. The natives depend on the walrus to a great extent for food and dog feed.

[6] For destruction of the animals and consequent starvation of the natives *see: Bureau of Education Reports,* 1890 and following years; *Reindeer Reports,* 1891, *et seq.,* Department of Interior. A description of this condition in 1890 is contained in *Bureau of Education Report,* 1890-1, p. 1291. *See* also "Franklin Papers," "Report Captain Maguire, H.M.S. Plover," pp. 905 *et seq.,* Parliament, London, 1855.

[7] Starbuck, *History of American Whaling,* p. 98.

[8] Walter S. Tower, *A History of the American Whale Fishery,* p. 130, Philadelphia, 1907.

[9] The mutinies occurred principally in the Southern seas. Starbuck, *op. cit.,* pp. 134-5.
The most notable encounter with the Alaska natives was that of the crew of the brig *W. H. Allen,* under Captain Gillie, in which fifteen natives were killed. This was about 1878. The fight was probably caused by the crew's getting the Eskimos intoxicated. "Report Captain Bailey," *U. S. R. C. S.,* p. 20, 1880; Nelson, *Western Eskimo,* p. 302; *Bur. Ed. Cir. of Inf. No. 2,* p. 12; W. T. Lopp, *Notes,* 1890; personal notes from Eskimos, 1917-1929, Andrews Collection.

[10] "Where the Ice Never Melts," *Scribner's Magazine,* April, 1891; Captain John A. Cook, *Pursuing the Whale.*

[11] *Report, Cruise U. S. Rev. Cutter "Bear" and Overland Expedition, 1899,* pp. 5 *et seq.*

[12] *Ibid.,* "Report, Lieut. D. H. Jarvis"; Lieut. E. P. Bertholf, later chief of the Coast Guard Service, and Surgeon S. J. Call of the same service, accompanied him.

[13] *Ibid.,* p. 84.

[14] *Ibid.,* pp. 85 *et seq.* A would-be noted Arctic traveler attacks the intentions of this expedition, in a work written twenty-three years after the work was done, and ten years after the death of Captain Jarvis, in an invidious paragraph, in *The Friendly Arctic,* pp. 580-581. The expedition

was made under orders, not for glory, or to go on the lecture platform, or to evade war duty. The attack was unwarranted and directed at an officer fulfilling his orders and performing duties requiring acts seldom adventured and never before except under the whip of necessity. It is an example of the sophistry of a half-truth. The truth consists of the fact the work was done and well done.

[15] The literature on whaling is voluminous. Arctic whaling along the Alaska shores is not covered by any one volume. Starbuck, *History of American Whaling,* is the epitome of all American work .to 1876, and the Bureau of Fisheries' *Fishery Industries of the United States,* 1886, continues the subject for ten years. There are interesting narratives such as *Pursuing the Whale,* and Aldrich, *Arctic Alaska and Siberia,* etc.

21

The Land of Furs

[1] "One was bribed off by the promise of double wages, but the other two continued their work. They were finally taken prisoners and sent off to Sitka by the first schooner that touched at the island." D. S. Jordan, *Fur Seals and Fur-Seal Islands,* Part 1, p. 27, Gov't Ptg. Off., 1898; W. H. Dall, *Alaska and Its Resources,* p. 241, Boston, 1870. For landing of parties *see* Jordan, *op. cit.,* pp. 26-7; *Fur Seal Arbitration,* vol. 5, p. 26.

[2] Some estimates are as high as 5,000,000 seals at the time of the transfer. These figures are quoted from *Seal Fisheries of Alaska, H. R. Hearings,* p. 271, Sixty-first Congress, Second Session, April 2, 1910. It states that it is likely that there were as many seals at the transfer as there were when Pribilof found the islands in 1786.

[3] The villages are of the same name as the islands. For description of the islands, charts, etc., *see* Jordan, *op. cit.,* which contains Steller's "Beasts of the Sea."

[4] "Report, Gen. O. O. Howard," *Ex. Doc. 83, Forty-fourth Congress, First Session,* p. 151.

[5] The general Government Reports give 100,000 taken in 1868; Captain Morgan states 240,000 taken. *Fur Seal Arbitration,* vol. 3, p. 63; but other records show differently. *See: Seal and Salmon Fisheries,* vol. 3, p. 529; *ibid.,* p. 323; *Fur Seal Arbitration,* "British Case," vol. 6, p. 194; *ibid.,* vol. 3, p. 157. Skins shipped 1868-9, 269,400, according to "Colyer's Report," *Report of the Secretary of Interior for 1869-70,* p. 1056.

[6] Both the Government and the sealers knew that if the killing continued the rookeries were doomed. There were rookeries in the South Seas, on Juan Fernandes, Kerguelan Land, in New Zealand, and others, from which millions of seal were taken and on which the seals were entirely exterminated. *F. S. Arb.,* vol. 2, pp. 374-5. Captain Morgan, one of the organizers of the company, was a whaler and sealer of the South Seas. Mr. Hutchinson was a shoe dealer of Massachusetts who became rich in the war trade. He learned about the seals from the R. A. Co. at Sitka. The

A. C. Co. was a strong corporation, organized in 1868, on capital partially from seals killed on the islands probably. *See: Fishery Industries of the U. S.,* pp. 382, *et seq.,* Washington, D. C., 1887.

[7] The bull seal never leaves his post at his harem from May until October, even to eat. Steller, "Beasts of the Sea," *Fur Seals and Fur-Seal Islands,* p. 179 *et seq.*

[8] *Fur Seal Arbitration,* 16 vols., Washington, D. C., 1895, describes the pelagic sealing minutely.

[9] "Fighting Bob" said of conditions: "The whole condition of Alaska, so far as the execution of the law is concerned, is a disgrace to our Government, and I shall so report; but it will not do any good." Commander Robley D. Evans, *A Sailor's Log,* p. 341, New York, 1918.

[10] The Convention for the Preservation and Protection of the Fur Seal was proclaimed December 11, 1911, *Treaty Series No. 564.*

[11] The literature of the seal and seal islands is voluminous. Besides the works cited there are hearings in Congress filling volumes. The Bureau of Fisheries issues a report annually giving full data of the work on the islands. *See: Alaska Fishery and Fur-Seal Industries,* Gov't Ptg. Off.

Prof. H. W. Elliott, for many years was chief authority of the sealing question, and his work appears in many hearings of Congress. *Our Arctic Province,* New York, 1887, was published by him.

[12] *See: U. S. Fisheries Report, 1905,* for take of sea otter in Alaska. The works relating to the sea otter are many, but most of them are in the nature of Government reports. Steller, "Beasts of the Sea," is the most valuable and interesting. It is in F. A. Golder and Leonard Stejneger, *Bering's Voyages,* vol. 2, New York, 1925, and in D. S. Jordan's *Fur Seals and Fur-Seal Islands,* Part 3, p. 210. Henry W. Elliott, *Our Arctic Province,* p. 127, has a description of the hunting. Edward W. Nelson, *Natural History Collections in Alaska, 1877-1881,* pp. 251-3, describes the animal and its habits.

[13] Letter of the Alaska Commercial Company, March 14, 1916, in Andrews Collection.

[14] *The Fisheries of Alaska,* p. 55, 1910, gives the catch for 1910.

[15] "Sea Otter, Forbidden To Kill," *Compiled Laws of Alaska,* Sec. 276, Chap. 4; Act, Aug. 24, 1912; Amendment Act, April 21, 1910. The sea otter has increased until the poachers are beginning to take them illegally. In 1935 eight skins were confiscated as contraband. *Alaska Seal and Fur-Seal Industries,* p. 62, 1935.

[16] *Report, Governor of Alaska, 1887,* pp. 31-4; *ibid.,* Appendix "A," pp. 41-8.

[17] "Fur-Seal and Other Fisheries of Alaska," *Fiftieth Congress, Second Session, H. R. Report 3883,* Gov't Ptg. Off., 1889.

22

The Rule of the Navy

[1] "The soldiers will have whiskey, and the Indians are equally fond of it. The free use of this by both soldiers and Indians, together with the other debaucheries between them, rapidly demoralizes both. "Colyer's Report," 1869; *ibid.*, statement of Williams, Appendix "B," p. 1007: "I look upon the different military posts in this department as disastrous and destructive." *Ibid.*, statement of E. J. Bailey, surgeon, U. S. A., Medical Director Department of Alaska, Appendix "E," p. 1023: "Their moral condition is low, and rendered worse by the proximity of the whites." *Ibid.*, statement of J. A. Tonner, Acting Assistant Surgeon, Appendix "E," p. 1024: "Within six months after the arrival of the troops at Sitka, the Medical Director informed me that nearly the whole of the Sitka tribe, some twelve hundred in number, were suffering from venereal diseases." *Ibid.*, statement of William S. Dodge, Appendix "M," p. 1030: "From a report of the Russian American Company on the sanitary condition of New Archangel and other posts from May 1, 1861, to May 1, 1862, it is learned . . . scorbutic and syphilitic diseases had almost entirely disappeared. In April, 1862, there was not a single case of the latter disease." Surgeon Rosse, *Report*, p. 17, Cutter *Corwin*, 1881; Tikhmenef, *Historical Sketch of the Russian American Company*, Part 2, p. 243.

[2] Report, M. P. Berry, Collector of Customs, Dist. of Alaska, Letter Files, July 10, 1877; "Report of Major John C. Tidball," *Ex. Doc. 5, Forty-Second Congress, First Session*, Appendix, states: "Indians, 365 men, 296 women, 260 children; total 921 in village Oct. 20, 1869. They stated 330 men, women and boys were absent hunting and fishing at that time."

"It is known by me, however, that De Ahna, after one day's experience as Collector of this District, did report to the Department, recommending the District be abolished." *Report of Wm. G. Morris, Special Agent, Treasury Department*, p. 41, Nov. 25, 1878.

[3] "Report, Commander L. A. Beardslee," p. 4, July 11, 1879; *Sen. Ex. Doc. 105, Forty-sixth Congress, Second Session*, p. 8, says: "The Indians entered the town."

[4] For the murder at Hot Springs and subsequent events, *see:* "Report Commander Beardslee," *op. cit.*, p. 4, p. 14 *et seq.*; for "Report, Capt. A'Court," *see* San Francisco *Chronicle*, March 18, 1879.

[5] *Ibid.*, p. 22 *et seq.*

[6] *Ibid.*, pp. 24 *et seq.*; the history of the case of Williams, or "Scotty," is given in some detail. *See* also court records, U. S. District Court, Deady, Judge.

[7] "Report, Commander Beardslee," *op. cit.*, p. 60.

[8] Among the killed at Wrangell was the "grandest Roman of them all," as John Muir termed Toyatte, a Christian chief of the Wrangell Indians. *See: Travels in Alaska* for Muir's account of his death. For Beardslee's account, *see: Sen. Ex. Doc. 71*, pp. 50 *et seq.*; S. Hall Young, *Autobiography*, pp. 221 *et seq.*, gives his version.

[9] John Muir, *Travels in Alaska*, p. 158; S. Hall Young, *Alaska Days with John Muir*, p. 114.

[10] William G. Morris, Letters, March 11, 1882; Customs Records of Alaska. The shaman was known as "One-Eyed Peter." Skondoo was another noted *Ekht*, or shaman, of the Thlingits.

[11] *Ibid.*, April 27, May 3, June 2, 1882.

[12] Veniaminof describes the practice in his works, *Letters about the Kolosh*, vol. 3, pp. 579 *et seq.*

Under U. S. dominion it has been practiced through all the years to some extent, but is dying out gradually, although in some of the villages it may still be found. For examples of it *see* "Morris, Report," p. 130, 1879; Morris, Letters, Customs Records of Alaska, 1882; "Cases at Klukwan," Skagway *Alaskan*, Feb. 11, 1902; "Cases at Hoonah," *ibid.*, Dec. 27, 1902; "Report, Commander Beardslee," *op. cit.*, Livingston F. Jones, *A Study of the Thlingits*, pp. 154 *et seq.*

[13] See William Ogilvie, *Early Days on the Yukon*, London and Toronto, 1913; MSS. Letter of Jack McQuesten, Andrews Collection.

[14] For Holt's crossing Chilkoot, or Dyea, Pass, 1872, *see: Geology Yukon Gold District*, U. S. G. S., Gov't Ptg. Off., 1898; *Alaska Coast Pilot*, p. 200, 1883.

[15] Fort Selkirk was captured and pillaged by the Chilkat and Chilkoot Indians in 1852; "Report of Geo. M. Dawson," *The Yukon Territory*, p. 349; Dall, *Alaska and Its Resources*, p. 115.

[16] Among those who crossed the pass in 1880 are Edmund Bean, Patrick McClinchey, Thomas Kiernan, Antone Marks, George Harkrader, John Lemon and others. McClinchey went over again in 1881. "Report, Commander Beardslee," *op. cit.*, gives a list of the names and the record of the crossing of the pass.

[17] "The Chilkats and the Chilkoots have for generations claimed the exclusive right to trade with the Stick Indians.... Their suspicion that Mr. Steele (who was not bound by promise) was endeavoring to establish the forbidden trade, had led them to appeal to me for assistance to prevent his doing so." "Report, Commander Beardslee, Sept. 1, 1880," *Boundary Case of the United States*, p. 371. In March, 1881, an expedition was made by G. C. Hanus, U. S. N., to Chilkoot to settle troubles between the natives. Of it he says: "Nearly all the trouble in this country is caused by hoochinoo, made from molasses." *Ibid.*, pp. 380, 381.

[18] Richard T. Harris and Joe Juneau discovered gold on Gold Creek in 1880. The mining district was organized by them Oct. 4, 1880. The first claim was filed by them on the same day. It is stated that they were grub-staked by George E. Pilz, of Sitka. Pilz was the first mining engineer in Alaska; in the Yukon in 1883, was in Fortymile in 1921. Biographical MS., George E. Pilz, 1921, copy, Andrews Collection. Pilz states that the Auk Indian, Kowee, was the real first discoverer of the gold. There are circumstances attached to the matter that indicate Kowee should be entitled to the credit of the discovery.

George E. Pilz was born in Saxony, 1845, was educated for a mining engineer, attended lectures given by Alexander von Humboldt at the Berlin University, mined coal near Leipzig, then came to America in 1867. From 1867 to 1877 he mined in California, Nevada, and Arizona. Then he went to Alaska through the influence of Nicholas Haley; and bought the Stewart, Haley, and Militid claims. He states that he outfitted Juneau and Harris for their prospecting when they discovered the mines at Juneau. Later he went to Dawson, down to Mexico and to South America, finally returning to Jack Wade Creek on the Fortymile. MS. George E. Pilz, copy in Andrews Collection.

[19] First export of canned salmon, 7,000 cases. "Morris Report," p. 115.

[20] If the white man had kept intoxicants out of the country there would have been little danger from the Indians. "From the first sergeant of a company down to the drummer boy, it may safely be said, a large number were either directly or indirectly interested in some soul-destroying still. . . . Following in the footsteps of the troops came the miners, who seem to have emulated the sons of Mars in the prosecution, performance, and mad riot of the quintessence of vicious enjoyment." "Morris Report," pp. 62, 63. Drinking, disease, and death took heavy toll, and no protection was afforded.

[21] Crime is low in proportion to the population in Alaska, especially murder and lynchings.

[22] For the destruction of Old Angoon, see "Morris Report," Customs Records of Alaska, Nov. 9, 1882.

Bitter feeling prevailed for many years among the Indians over the destruction of the houses. The Indians say that the soldiers looted the houses before the bombardment, and took quantities of blankets and furs. Over the door of Kah Chukte, a chief or the tribe, living in Killisnoo in 1892, was the legend:

> "Stores of furs and blankets pillaged
> By the 'Adams' pirate crew,
> Though Kah Chukte ever neutral,
> Dwelt afar from Hootznahoo."

Pilz says in his MSS.: "So Captain Berryman (Merriman, CLA,) steamed in front of the 'Hoochinoo' village, sent a squad of marines ashore to guard the back of the village and the gang of sailors on the beach to gather all the canoes and tie them together and send them adrift on Chatham Straits. Then he opened fire on the village with his small guns and two gatlings. Not being able to set it afire, he sent sailors again ashore to set fire to the whole village, and as it was in the fall when the Indians had all their winter supplies, consisting of dried salmon, fish, and seal-oil and whale blubber, the village made a fine bonfire, and everything was burned down." Pilz MSS., p. 18.

23

The Pioneers of the Yukon

[1] The account of the voyage is in *Narratives of Exploration,* War Department, p. 19, Gov't Ptg. Off., 1900. The *Youkon* was licensed in

Sitka as written here, but is generally known as the *Yukon,* and was still
running in 1886. Henry F. Allen, "Military Reconnaissance of the Copper
River," *Narratives of Exploration,* pp. 452 *et seq.* Finally it was put up
for the winter in a slough below Fort Yukon in the late eighties and sank
there. Moore, MS., Andrews Collection.

The *Youkon* was the first steamer on the waters of the river. A small
steamer, the *Wilder,* had been brought to St. Michael by the Western
Union Telegraph Company in 1866. It was run as far as Unalakleet, but
never went to the Yukon. Whymper, *Travels in the Territory of Alaska,*
New York, 1869; Dall, *Alaska, etc.,* p. 8.

² The names of the crew and of the fur traders on the boat were:
Captain Benjamin Hall, master; John R. Forbes, engineer; Frederick M.
Smith, superintendent; Ferdinand Westdahl, chief trader; Michael Labarge,
chief trader; John Godfrey, trader; Robert Bird, trader; Lewis B. Parrott,
Charles P. Raymond, John J. Major and Michael Foley, passengers. Two
traders, Robert and Moses (Moses Mercier?) were met with on the Yukon
near Fort Adams. *Narratives of Exploration,* pp. 21-22.

³ Mercier was at Fort Yukon in 1873. McQuesten, MSS., copy in
Andrews Collection. John Clark was stationed at Anvik, and Roberts at
Ft. Adams, near the mouth of the Tanana. *Narratives of Exploration,* p.
24. Ogilvie, *Early Days on the Yukon,* pp. 64-5, says Moses Mercier was
in charge at Ft. Yukon, then moved his post up to what he called Belle Isle
(now Eagle), "about 190 miles up the Yukon."

⁴ McQuesten, Al Mayo and J. McKniff were on the Hay River, Canada,
in 1871, and there first heard of the transfer of Alaska. They concluded
they would go to the Yukon River to look for gold. They arranged with
the agent for the Hudson's Bay Company to go by way of Peel River. In
the spring of 1873, A. Harper, G. Finch, and A. Gesler came down the
Nelson River from St. John on the Peace River. They all went down to
Fort Simpson. From there Harper and his party went on, while McQuesten
et al. stayed a month on business, then followed. At this place George
Nicholson joined them. They arrived at Fort Yukon in August, 1873.
MSS. Letter, L. N. (Jack) McQuesten to Albert McKay, July 1, 1905,
copy in Andrews Collection. The Alaska Commercial Co. states that
McQuesten was with them for eight years to 1882, thereafter was a free
or independent trader. *Fur-Seal Fisheries of Alaska,* p. 326. This arrange-
ment continued until about 1896. All traders on the Yukon had similar
arrangements. *See ibid.* In 1889 there were eight stations on the river: Fort
Reliance, Tanana, Novikakat, Nulato, Anvik, Mission, Andrievski, and
Kotlik. *Ibid.,* p. 380. The traders were A. Fredericks, A. Harper, L. N.
McQuesten, A. Mayo, A. Belkoff, G. Kokerine, John Beaudoin, Dennis
Belkof. *Ibid.,* p. 326. Stewart Menzies, MSS., Andrews Collection. Distances were estimated up and down the river from Fort Reliance, estab-
lished by McQuesten.

"To the best of my recollection, from conversations with Arthur
Harper, Jack McQuesten, and Al Mayo, the last mentioned gentleman
landed at Ft. Yukon, Sept. 3, 1873, in company with Jack McQuesten."
Stewart Menzies, MSS., Andrews Collection.

[5] McQuesten says 12 men, MS. Letter. Among them were Jos. Ladue, J. Rogers, and Joseph Paris. McQuesten, MSS., G. F. Spangenberg, Chas. Powell, Louis St. Louis, Pete Skogland, Tom Reynolds, Jim Miller, J. (?) Carr, came in over the pass in a party. Part of those who came left Tombstone, Arizona, with the Scheiffelin party. Geo. F. Spangenberg MSS., Andrews Collection. Schwatka mentions Scheiffelin at Nukluklayet, Allen, *Military Reconnaissance in Alaska*, Gov't Ptg. Off. 1885; *Narratives of Exploration*, p. 320.

[6] Scheiffelin sold the *New Racket* to McQuesten and Harper. Schwatka, *Narratives of Exploration*, p. 321; Stewart Menzies, MSS., April 14, 1916, p. 4. On the *New Racket* were Ed Scheiffelin, Eff Scheiffelin, Jack Young, Chas. Sowerby, and the engineer. Ed Scheiffelin was the founder of Tombstone, Arizona. Spangenberg, MSS.

[7] The Marks party consisted of Charles McConkey, Dick Poplin, and Ben Beach. George Marks, MS., Andrews Collection. Poplin went out over the Dyea Pass in 1884 and returned in 1885. McQuesten, MSS., p. 8.

[8] *Ibid.*, p. 8.

[9] *Ibid.*, p. 10.

[10] *Ibid.*, p. 10.

[11] Fortymile. *Ibid.*, p. 11. Sometimes called Shitando River. News of the strike was sent over the pass by George Williams, who volunteered to go, to notify McQuesten, in San Francisco, to buy more supplies. Williams froze on the trail so badly that he died at Dyea soon after arriving. An Indian carried him in. For a description of strike and output, Spurr, *Geology of the Yukon Gold District*, pp. 115 *et seq.*, U. S. Geological Survey.

[12] McQuesten, MSS., p. 12. Spurr, *op. cit.*, p. 117, says O. B. Miller discovered it in 1892.

[13] McQuesten, MSS., p. 12. Spurr, *op. cit.*, p. 118, says Pitka and Sorresco were Russian half-breeds. Ogilvie, *Early Days on the Yukon*, p. 67.

[14] *Narrative of Exploration*, pp. 285-323; Schwatka, *Summer in Alaska*, St. Louis, 1893; *Military Reconnaissance in Alaska*, Gov't Ptg. Off., 1885.

[15] Henry T. Allen, *Report of an Expedition to the Copper, Tanana, and Koyukuk Rivers*, Washington, D. C., 1887.

[16] *Fur-Seal Fisheries of Alaska*, p. 381.

[17] Dall, *Alaska and Its Resources*, pp. 501-2. At present there are probably more than fifty thousand muskrats and two thousand fox taken in the Kotzebue region, besides lynx, mink, ermine, and beaver.

For the work of Dr. Simpson, *see* "Search for Sir John Franklin," *Parliamentary Papers*, p. 91, 1852.

[18] For note on old trade trail from Kikiktarik to the mouth of Coleville River, *see* "Franklin Papers," pp. 905 *et seq.*, 1855.

[19] Lieut. George M. Stoney, *Naval Explorations in Alaska*, Annapolis, 1900.

[20] Lieut. Cantwell's report is in *Cruise of the "Corwin,"* for 1884, Gov't Ptg. Off., 1889; *Cruise of the "Corwin"* in 1885, Gov't Ptg. Off., 1887.

[21] The sources of information of the North are meagre. There are bits of history to be gathered from the records of the whalers, the explorers, the traders, the reports of the Bureau of Education, etc. These are: *The Voyage of the "Herald,"* 2 vols., London, 1853; Beechey, *Narrative,* 2 vols., London, 1831; *The Tents of the Tuski,* London, 1853; Collison, *Journal of H.M.S. "Enterprise"*; Knud Rasmussen, *Across Arctic America;* McClure, *Discovery of the Northwest Passage,* London, 1865; Thomas Simpson, *Narrative of Discoveries,* London, 1843; *U. S. Geological Survey Reports;* Bull, *Geology and Mineral Resources of N.W. Alaska,* 1930, etc.

[22] The date of Mrs. Bean's murder is not given, but it was first reported by Captain Bailey in his "Report, 1880," *Revenue Service,* p. 16. See: *Bureau of Education Report,* 1896-7; Schwatka, *Narratives of Exploration,* p. 347; Allen, *op. cit.; Narratives of Exploration,* p. 452.

[23] MSS., Captain W. D. Moore, U. of W. Library Collection. Captain Moore and "Jack" McQuesten were both present at the trial.

24

Missions and Schools

[1] A well-developed trade in contraband in whiskey and opium flourished, and its membership was hard to trace. One seizure of thirty-eight thousand dollars in value was made. An inquiry concerning some detail, of one who knew, in recent years, elicited the answer, "Better to let sleeping dogs lie." E. R. Scidmore, *Appleton's Guide to Alaska,* p. 65; B. C. *Daily Colonist,* Jan. 19, 1886; Lewis and Dryden, *Marine History of the Pacific,* p. 209.

[2] The different voyagers of early companies gave shares to different dignitaries of Church and State. *See* Bancroft, *History of Alaska,* p. 186.

[3] The Rev. John G. Brady and Miss Fannie Kellogg founded the Sitka Mission, April 11, 1878. The Rev. Brady was afterward the fifth Governor of Alaska.

The Wrangell Mission was established by Mrs. A. R. McFarland, a missionary worker, under direction of Dr. Sheldon Jackson. They arrived at Wrangell, August 10, 1877.

[4] *The Presbyterian Church in Alaska, Its Rise and Progress,* p. 5, Washington, 1886; *Reports of Bureau of Education for Alaska;* Sheldon Jackson, *Alaska,* pp. 202 *et seq.;* Mrs. Eugene Willard, *Life in Alaska,* pp. 13 *et seq.;* Julia McNair Wright, *Among the Alaskans,* pp. 163 *et seq.*

[5] *The Presbyterian Church in Alaska,* p. 5.

[6] *Reports of Bureau of Education for Alaska,* 1887, p. 4, gives seven schools established.

[7] *Ibid.,* 1886, pp. 53 *et seq.* Allen, "Military Reconnaissance of the

Copper River," *Narratives of Explorations,* War Department, pp. 481, 415. Sims died at Rampart House May 25, 1885, and was buried there. Hudson Stuck, *Voyages on the Yukon,* p. 236. McDonald is said to have made a translation of the Bible into the native language. He returned to the Mackenzie in later years. *Ibid.,* pp. 85-6. He discovered gold on the Yukon in 1862-3. Ogilvie, *Early Days on the Yukon,* pp. 86-7.

[8] *Report of Bureau of Education for Alaska,* 1886, Appendix 1, pp. 55 *et seq.*

[9] It is said that the first Catholic missionary went to the Yukon in 1871, Juneau Empire, 1916, Dev. Ed.

[10] *Report, Governor of Alaska,* 1885, p. 4.

[11] *Report of Bureau of Education for Alaska,* 1886, pp. 79 *et seq.,* Appendix K. An old Indian woman wanted to sell a girl to a miner or trader; the court ordered the girl delivered to the woman. *Ibid.,* p. 80.

[12] *Report of Bureau of Education for Alaska,* 1885-6; Sitka *Alaskan,* Jan. 29, 1887, and *Education in Alaska,* 1894-5, p. 1432. Town of Saxman named for Prof. Saxman.

[13] *Report of Bureau of Education for Alaska,* 1893-4, pp. 1451 *et seq.*

[14] *Report of Bureau of Education for Alaska,* 1899, p. 1386.

[15] For the progress of the Metlakatla community, *see* John W. Arctander, *The Apostle of Alaska;* Henry S. Wellcome, *The Story of Metlakatla; Reports of Bureau of Education for Alaska.*

[16] Among the new books of this time were: Eliza Ruhama Scidmore, *Alaska and the Sitkan Archipelago;* Charles Hallock, *Our New Alaska,* 1886; Edward Perrepont, *Fifth Avenue to Alaska,* 1885; H. W. Seton Karr, *Shores and Alps of Alaska,* 1887; Henry W. Elliott, *Our Arctic Province,* 1887.

[17] Statement of I. C. Dennis, "Morris, Report," p. 153, *Ex. Doc., Forty-Fifth Congress, Third Session, H. R.*

25

The Fight for a Government

[1] The first law on townsites was passed in 1891, Mar. 3, *Compiled Laws,* Sec. 85, but it was not until 1900 that actual title could be secured. A law was made in 1891, but was not satisfactory, *Comp. Laws,* Sec. 90. Another provision was enacted Mar. 14, 1898, *Comp. Laws,* Sec. 92. The mining laws were extended in the law of June 6, 1900, *see: Charlton Code,* p. 73; a civil code was also passed, the *Carter Code, see: Charlton Code,* p. 65.

[2] "Colyer, Report," *Report of the Secretary of Interior for 1869-70; Alaska Times; Ex. Doc. 5, Forty-second Congress, First Session;* San Francisco *Evening Bulletin,* San Francisco, Oct. 21, 1879; I. C. Dennis in "Morris, Report," p. 153 of Appendix.

[3] Forts were placed at Kodiak and Kenai, where for over half a century there had not been a suspicion of a difficulty with inoffensive Aleuts, and

they were abandoned within about two years. At Wrangell a fort was built in 1868-70, occupied, then abandoned in 1870, reoccupied in 1875, abandoned June 11, 1877. For the treatment of the Aleuts by the soldiers *see* description of the little girl crying at the door of the house while the drunken soldiers abused the mother inside. "Colyer, Report," *loc. cit.,* p. 985.

[4] Receipts and expenditures of the Government relating to seal fisheries of Alaska, 1871-1887, as follows:

Receipts from tax on seal skins and rental $5,028,536.50
Sales of skins by Government agents, 1874 .... 29,529.17
Forfeitures of skins unlawfully taken, 1886 .... 1,000.00

$5,059,065.67

Expenditures:
Buildings at Seal Islands, 1872 .... $ 6,000.00
Collecting information concerning 787.51
Salaries and Expenses, 1876-1887 ....   129,305.81
Protection sea otter and seal 163,808.62
Net profit 4,759,163.73

$5,059,065.67

Fur-Seal Fisheries, p. 415, 1889.

[5] In 1888 the Alaska Commercial Co., "on the Karluk River packed 101,000 cases of 48-one-pound cans each ... over 1,200,000 blue-backs or red salmon." "Report, Joseph Murray," *Seal and Salmon Fisheries,* p. 424, 1889.

[6] The Rock Springs massacre in Wyoming, also Chinese riots in Los Angeles, Cal., 1871; S. F. *Evening Bulletin,* Oct. 25, 1871.

[7] *Seal and Salmon Fisheries,* vol. 1, p. 5.

[8] *House Journal, Forty-seventh Congress, First Session.*

[9] "Morris, Report," p. 123; *House Report 560, Part 2, Forty-seventh Congress, First Session.*

[10] The minority report of the committee said: "We know of no other way in which Congress can be informed concerning the business affairs and governmental interests, than by permitting it to be represented. . . . We therefore recommend the passage of the bill as reported by the Committee, with the provisions for Delegate." *House Journal, Forty-seventh Congress, First Session.*

[11] *The Presbyterian Church in Alaska, Its Rise and Progress,* pp. 2, 3.

[12] Bancroft, *History of the United States,* vol. 1, pp. 239, 244, 246, New York, 1868. He says: "The charter plainly gave legislative power to the whole body of the freemen," etc.

[13] Andrew T. Lewis was the clerk of the court; Munson C. Hillyer, U. S. Marshal; Edward W. Haskett, District Attorney. Arthur K. Delaney, *Alaska Bar Association and Sketch of the Judiciary;* Andrew T. Lewis, MSS., Andrews Collection; Bancroft, *History of Alaska,* p. 728; Jeannette Paddock Nichols, *Alaska,* Cleveland, Ohio, 1924. The Oregon

Code was adopted for law, thus using a statute of a State for a Territory over one thousand miles distant.

The granting of the measure of government for Alaska was owing to the untiring efforts of Sheldon Jackson, General Agent of Education for Alaska.

[14] The first miners' meeting held in the Territory is said to have been in the "Flag of All Nations," to frame mining laws for Juneau District in 1881. *Alaska Morning Record* (Special mining number), 1898.

There is understood to have been a miners' meeting held in 1880 when Juneau and Harris named the mining district and the townsite. A meeting was held about 1881 to draft mining laws, held in the house of P. McClinchy, date not given. At an adjourned meeting, Feb. 28, a meeting was held at the house of William Newcomer. Delaney and Gamel, *Mining Laws, Harris Mining District*, Juneau.

[15] Delegates sent: Mottram D. Ball, 1878; Miner W. Bruce and C. W. Garside, 1889; James Carroll, 1890; T. S. Nowell, 1894; J. G. Price, 1899; J. W. Ivey, 1902.

[16] J. P. Nichols, *Alaska Under the Rule of the United States*, Cleveland, 1924.

[17] "Sec. 14, of the act of May 17, 1884, prohibits the importation, manufacture, and sale of intoxicating liquors in Alaska, excepting for medicinal, mechanical, and scientific purposes." *Report, Governor of Alaska, 1888*, p. 49.

[18] *Census Report, Ivan Petrof, 1880.*

[19] Mail routes in Alaska: Only two. *Report, Governor of Alaska, 1888*, pp. 48-9.

[20] "Establishment of Education," *Report for Alaska, 1894-5, Interior Department*, p. 1451; "Decennary Review" of Dr. Sheldon Jackson.

In 1869 Vincent Collier recommended appropriation of $100,000.00 for education.

In 1870 John Eaton, Commr. of Ed., asked for appropriation of $100,000.00.

In 1882 President Arthur recommended an appropriation of $50,000.00.

In 1883 thousands of circulars were sent out asking for education and government. *Report of Bureau of Education*," pp. 1143-7.

26

The Progress of Thirty Years

[1] "Mineral Resources of Alaska," U. S. *Geological Survey Bulletin 714*, p. 61, 1919.

[2] *Report, Governor of Alaska, 1897*, p. 26; *ibid.*, p. 22.

[3] *Report, Fisheries of Alaska, 1897*, Bureau of Fisheries, p. 17.

[4] *Report, Governor of Alaska, 1896*, p. 11; *ibid.*, p. 44.

[5] "Report, Captain Hooper, R. C. Service," *Sea Otter Banks of Alaska*, p. 16, 1897. Also *see: Report, Fisheries of Alaska, 1907*, pp. 31-2.

[6] *Fur Seals and Fur-Seal Fisheries, 1896-7*, p. 149.

[7] *Report, Census, 1890*, p. 255; *Report, Fisheries of Alaska, 1905*, pp. 31-2. This latter reference includes the pelagic sealing.

[8] George C. Pilz, first mining engineer at Sitka after the transfer, claims to have outfitted Juneau and Harris, who are understood to have made the discovery, and who established the town of Juneau. They were from Sitka. MSS. of George E. Pilz, copies in Andrews Collection; *Alaska Mining Record*, Feb., 1895, Juneau, Alaska, copy in Andrews Collection. Pilz states that the Auk chief, Kowee, was the actual discoverer of the gold.

[9] *Report, Governor of Alaska, 1886;* The Sitka *Alaskan*, Dec. 25, 1886.

[10] Cession Papers, Russian America, *Ex. Doc. 177, Fortieth Congress, Second Session*, H.R.

[11] The *Reliance* was ordered to Kotzebue Sound, April 18, 1870. *Fur Seal Arbitration*, vol. 8, p. 392, Washington, D. C., 1895. The captain was ordered to "keep a very accurate journal of everything transpiring on this voyage."

[12] The early work of the Geological Survey is in *U. S. Geological Survey Bulletin 84;* "St. Elias Expedition," *Thirteenth Annual Report, U. S. Geological Survey; Seventeenth Annual Report U. S. Geological Survey*, Part 1; *Eighteenth Annual Report, U. S. Geological Survey*, Part 3; *Geology of the Yukon Gold District*, 1897; "Glacier Bay," *Thirteenth Annual Report, loc. cit.*, Part 1; H. F. Reid in *National Geographic Magazine*, March 21, 1882.

[13] Gold was first found in the Cook Inlet region in 1888 by George Palmer, on Palmer Creek. The production of the region has been perhaps $2,000,000 to the present time.

[14] A. E. Nordenskiold, *Voyage of the "Vega,"* New York, 1882.

[15] *Report, Governor of Alaska, 1892;* thirteen steam vessels are listed in U. S. Customs Office Reports for District of Alaska.

[16] *List of Merchant Vessels in U. S., 1899*. The *Youkon*, the first steamer on the river, was laid up for the winter below Fort Yukon, frozen to the bottom. When the water rose in the spring, the ship filled and became a total wreck. Letter, Captain W. D. Moore, Andrews Collection.

[17] Alaska *Times*, May 14, 1869.

[18] *Report, Governor of Alaska, 1892*, pp. 49-50.

[19] The first lights, or lighthouses, recorded in the *Light List of the Pacific Coast*, 1914, are of 1902: Mitkof Island, Five Fingers Island, Sentinel Island, and Killisnoo. The Castle, where the first light shone, was burned in 1894.

[20] "Dixon's Entrance to Yakutat Bay," *Pacific Coast Pilot of Alaska*, Third Ed., Part 1, Gov't Ptg. Off., 1891.

[21] Letters of Collector, Customs Records, Alaska.

[22] "Report, Commander L. A. Beardslee," *Sen. Ex. Doc. 71*, March 3, 1880; *ibid.*, January, 1882.

[23] *Report of Bureau of Education for Alaska*, 1890.

[24] *Preliminary Report of the General Agent of Education for Alaska, 1896-7*, pp. 1613-15, Gov't Ptg. Off., 1897.

[25] *Rules and Regulations, Reindeer Service*, 1907.

[26] "Introduction of Reindeer into Alaska," *Preliminary Report of the General Agent of Education for Alaska*, Gov't Ptg. Off., 1890.

[27] *Report of Bureau of Education for Alaska*, 1890.

[28] *Rules and Regulations, Reindeer Service*, approved by the Secretary of the Interior, June 10, 1907.

[29] *Report of Bureau of Education for Alaska*, 1896-7, p. 1630.

[30] First base line surveyed in 1905. *Report, Governor of Alaska, 1905*.

[31] Captain James Carroll, of the Pacific Coast S.S. Co., was one of the outstanding characters of the time. He was reputed to have been connected with sundry matters, of which one of his friends remarked, upon inquiry, "Better to let sleeping dogs lie." He was, however, one of the capable men of that time in Alaska. The Sitka *Alaskan*, May 23, 1891.

[32] The mails to and from the Yukon by way of the Dyea Pass were carried privately by the miners, often at a cost of $1.00 for each letter. It is stated that there were one thousand miners in the Yukon Valley in 1895. The Sitka *Alaskan*, August 24, 1895.

[33] *Report of Bureau of Education for Alaska*, 1896-7.

[34] "The Fur-Seal and Other Fisheries of Alaska," *Ex. Doc. 3883, Fiftieth Congress, Second Session, H.R.*

[35] Nichols, *Alaska Under the Rule of the United States*, Cleveland, 1924; Clark, *History of Alaska*, New York, 1930.

27

Following the Lure of Gold

[1] John F. Miller, C. F. Treat, Ronald M. Crawford, Black Sullivan, and others landed from the *Mexico* at Dyea, March 29, 1897. Dawson *Daily News*, April 11, 1901; Dawson *Nugget*, May 28, 1897. Crawford and Treat reached Dawson, May 28.

[2] Seattle *Post-Intelligencer*, July 17, 1897.

[3] There were many books published describing the gold rush to the Klondike. Perhaps the best of them is that of Tappan Adney, *The Klondike Stampede*, Harper Bros., New York, 1900. Among others are: Ogilvie, *The Klondike Official Guide*, 1898; Palmer, *In the Klondike*, New York, 1899; Haskell, *Two Years in the Klondike*, Hartford, 1898. Twenty thousand people are estimated to have been in Dawson and on the surrounding creeks during the height of the working of the mines. A pictorial presentation of the scenes on the trails is contained in Frank

LaRoche's *Klondike, A Series of Photographic Views*, W. B. Conkey & Co., 1898.

[4] In the last days of July, 1897, the first boats of the stampede landed at Skagway and Dyea. On October 21 Skagway "had grown from a concourse of tents to a fair-sized town, with well-laid-out streets and numerous frame buildings, stores, saloons, gambling houses, dance houses, and a population of about 2000." Three wharves were nearly completed, and a wagon road was begun. *Report, Northwest Mounted Police*, 1897, p. 26.

[5] The Sitka *Alaskan*, June 26, 1886. He died August 31, 1916. *All Alaska Review*, Nov. 16, 1916. *"Skookum"* means "strong" in the Chinook Indian dialect.

[6] Ogilvie paid ten cents a pound in 1887. *The Klondike Official Guide*, p. 17. Adney, *The Klondike Stampede*, p. 83, says: "A little while ago . . . twenty cents a pound, then twenty-five cents. . . . Just now $650 was paid for 1000 pounds." This was August 25. Later it as one dollar a pound from Dyea to Lindeman.

[7] The White Pass had been little traveled before 1897, as most of the travel went by the Indian trail over the Chilkoot, or Dyea, Pass. From Skagway to Bennett is about forty miles by trail, from Dyea to the same place, where the trails joined at the lake is about thirty miles.

[8] Keeler's pawnshop was one of the show places of Skagway. His advertisement read, "Keeler, The Money King, Barrels of Money."

[9] The Skagway *News*, M. L. Sherpy, editor and proprietor. Across the top of the first page was the legend in red ink, "The nearest newspaper to the Klondike Gold Fields." Andrews Collection.

[10] Inspector Steele says of Skagway at this time, "Little better than a hell on earth." *Report, Northwest Mounted Police*, 1898, p. 4.

[11] The first Commissioner at Dyea was John U. Smith, which is sufficient recommendation. The first marshal was killed by a barkeeper named Fay. *Stikine River Journal*, Wrangell, Alaska, Feb. 5, 1898. For a civil authority in the Yukon *see* Ray's Report in *Narratives of Exploration, War Dept.*, p. 547, 1899.

[12] Inspector Constantine was sent to Fortymile, Fort Constantine, in 1895. Hayne and Taylor, *The Pioneers of the Yukon*, London, 1897; Ogilvie, *Guide to the Yukon*, p. 12.

[13] Skagway *Weekly News*, file, Andrews Collection; *Alaska-Yukon Magazine*, September, 1908, p. 409.

[14] Major Walsh; Inspectors Norwood and McGregor, Inspector Scarth and nineteen men; N. W. M. P. Inspector Harper with twenty men; Inspector Strickland with five men; Inspector Wood and ten men. *Report, Northwest Mounted Police*, 1897; *ibid.*, 1898, pp. 32 *et seq.*; pp. 67 *et seq.*; p. 74. Judge McGuire, Crown Prosecutor Wade, and a party went to Dawson on October 30, 1897. "Report, Inspector Strickland," *ibid.*, p. 82.

[15] No steamers were on the upper river during 1897. The number of

small boats going down in 1897 is not recorded. "Six to ten boats are leaving daily." Adney, *The Klondike Stampede*, p. 120.

[16] The Chilkoot Railroad and Transport Company began work on the tramway in December, 1897. Z. T. Wood, *Report, Northwest Mounted Police*, 1898.

[17] There were estimated to be thirty-five hundred people on the trail to the Copper River, en route for the Klondike in 1898, according to the report of Captain W. R. Abercrombie. *Narratives of Exploration, War Dept.*, p. 588.

28

St. Michael and the Yukon

[1] Seattle *Post-Intelligencer*, July 16, 1897.

[2] The *Portland* left Seattle July 21; the *Cleveland* left San Francisco on July 23; the *Eliza Anderson* on August 11; the *Humboldt* on August 13. The *Politofski* and others followed. *Ibid.*, files; Seattle *Times*, files.

[3] One agent escaped and left for Seattle on the *Charles Nelson*. Seattle *Post-Intelligencer*, files, Sept. 11, 1897. "Report of Captain P. H. Ray, U.S.A.," *Narratives of Exploration, War Dept.*, p. 522, 1899. "Report of Lieut. W. P. Richardson," *ibid.*, p. 522.

[4] "Report of Captain Ray," *ibid.*, pp. 519-560.

[5] *Report, Northwest Mounted Police*, 1897, p. 309. The police in Dawson had a very effective custom of putting offenders on the woodpile to saw wood. "Report of Captain Ray," *Narratives of Exploration*, p. 547.

[6] *Ibid.*, p. 531; statements of personal witnesses; Adney, *The Klondike Stampede*, p. 191; "Report, Sam C. Dunham," *Department of Labor Bulletin No. 16*, p. 366.

[7] Telegram, Portland Chamber of Commerce, Nov. 29, 1897; "Report, E. H. Wells," *Narratives of Exploration*, pp. 511 *et seq.*

[8] "Introduction of Domestic Reindeer into Alaska," Gov't Ptg. Off., 1898.

[9] The deer were gelded sled deer. The moss brought for food was exhausted. Many died at Haines; the remainder were driven up the Chilkat River to the divide where the moss grew. There they were recruited during the summer, then driven by way of Dawson and Circle to the mouth of the Tanana River where they were sold to a mission. These deer form no part of the reindeer herds of Alaska at this time. *See ibid.*

[10] "Report, Captain Ray," *Narratives of Exploration*, pp. 543 *et seq.* Notes from eyewitnesses E. L. Range and O. F. Horn.

[11] "Report, Captain Ray," *loc. cit.*

[12] Statements of witnesses present. Notes and MSS. in Andrews Collection.

29

The Trails of Ninety-eight

[1] "Report, Supt. Wood," *Northwest Mounted Police*, 1898, p. 37. The Dyea Pass was sometimes called the Poor Man's Pass because a man could pack his outfit over it himself. *Ibid.*, p. 90.

[2] Seattle *Post-Intelligencer*, May 28, 1898, p. 7.

[3] Fifty-four bodies were recovered within a few days, two others when the snow melted in the spring. *Dyea Trail Newspaper*, April 4, 1898, Spl. Ed., Andrews Collection; *Report, Northwest Mounted Police*, 1898, p. 90.

[4] *Ibid.*, p. 39; Skagway *Alaskan*, August 9, 1898.

[5] The *A. J. Goddard* was built on the lake at Bennett, and was the first steamboat to pass down the river. *Report, Northwest Mounted Police*, 1898, pp. 83-4. The *Goddard* and the *Kilbourne* were built by the Upper Yukon Co.; the *Ora, Flora,* and *Nora* by the Bennett Lake and Klondike Nav. Co.; the *Olive May* by the Kerry Mill Co. *See* also: *Alaska-Yukon Gold Book*, p. 33; "Report, Supt. Steele," *Northwest Mounted Police*, 1898, p. 17.

[6] The first sawmill was at Bennett in 1897, capacity about one thousand feet per day, lumber $70 per M., "Report, Insp. Scarth," *Northwest Mounted Police*, 1897, p. 147. In 1898 the Kerry Mill Co. had a small mill on Lake Nares, J. R. Kerry had one on the same lake, and Racine's mill was at head of Windy Arm. *Report, Northwest Mounted Police*, 1898, p. 84.

[7] Seattle *Post-Intelligencer*, July 18, July 20, and July 26, 1898.

[8] The *F. K. Gustin*, the *D. R. Campbell*, the *Mary E. Graff*, the *Oil City*, the *J. P. Light*, and others were of this fleet. Seattle *Post-Intelligencer*, July 23, 1898, p. 12. Nearly all these steamers were lying on the ways at St. Michael in 1923—a veritable boneyard of ships.

[9] Seattle *Post-Intelligencer*, June 6, 1898. The *Laurada* was later wrecked in the Bering Sea.

[10] *Ibid.*, July 11, 1898.

[11] The *Guardian, Helen, Penelope, Northern Light, Leslie D, Catherine Sudden,* and others went to Kotzebue. The *Jane Grey* foundered at sea with the loss of thirty-four people. *Ibid.*, June 12, 1898; Grinnell, *Gold Hunting in Alaska*, p. 12.

[12] Captain Abercrombie, Captain E. F. Glenn, Lieut. Castner, and others made the explorations in the Copper River region. *See: Narratives of Exploration, War Dept.*, 1899. *Ibid.*, p. 589. From the Copper River country 306 men were fed by the army at Liscum. In August-October, 1898, 121 men were carried out free by the Pacific Steam Whaling Co., and 185 went out second class at $5.00 to $25.00. The Christian Endeavor built a refuge station on the glacier during the winter. Seattle *Post Intelligencer* files, 1898.

[13] *Ibid.*, advertisement, May 5, 1898.

[14] Willis Thorp and F. P. Kendall took ninety head of cattle by the Dalton Trail. *Ibid.*, Sept. 3, 1897. *Alaska Mining Record*, Feb. 10.

[15] *Reindeer Report*, 1898, p. 41.

[16] Seattle *Post-Intelligencer*, June 28, 1898; *ibid.*, May 24, 1898.

[17] "Report of Supt. Steele," *Northwest Mounted Police*, 1898, pp. 18, 21-2.

[18] *Ibid.*, p. 21.

30

"Soapy" Smith and His Gang

[1] S. H. Graves, *On the White Pass Payroll*, p. 16.

[2] The letters appeared in the *Alaska-Yukon Magazine* in two numbers: Dec., 1907, and Jan., 1908, then suddenly stopped without an excuse, evidently leaving many unpublished. Marshal Tanner states that the letters were stolen from him. MSS. notes by J. M. Tanner, who made most of the arrests, and afterward was appointed U. S. Marshal for the division.

[3] *Alaska-Yukon Magazine*, Jan., 1908, p. 386. Marshal Rowan was killed by Fay, a barkeeper, and his successor was considered an accomplice of the outlaws.

[4] *Ibid.*, p. 387; *Alaska Miner*, March 12, 1898.

[5] The Tanner MSS. state: "The Committee sent nine out of town on the British boat *Tartar*, among them being the New York *World* reporter and the editor of the *Daily Alaskan.*"

[6] Frank H. Reid came to Oregon from Minnesota and taught school in Linn County in 1877. The writer was one of his pupils. In 1878 he enlisted in Mart Brown's Company of Volunteers for the Piute Indian War and served through that campaign. From Oregon he went to Washington, and from there to Alaska in 1897. He was a civil engineer and surveyed the town plat of Skagway.

[7] Skagway *Alaskan*, July 12, 1898; the Tanner MSS.; Court Records of Skagway and Sitka. Case No. 1014 and Case No. 1015 Com. Ct., Skagway.

[8] Many original sources have been consulted for the data for this account, but they could not be used in detail. Tanner MSS.; *Stikine Journal*, files; The Sitka *Alaskan*, files; personal statements of: Dr. F. B. Whiting, attending physician; E. R. Peoples, undertaker; Theodore Johnson, O. J. Laird, W. J. Rogers, and other witnesses.

Bowers, Foster, and "Old Tripp" were given jail sentences of one year each at Sitka, while Turner Jackson went to McNeill's Island, and Bronson's case was found "not a true bill."

"Soapy's" name was Jefferson R. Smith. His wife came out from St. Louis after his death to inquire regarding the tragedy and financial matters relating to the estate.

A cross, made of tin discs nailed to the boards of the dock was placed by two women at the spot where the shooting occurred, and the discs of same were carried away, one by one, by souvenir collectors, and finally it is said that one of the collectors took the wooden headboard from "Soapy's" grave.

31

The Building of the White Pass Railway

[1] E. C. Hawkins was Chief Engineer and General Manager. John Hislop and Alfred Williams were Assistant Engineers; Hislop was accidentally killed at Chicago soon after the completion of the railway. Hawkins and Williams were afterward engaged in the building of the Copper River & Northwestern Railway. Mr. Hawkins died in New York, April 9, 1912, aged 51 years. Mr. Williams passed on in Seattle, Washington, November 13, 1913.

[2] Seattle *Post-Intelligencer*, July 27, 1898, p. 12.

[3] The Pacific & Arctic Ry. & Nav. Co., in U. S. Territory, the British Columbia and Yukon in British Columbia, and the British Yukon Railroad in Yukon Territory, 110.4 miles total. It was financed by Close Bros.

[4] Michael John Heney died in 1910. *Alaska-Yukon Magazine*, Nov., 1910.

[5] At Skagway, Corporal D'Amour, with his scarlet coat, shiny boots, and riding crop, paraded the docks each morning.

[6] *The Joint Report of the Commissioners on the Boundary* was made Dec. 31, 1895. When the railroad builders reached the summit with the construction they were halted and told that they could go no farther, as that was British territory. Graves, *On the White Pass Payroll*, p. 30.

The local story is that Heney sent "Stikine Bill" as an ambassador to the summit, where the guard was pacing a beat to stop the workers. Bill took a bottle of "Scotch" in each coat pocket, and a box of cigars under each arm. When the guard woke up a day or so later the construction gang was working a mile down the shore of the lake.

[7] Skagway *Alaskan*, Feb. 21, 1899.

[8] *Alaska Weekly*, annual list of pioneers who cross the Divide.

32

The Golden Sands of Nome

[1] The revenue cutter *Reliance* was the first to enter the Arctic Ocean, going under orders of May, 1870. *Fur Seal Arbitration*, vol. 8, p. 391.

[2] *The Yukon Territory*, p. 95, Ottawa, 1926.

[3] A party including D. B. Libby, who had been with the Western Union Telegraph Russian Extension of 1866, L. S. Melsing, A. P. Mordaunt, and H. L. Blake discovered gold in Ophir Creek in March, 1898, but the discovery that attracted the attention of the world was that of Lindeberg *et al.*, in September. Lindeberg was a reindeer herder brought from Norway, and who left the Government service the day after reaching St. Michael. Lindbloom was a sailor who had deserted from the bark *Alaska*, whaling in those waters. Brynteson was a Swedish miner. *U. S. Geological Survey Bulletin 328*, p. 17.

[4] E. S. Harrison, *Nome and The Seward Peninsula*, p. 51.

[5] Judge William B. Morrow, "The Spoilers," *California Law Review*, January, 1916, p. 99; Harrison, *op. cit.*, p. 51.

[6] *Ibid.*, p. 52.

[7] S. C. Dunham, *The Goldsmith of Nome*, p. 46, says: "The landscape from sea-beach to skyline was staked. . . . "

[8] Harrison, *op. cit.*, p. 51.

[9] A man, going up on a steamer, carried a garden rake and a sugar sack. Being asked what they were to be used for, he replied: "To rake up the nuggets, and the sack to carry them."

[10] Morrow, *op. cit.*, pp. 89 *et seq.*; Rex Beach, *The Spoilers*.

[11] H. L. French, *Seward's Land of Gold*, p. 16. The storm tore away a corner of the graveyard on Belmont's Point and dragged the frozen bodies out into the sea. A similar storm followed ten years later.

[12] Esther Birdsall Darling, *The Great Dog Races of Nome*, 1916; Darling, *Baldy of Nome*; Lafe Spray, "The Arctic Derby," *Alaska-Yukon Magazine*, June, 1910.

[13] "The Gold Placers of the Seward Peninsula," *U. S. Geological Survey Bulletin 328*, pp. 16 *et seq.*; Lanier McKee, *The Land of Nome*; "The Yukon and Nome Gold Regions," *Department of Labor Bulletin No. 29*, 1900; *Reconnaissance of the Cape Nome, etc., Gold Fields*, U. S. Geological Survey, Washington, D. C.

[14] "The Future of Alaska Mining," *U. S. Geological Survey Bulletin 714A*, p. 10. Captain Smith's colony nearly starved in the fertile state of Virginia. LaSalle's colony perished in bountiful Texas. They did not know the riches that lay around them, nor how to get them.

33

Fairbanks—In Alaska's Golden Heart

[1] "Report, Lieut. Castner," *Narratives of Exploration, War Dept.*, p. 692.

[2] "Geology of the Fairbanks District," *U. S. Geological Survey Bulletin 525*, p. 86.

[3] Captain Sam Lancaster, of the steamer *Louise*, says that this statement is incorrect; that the earnings of the *Isom* are exaggerated; and further, that she got stuck on the flats on her maiden voyage and would not have reached Dawson in that season had not the *Susie* and the *Sarah* gone to her rescue and pulled her off.

[4] "Colors" are the fine grains of gold that lie in the sand and will show in "panning" or washing the earth in a gold pan, when all other material is washed out.

[5] Statements of the amount of gold mined, and amount remaining in the gravels is in *U. S. Geological Survey Bulletin 714*, 1921, and in subsequent years in the "Mineral Resources of Alaska," *ibid.*

[6] The *U. S. Geological Survey Bulletins for Alaska* are the authority on the mineral production. The *U. S. Department of Agriculture Reports* give the agricultural progress. The publications of the Alaska Agricultural College and School of Mines give local information, as do the files of such newspapers as the Fairbanks *Times, Farthest North Collegian*, Fairbanks *News*, Tanana *Daily Miner*, and Fairbanks *Daily News Miner*. The *Hearings of the House of Representatives* tell of the struggles for roads and railways.

34

Copper, Coal, and Railways

[1] "Nicolai's house is supposed to be in the heart of the mineral region, and by him we were shown the locality of a vein which at that season of the year, April, was above the snow-line." "He had bullets of copper in his possession." Lieut. Allen, *Reconnaissance in Alaska*, p. 158. Millard, McClellan, McCarthy, Gates, and McNeer were the first discoverers. Valdez *Prospector*, Mining Edition, January 15, 1909.

[2] In 1916 there were 617,264 tons of ore valued at $29,484,291 mined in Alaska, most of which came from the properties of the Kennicott group. Alfred H. Brooks, *The Alaska Mining Industry in 1919*, p. 69. Over four times the cost of the whole Territory from one copper mine in one year.

Bogenoff ascended the Copper River for one hundred and fifty miles before 1805. Lisianski, *Voyage Round the World, 1803-1806*, p. 188.

[3] "A bell was cast by our Shaposhnikof for the church here of weight 5 *poods* 3 *funt* (203 lbs)." "About the American copper here it has been my intention to gather it on the Copper River; but to the present time the Lebedef people have prevented and I do not know when it will be better." Letter, Baranof to Shelekof, May 20, 1795. Tikhmenef, *Historical Sketch of the Russian American Company*, Part 2, p. 94, Appendix.

The first shipment of copper from Alaska was from the Baronovich Mine at Kasaan Bay in 1880. *U. S. Geological Survey Bulletin* 642, p. 18.

[4] The size of these sheets, called *tows*, was about fifteen by twenty-six feet, according to the *Coast Pilot of Alaska*, p. 36, 1869. Scidmore, *Appleton's Guide to Alaska*, p. 46. One is occasionally seen to the present time.

[5] "Viewing the Copper River Spectacle," *Alaska-Yukon Magazine*, October, 1910, p. 1; "The Winter's Crucial Battle on Copper River," *op. cit.*, June, 1910, p. 27.

[6] *See* Rex Beach, *The Iron Trail*, for the story of the war of the railways; "Alaska Pacific and Terminal Co. Hearing," *H.R. Hearings, Sixtieth Congress, First Session*, p. 20.

[7] Mr. G. W. Perkins, of the Morgan branch of the Alaska Syndicate, came to Alaska in 1909. "Speech of James Wickersham," *Sixty-third Congress, Second Session*, p. 101.

[8] *See* Orders reserving Chugach and Tongass Nat. Forests, Coal Lands withdrawal, etc., in Alaska. First forest withdrawal, Aug. 20, 1902;

Chugach Res., July 23, 1907; Bird Res. made, Mar. 4, 1909; Bering Sea Reserve, Feb. 27, 1909; Coal Lands withdrawn, Nov. 12, 1906; Aleutian Is. Reserve, March 3, 1913.

[9] The Alaska Railroad Commission, Dr. Alfred H. Brooks, *et al.*, first made a report on preliminary work, then the Engineering Commission estimated the cost at $35,000,000. The first and second estimates are summed up in *H. R. Hearings, Sixty-seventh Congress, First Session*, Oct. 7, 1921. The first report of the Engineering Commission is in *Ex. Doc. 610*, Part 2, *Sixty-fourth Congress, First Session, H. R.*, 1916.

Judge James Wichersham, Delegate from Alaska for eight years, was the chief supporter of the measure. His speech urging it is in *Congressional Records, Sixty-third Congress, Second Session*, 1914.

[10] "Mineral Industries of Alaska," *U. S. Geological Survey Bulletin 813*, p. 23; Alfred H. Brooks, "The Development of Alaska by Government Railroads," *Quarterly Journal of Economics*, May, 1914; Brooks, "The Value of Alaska," *National Geographic Review*, January, 1925, pp. 25-50.

35
Forty Years of Development

[1] Old Ben Downing was one of the veteran mail carriers of Yukon. He established the winter route and built the roadhouses. Mail abandoned by carrier, *Narratives of Exploration*, p. 588. The first post office at Skagway was opened by Dr. Runnels, and he charged twenty-five cents a letter for delivering it. Dyea office opened for money orders Apr. 14, 1898. Seattle *Post-Intelligencer*, Spl. Ed., July 1, Klondike Ed.

[2] "Laws, Postal Service," *Compiled Laws of Alaska*, p. 83; *U. S. Official Postal Guide*.

[3] *Charlton Code*, pp. 74-5.

[4] *Ibid.*, p. 8. The Curry bill was introduced following plans of Secretary Lane for new adjustment. By political manipulation it came to naught as a bill, but resulted in some benefits. *Hearings of the Committee on Territories, Sixty-seventh Congress, First Session, H. R.*, 1921.

[5] *Ibid., H. R.*, 5694. Table showing necessity for co-ordination. P. 7.

[6] *Compiled Laws of Alaska*, pp. 262 *et seq.*

[7] The rebate on the fish tax was that the fish be exempt at the rate of ten cases of canned salmon to every thousand red or king salmon fry liberated. *Compiled Laws of Alaska*, p. 198.

This meant that the canners had depleted the waters by overfishing and were to be excused from taxes on consideration of replenishing the water with young salmon to catch when they returned from sea. It was equivalent to a farmer being relieved of his tax on land if he would manure it.

[8] The first Act of the Legislature was to extend the elective franchise to women in the Territory of Alaska. *Session Laws, Alaska*, 1913, p. 1.

The granting of a Legislature was chiefly due to the efforts of the Hon. James Wickersham, Delegate from Alaska.

[9] The publications also include an excellent line of topographical maps, covering all parts of the Territory. There is also an *Index of Publications, U. S. Geological Survey,* Gov't Ptg. Off., 1916.

[10] Morris, "Report on Customs District, etc.," *Ex. Doc. 59, Forty-fifth Congress, Third Session, H. R.*

[11] Message of the President, *Ex. Doc. 146, Fiftieth Congress, H. R.,* 1889.

[12] Canada claimed the Port of Skagway, commanding the trade to the Klondike Mines. A Mounted Police was stationed there to show authority. He paraded the docks in uniform each morning. A customs officer was stationed there nominally to facilitate passage of Canadian freight. He raised the Canadian flag over his office, which was resented by the people. George Miller, a brother of Joaquin, the "Poet of the Sierras," cut it down, and excitement ensued. The next move was stopping convoys on the trail in 1899 in U. S. Customs Transfer of Liquors. The liquors were held at Skagway awaiting unobstructed passage, which modified their obstinacy through the desires of the stomach, and business was resumed. Customs Records, Skagway, Alaska.

The proceedings are in *Boundary Tribunal,* Case, Counter Case, Argument, etc., and atlases of maps, Washington, 1903.

[13] *Compiled Laws of Alaska,* p. 73.

[14] *Ibid.,* p. 86; *Annual Report, Alaska Road Commission.*

[15] *Report, Governor of Alaska,* 1918, p. 12.

[16] *Ibid.,* 1919, p. 9.

[17] *Report, Office of Indian Affairs,* 1936.

[18] *Bulletin of the Bureau of Education,* 1930.

[19] *See: Alaska Weekly,* March 20, 1931, for statement of Dr. A. H. Anderson before Legislature of Alaska. The annual reports of the Bureau of Education from the preliminary report of 1886 to 1918, contain much valuable historical material not to be had from any other source. In 1918 the reports were discontinued. The educational work in Alaska has had the poorest support in its work of any of the branches of Government work in Alaska in Governmental appropriations. In 1923 the M.S. *Boxer* was first provided for the service in the outlying districts. In that year the Bureau of Fisheries operated ten boats in Alaskan waters.

[20] The story of the reindeer from 1891, the inception of the industry, to 1906, is in the Annual Reports of the Reindeer Service, published by the Interior Department. From 1907 to 1918 it may be gleaned from the *Bureau of Education Annual Reports.* Thenceforward it is only in the MSS. records of the Bureau of Education as transferred to the Bureau of Indian Affairs. The encroachment of the white interests upon the native industry is a long and intricate story. A hearing was held in

Washington, D. C., in 1931, which partly shows the situation of the Eskimos and their reindeer but does not give space to the history of the encroachments and obstacles. *Hearings of the Reindeer Committee*, Washington, D. C., 1931.

[21] The Territorial Department of Education at Juneau, Alaska, issues an interesting and informative monthly publication, the *Alaska School Bulletin*, containing data on the work of this department.

[22] The first newspaper in Alaska was the *Alaska Times*, established May 1, 1868, at Sitka, by W. S. Dodge—Thomas G. Murphy, Editor. The first paper published in Northwestern Alaska was the *Eskimo Bulletin*, printed and illustrated by Eskimos and edited by William T. Lopp, at Cape Prince of Wales. The first in the Yukon Valley was the *Yukon Press*, at Fort Adams, Jan. 1, 1894, by Gordon C. Bettles and George T. Howard —Manager, Jules L. Prevost. James Wickersham, *Bibliography Alaskan Literature*, 1927.

The Esquimaux, a monthly paper, published at Libbysville, Port Clarence, R. A., first issue dated October 14, 1866, by the working party of the Western Union Telegraph Company, Russian Extension, was the only paper published in the Russian Colonies before the transfer to the U. S.

[23] For the Sitka Library, *see* Khlebnikof's letter in *Materialui dlya Istorii Russkikh Zaselenii, etc.,* Part 3, p. 117.

[24] Nadia Lavrova, "Rare Rezanof Russian Books Found in San Francisco," San Francisco *Chronicle,* June 10, 1934.

[25] *The Esquimaux*, published by the Russian Extension, Western Union Telegraph Company at Libbysville, R. A., Feb. 3, 1867.

36
The Alaska of Today

[1] *Alaska Weekly,* November 27, 1942.

[2] T. A. Bean, "Food Fishes of Alaska," *Fur-Seal Fisheries of Alaska,* pp. 40 *et seq.*

[3] E. W. Allen, *North Pacific,* pp. 177 and 227, New York, 1936.

[4] Of the 29,283 persons who prepared the products of the Alaskan Fisheries in 1929, 5,365 were resident natives, the others are about 4,000 white men who live in Alaska, and the white men, Filipinos, Japanese, Chinese, Mexicans, and others, who come from the States and return there. The earnings average about $300 per capita, of which the larger earnings go to the skilled employees, superintendents, overseers, bosses, engineers, etc., who mainly come from the U. S.

[5] "Memorandum for the Press," *U. S. Geological Survey,* May 28, 1937, gives the gold product of Alaska at this amount.

[6] *U. S. Geological Survey Bulletin 772;* Alfred H. Brooks, "Estimate of Coal," *The Value of Alaska,* p. 44.

[7] *Soil Reconnaissance in Alaska,* p. 184, Department of Agriculture, 1915; for Cook Inlet-Susitna Region *see: ibid.,* p. 102; Annual Reports

of the Department of Agriculture for Alaska; *Soil Reconnaisance in Alaska,* 1913; *Grass Lands of the South Alaska Coast,* Department of Agriculture, 1905; *The Grasses of Alaska,* vol. 13, Part 3, U. S. National Museum, 1910.

In 1897 Congress appropriated $5,000 for investigation of the agricultural resources of Alaska, and the next year Professor C. C. Georgeson was made Special Agent of the Agricultural Department for Alaska. He laid the foundation for the work, and occupied the position for many years. His printed reports begin with 1901.

[8] *Alaska Bureau, Seattle Chamber of Commerce Bulletin,* 1930. The seal herd on the Pribilof (Seal) Islands is computed to be 1,550,913. The sea otter have increased until they are again the object of illicit hunting. The killing of the otter is forbidden by the Treaty of July 7, 1911, and the laws thereunder. *Annual Report, U. S. Bureau of Fisheries,* 1935.

[9] For information on reindeer handling see: *Reindeer Reports, Bureau of Education in Alaska,* Washington, D. C., 1890; *Rules and Regulations of Reindeer Service in Alaska,* Washington, D. C., 1911; *Hearings of the Reindeer Committee, in Washington, D. C., Department of the Interior, Office of the Secretary,* February-March, 1931, 9 meetings, 2 volumes; *Appropriations Hearings of the Interior Department, on Reindeer,* 1931 to 1943, House of Representatives and Senate; *Congressional Record, 75th Congress, 1st Session,* pp. 1 to 8, August 20, 1937; *Senate 1st Session,* p. 12117, *et seq.; Survey of the Alaska Reindeer Service,* 1831-1933, Washington, D. C., 1933; *The New Outlook,* August, 1933, "Coming Storm Over Alaska," by Trumbull White; *Turi's Book of Lapland,* by John Turi, New York, Harper and Brothers; *Hearings, Sub-Committee on Indian Affairs, U. S. Senate, 74th Congress, 2nd Session,* Part 36, "Reindeer," Washington, 1939, Ryan's Report, p. 20087.

[10] *Report, Governor of Alaska, 1929,* p. 58, gives 85,000,000,000 feet of timber in the forest reserves of Alaska.

The West Coast Lumberman, May, 1923, estimates Alaska's total timber at 150,128,000,000 feet.

The *World Almanac,* 1930, p. 351, quotes standing timber:

	Feet
Oregon	396,000,000,000
California	290,000,000,000
Washington	256,000,000,000
Idaho	81,310,000,000

[11] *Report, Governor of Alaska, 1930,* estimates:

	Feet
Chugach National Forest, Alaska	6,260,000,000
Tongass National Forest, Alaska	78,500,000,000

[12] *Ibid.,* p. 68.

[13] "Report, Collector of Customs for Alaska," Jan. 1, 1931.

[14] *Fifteenth Census, Population Bulletin,* Series 1, Table 1, 1930. This does not give the different peoples. *Fourteenth Census, Population Bulle-*

tin, Table 1, gives: White, 27,883; Indian, 26,558; Chinese, 56; Japanese, 312; Negro, 128; all other, 99. Total, 55,036. The increase was 4,242.

The linguistic stock of the natives is given as:

	1920	1930
Aleut	2,942	------
Athabaskan	4,657	4,935
Eskimoian	13,698	19,023
Haidan	524	588
Thlingit	3,895	4,462
Tsimpsien	842	845
Total	26,558	29,853

The Sixteenth Census, 1940, p. 9, "Population," differs from the 1930 census in its linguistic classification of the Indian people. It combines the Athabaskan, Haidan, Thlingit, and Tsimpsien all under one heading as "Indian," while it lists the Aleut and Eskimo separately. The reason for this is not clear, but it will be followed. The figures are as follows:

Aleut	5,599
Eskimo	15,576
Indian	11,283
Total	32,458
Non-white (Japanese, Chinese, *et al.*)	896
White	39,170
Total	72,524

Non-white

Chinese	56
Japanese	263
Negro	141
Filipino	403
Hawaiian	22
Korean	6
Polynesians	3
Other and Unknown	2
Total	896

[15] "Report, Collector of Customs for Alaska," Jan. 1, 1936.

[16] "Memorandum for Press," *Geological Survey*, May 28, 1937.

[17] "Grasslands of the South Alaska Coast," *Department of Agriculture Bulletin No. 82*, 1905.

37
The Alaska of the Future

[1] *World Almanac*, 1931, p. 691; W. E. Curtis, *Denmark, Sweden, and Norway*.

[2] The area and population of the Scandinavian countries are as follows (*World Almanac*):

	Sq. Miles	*Population*
Denmark	16,570	3,434,555
Finland	149,641	3,582,406
Norway	124,964	2,772,000
Sweden	173,157	6,120,080
Totals	464,332	15,909,041

Alaska—590,000 sq. miles; population, 59,278. *Fifteenth Census, Population Bulletin,* 1930, Table 1.

[3] *Ibid.,* 1931.

[4] *Ibid.,* 1931, p. 193.

[5] Brooks, "The Future of Alaska," *Annals of American Geographers,* December, 1925; Brooks, "The Value of Alaska," *American Geographical Review,* January, 1925.

Jeannette Paddock Nichols, *Alaska—A History.* Especially valuable on political subjects relating to Alaska under United States' rules.

Among those who have written feelingly of Alaska are Charles Sumner, William H. Dall, William Gouverneur Morris, Charles Hallock of *Forest and Stream,* Governor Brady, Governor Swineford, Judge Delaney, Judge Wickersham, Ella Higginson, Barrett Willoughby, Mary Lee Davis, and too many others to name in this brief space.

STATISTICAL AND CHRONOLOGICAL DATA

Chief Managers of the Russian American Company:
  Alexander Andreevich Baranof—1790 to January 11, 1818.
  Leontii Andreanovich Hagemeister—Jan. 11, 1818, to Oct. 24, 1818.
  Semen Ivanovich Yanovski—Oct. 24, 1818, to Sept. 15, 1820.
  Matvei Ivanovich Muravief—Sept. 15, 1820, to Oct. 14, 1825.
  Peter Egorovich Chistiakof—Oct. 14, 1825, to June 1, 1830.
  Baron Ferdinand VonWrangel—June 1, 1830, to Oct. 29, 1835.
  Ivan Antonovich Kupreanof—Oct. 29, 1835, to May 25, 1840.
  Adolf Karlovich Etolin—May 25, 1840, to July 9, 1845.
  Michael Dmitrievich Tebenkof—July 9, 1845, to Oct. 15, 1850.
  Nikolai Yakovlevich Rosenberg—Oct. 14, 1850, to Mar. 31, 1853.
  Alexander Ilich Rudakof—Mar. 31, 1853, to April 22, 1854.
  Stephen Vasili Voevodski—April 22, 1854, to June 22, 1859.
  Ivan Vasilivich Furuhelm—June 22, 1859, to Dec. 2, 1863.
  Prince Dmitri Maksoutoff—Dec. 2, 1863, to Oct. 18, 1867.
Governors of Alaska under the United States:
  John H. Kinkead, appointed July 4, 1884, from Nevada.
  Alfred P. Swineford, appointed May 8, 1885, from Michigan.
  Lyman E. Knapp, appointed April 12, 1889, from Vermont.
  James Sheakley, appointed June 28, 1893, from Alaska.
  John G. Brady, appointed June 23, 1897, from Alaska.
  Wilford B. Hoggatt, appointed March 2, 1906, from Alaska.
  Walter E. Clark, appointed May 20, 1909, from Connecticut.
  John F. A. Strong, appointed May 1, 1913, from Alaska.
  Thomas Riggs, Jr., appointed April 12, 1918, from Alaska.
  Scott C. Bone, appointed June 16, 1921, from New York.
  George A. Parks, appointed June 16, 1925, from Alaska.
  John W. Troy, appointed April 19, 1933, from Alaska.
  Ernest Gruening, appointed _____, 1940, from Washington, D. C.

BIBLIOGRAPHY

Bibliography

Academy of Science, U.S.S.R.—*Pacific Russian Scientific Investigations,* Leningrad, 1926.

Agricultural College—*The Farthest North Collegian,* Fairbanks, Alaska.

Alaska Commercial Company—*Memorial, Farewell on Retirement,* 1940.

———— Letter in re sea otter.

Alaska Herald, San Francisco, California.

Alaska Mining Record, Special Mining Number, 1888.

Alaska-Yukon Magazine, Letters: "Correspondence of a Croop, 1907-8."

Allen, Edward W.—North Pacific, New York, 1916.

Allen, Lieutenant Henry F.—*Military Reconnaissance Copper River,* 1886.

Andrews, C. L.—Translation of Song of Baranof, in *Nuggets of Verse.*

Arctander, John W.—*The Apostle of Alaska,* New York, 1909.

Baily, Captain G. W.—"Alaska and Its People," *Senate Executive Document No. 132, 46th Congress,* Washington, D. C.

Baker, Marcus—*Dictionary of Alaska-Geographic,* Washington, 1906.

Bancroft, H. H.—*History of Alaska,* San Francisco, 1885.

Baranof, Alexander—"Letters to Shelekof," in Tikhmenef.

Barnes, Kathleen, and Gregory, Homer E.—*North Pacific Fisheries,* New York, 1939.

Barrington, Daines—*Miscellanies,* "Voyage of Quadra."

Beach, Rex—*The Spoilers,* Sewards.

———— *The Iron Trail,* fiction, Copper River Railway.

Bean, Professor T.A.—"Food Fishes of Alaska," in *Fur-Seal Fisheries of Alaska.*

Beechey, Frederick Wm.—*Narrative Voyage to the Pacific and Bering Strait,* London, 1931.

Beardslee, Captain L. A.—*Report, January 15, 1879,* Washington, D. C.

———— Report, April 28, 1881, *Senate Executive Document No. 71, 47th Congress, 1st Session.*

Belcher, Sir Edward—*Narrative Round the World Voyage,* London, 1847.

Benyowski, Maurice A.—*Memoirs and Travels,* London, 1780.

Berkh, Vasili M.—*Kronologicheskaya Istorii Aleutskikh Osstrovof (Chronological History of the Aleutian Islands),* St. Petersburg, 1823.

Biological Survey Reports, 1900 to 1926, "Reindeer," etc.

Borrowe's Report, *Executive Document No. 67, 41st Congress.*

Boundary Tribunal, Report, Government Printing Office, 1903.

Brooks, Alfred H.—"Report of the Railroad Commission," *H. R. Hearings, 67th Congress,* October, 1921.

——— "The Future of Alaska," 1923, in *Annals of American Geographers,* December, 1925.

——— "The Value of Alaska," in *Geographic Review,* New York, January, 1925.

Bureau of Education—*Reports,* 1882 to 1918.

Bureau of Fisheries—*Reports,* 1888 to 1940.

Bureau of the Census—*Reports,* 1880 to 1940.

California Historical Society—*Russians in California,* San Francisco, 1933.

Campbell, Robert—MS. *Journal, Discovery of the Stikine Headwaters.*

Clark, Henry W.—*History of Alaska,* New York, 1930.

Cleveland, Richard, *Narrative of Voyages,* Cambridge, 1842.

Coast Pilot, Part I, 1869.

Collector of Customs—*Letters—1867 to 1882.*

——— *Records on Shipping—1886 to 1903.*

——— *Annual Reports, Imports and Shipments, 1904 to 1940.*

Collinson, Captain Richard—*Journal of the "Enterprise," 1850-55,* London, 1889.

Colyer, Vincent—"Report," *H. R. Document, 2nd Session, 41st Congress,* Report of Secretary of Interior.

Cook, Captain James—*Voyage to the Pacific,* 3rd Voyage, 1785 edition.

Cook, Captain John A.—*Pursuing the Whale,* New York, 1926.

Coxe, Dr. William—*Account of the Russian Discoveries between Aria and America,* London, 1780 and 1803.

Curry, Charles F.—"The Curry Bill," *H. R. 5694 67th Congress, 1st Session,* to co-ordinate national Interests in Alaska.

Dall, Wm. H.—*Alaska and Its Resources,* 1879.

Darling, Esther Birdsall—*The Great Dog Races at Nome.*

——— *Balsy of Nome.*

Davidof, Gavril, Khvostof and Davidof—*Dvukratnoe Puteschestvie iv Ameriku (Two Voyages in America),* 2 vols., St. Petersburg, 1810.

Davidson, George—*Landfalls of Bering and Chirikof,* San Francisco, 1901.

——— *The Alaska Boundary,* San Francisco, 1903.

Davis, Mary Lee—*Uncle Sam's Attic,* and other works.

Dawson, George M.—*The Yukon Territory,* London, 1898.

Delaney, Judge A. K., and Gamel—*Mining Laws, Harris Mining District,* Juneau.

——— *History of the Alaska Judiciary.*

Dixon, Captain George—*Voyage Round the World,* London, 1789.

Dodge, Colonel W. S.—Letter, *Customs Record,* January 16, 1878.

Douglas, Sir James—MS. Journal, Photostat, *To Alaska to Establish First, Durham and Stikine.*

Dunham, S. C.—*Report, Klondike Mines,* Bulletins No. 16 and No. 19, Dawson, Forty Mile, Circle, etc., Washington, D. C., 1898.

——— *Report, Nome Gold Fields,* Bulletin No. 29.

The Dyea Trail, Newspaper of Dyea.

Elliott, Professor H. W.—*Our Arctic Province,* New York, 1887.

Farrar, Victor J.—"The Background of the Purchase of Alaska," *Washington Historical Quarterly,* April, 1922.

French, L. H.—*Seward's Land of Gold.*

Geological Survey—*Reports* from 1892 to present time.

Golder, Professor F. A.—*Russian Expansion on the Pacific,* 1914.

——— *Guide to Materials for American History in Russian Archives,* Washington, D. C.

Golovin, Paul N.—*Obzor Russkikh Kolonii in Amerika (Review of Russian Colonies in America),* St. Petersburg, 1862.

Golovnin, Vasili M.—*In Materialui dlya Istorii Russkikh Kolonii ivkpo Beregam Vostochnoi Okean (Materials for the History of the Russian Colonies in the Dhores of the Eastern Ocean),* Parts 1, 2, and 4, St. Petersburg, 1861.

Government Documents—*Alaska Boundary Tribunal,* Washington, D. C., 1904.

——— *Also British Case.*

——— *Fisheries Industry,* Section 5, Vol. 2.

——— *Fur-Seal Arbitration,* 16 vols., Washington, D. C., 1895.

Government Publications—*Report, National Museum,* Washington, D. C., 1889.

——— *Cession Papers,* Doc. 177, Washington, D. C., 1867.

Governor of Alaska—*Reports,* 1884 to 1942.

Gowen, Herbert H.—*The Napoleon of the Pacific,* New York, 1919.

Graves, S. H.—*On the White Pass Payroll,* Chicago, 1898.

Greenhow, Robert—*History of California,* London, 1844.

Gregory, Homer E.—*North Pacific Fisheries,* New York, 1939.

Hallock, Charles—*Our New Alaska,* 1886.

Harrison, E. S.—*Nome and the Seward Peninsula,* Seattle, 1906.

Haswell, ——,—Journal, *To the Northwest Coast.*

Heceta, ——,—*Diario del Viage, 1775,* MS., Bancroft Library.

Hooper, Lieutenant W. H.—*Ten Months Among the Tents of the Tuski,* London, 1853.

Howard, General O. O.—Report, *Executive Document No. 83, 44th Congress, 1st Session.*

Irving, Washington—*Astoria.*

Ivanisintzof, N.—*Russkaya Krugosvyetniya Puteschestviya Vokrug Svye-tniya, 1803 to 1849,* St. Petersburg, 1872.

Jarvis, Lieutenant D. H.—*Report of Overland Express to Barrow,* Washington, 1898.

Jones, Livingstone A.—*A Study of the Klingits,* New York, 1914.

Khlebnikov, Kyril—(Letters in *Materialui*) *Materialui Dlya Russkikh Zaselenie,* Parts 3 and 4, St. Petersburg, 1862.

Kruzenstern, Captain A. J.—*Voyage Round the World,* London, 1813.

Langsdorff, G. H. von—*Voyages and Travels,* London, 1813.

LaPerouse, J. F. de G.—*Voyage Round the World,* 2 vols., London, 1798.

Lewis and Dryden—*Marine History of the Northwest,* Portland, Oregon, 1893.

Lisianski, Urey—*Voyage Round the World,* London, 1812.

Malaspina, Alessandro—*Viaje Politic-Scientifico,* Madrid, 1885.

Marchand, Etienne—*Voyage Round the World,* 2 vols., London, 1801.

Marks, George—MS. *Journey Down the Yukon in 1883.*

Materialui (Materials for History of Russian Colonies), St. Petersburg, 1862.

Maurelle, ____—*Journal,* Bancroft Library.

Meany, Edmund S.—*Vancouver's Discovery of Puget's Sound,* New York, 1907.

Meares, James—*Voyages made in 1878-9,* London, 1791.

McClintock, Captain F. L.—*Narrative of the Fate of Sir John Franklin,* Boston, 1859.

McQuesten, L. N.—Letter, July 1, 1905. MS.

Morris, Wm. Gouverneur, Report of Customs District, *Executive Document, 45th Congress, 3rd Session,* 1879, House Document.

Morrow, Wm. B.—"The Spoilers," *California Law Journal,* 1916.

Muir, John—*Travels in Alaska,* "Cruise of the Corwin."

Muller, G. F.—*Voyages from Asia to America,* London, 1803.

Munro, Harold—*Tales of an Old Seaport,* "Nor'West John," Princeton Press, 1917.

Murray, Alexander H.—*Journal of the Yukon,* Ottawa, 1910.

Nelson, Edward W.—*The Western Eskimo,* Government Printing Office, Washington, D. C.

Nordenskjold, A. F.—*Voyage of the "Vega,"* New York, 1882.

Northwest Mounted Police—Reports, 1897, 1898, and 1899.

Ogilvie, Wm.—*Early Days on the Yukon,* London, 1913.

———— *Official Guide to the Klondike,* 1898.

Osborne, Captain Sherard, *The Discovery of a Northwest Passage,* London, 1855.

Parliamentary Papers—*Franklin Papers; Further Correspondence Connected with; Further Papers in the Search,* London, 1850, 1852, 1854, and 1855.

Perez, Juan—*Diario,* MS., Bancroft Library.

Petrof, Ivan—*Census Report, 1880.*

Pierrepont, Edward—*Fifth Avenue to Alaska,* 1883.

Pilz, George E.—MS. *Reminiscences, First Mining Engineer in Alaska.*

Portlock, Nathaniel—*Voyage Round the World*—London, 1789.

Rasmussen, Knut—*Across Arctic America.*

Ray, Captain P. H.—*International Expedition to Point Barrow,* Washington, D. C., 1900.

Raymond, Captain Charles P.—*Reconnaissance of Yukon River,* 1869.

Reports of Reindeer Service, 1890 to 1906.

Revenue Cutter Service—*Reports, 1880-1917.*

Rezanof, N. P.—Letter to Directors, 1805, in Tikhmenef's *History.*

Richardson, ____—*Polar Regions.*

Roquefeuil, M. de—*Voyage Round the World,* London, 1823.

Russian American Archives—*Alaska under Russia,* Washington, D. C.

Russian Hydrographic Office—*Sarychev's Atlas,* 1826.

Sarychef, Gavrila A.—*Account of Billings' Expedition,* London, 1886.

Schwatka, Frederick—*Military Expedition on the Yukon,* 1883.

Scidmore, Eliza Ruhamah—*Appleton's Guide to Alaska,* New York, 1898.

Seaman, Barthold—*Voyage of the "Herald,"* London, 1853.

Seattle Post Intelligencer—"Klondike," July 17, 1897.

Shelekof, Gregorii I.—*Stranstvovanie Iz Okhotska k Amerikanskoi Beregam (Voyage from Okhotsk to the American Shores),* St. Petersburg, 1793.

Sherpy, M. L.—*Skagway Daily News.*

Simpson, Sir George—*Journey Round the World,* London, 1847.

Simpson, Thomas—*Narrative of Discoveries on North Side of America,* London, 1843.

Skagway Alaskan, "Items on 'Soapy' Smith Case, 1898."

Spangenberg, G. F.—MS., *On the Yukon in 1882.*

Spurr, Josiah Edward—*Geology of the Yukon District,* Washington, D. C., 1897.

Starbuck, ____—*History of American Whale Fishery.*

Stellar, George Wm.—*Journal of Voyage, Petropaulovsk to America,* American Geographic Society, New York, 1925.

Stoney, Lieutenant George M.—*Navak Explorations in Alaska,* Annapolis, 1900.

Tanner, Josiah—MS. on Reid-Smith duel.

Tidball, Major J. C.—Report and Census of 1877, *Executive Document 5, 42nd Congress, 1st Session.*

Tikhmenef, P.—*Istoricheskoe Obozryenie Obrazovaniya Rossiisko Amerikanskoi Kompanii (Historical Sketch of the Beginnings of the Russian American Company)*, St. Petersburg, 1861-63.

Tower, Walter S.—*A History of the American Whale Fishery*, Philadelphia, 1907.

U. S. Army—*General Orders, Secretary of War, to Abandon Alaska.*

U. S. Fisheries—*Fur Seal and Fur-Seal Islands of North Pacific Ocean*, Government Printing Office, 1899.

U. S. Geological Survey—Reports, 1896 to date.

U. S. Laws for Alaska: *Compiled Laws of Alaska* (Charlton Code & Deady Code), Washington, D. C., 1913.

Valaam Monastery—*Ocherk iz Istorii Amerikanskoi Pravoslavnoi Dukhovnoi Missii, Kadyakskoi Missii (Sketch from the History of the American Orthodox Religious Mission, Kodiak Mission)*, 1794-1837, St. Petersburg, 1894.

Vancouver, George—*Voyage of Discovery to the North Pacific Ocean*, London, 1801.

Veniaminof, Ivan—*Works of Innocent, Metropolite of Moscow.*

Welcome, Henry W.—*The Story of Metlakatla*, New York, 1887.

Whymper, Frederick—*Travels in the Territory of Alaska, New York*, 1869.

Wickersham, Judge James—Speech, 63rd Congress, 2nd Session, 1909.

———— Speech on Railway, 2nd Session.

———— *Old Yukon*, Washington, D. C., 1938.

Willard, Mrs. Eugene—*Life in Alaska*, Philadelphia, 1884.

Wright, Julia McNair—*Among the Alaskans*, Philadelphia, 1883.

Young, S. Hall—*Autobiography*, New York, 1927.

Zagoskin, Lieutenant L.—*Pyeshekhodniya Opis Chasti Russkikh Vladenie iv Amerike (Pedestrian Exploration of Parts of the Russian Possessions in America)*, St. Petersburg, 1847.

Index

ARC

SIBERIA

BERING

ST. LAWRENCE I.

NUNIVAK I.

ALASKA PEN

ALEUTIAN ISLANDS UNALASKA

PACI